Policing Africa

Policing AFRICA

Internal Security and
the Limits of Liberalization

ALICE HILLS

HV
8267
.A3
H55
2000
West

LYNNE
RIENNER
PUBLISHERS

BOULDER
LONDON

Published in the United States of America in 2000 by
Lynne Rienner Publishers, Inc.
1800 30th Street, Boulder, Colorado 80301
www.rienner.com

and in the United Kingdom by
Lynne Rienner Publishers, Inc.
3 Henrietta Street, Covent Garden, London WC2E 8LU

© 2000 by Lynne Rienner Publishers, Inc. All rights reserved

Library of Congress Cataloging-in-Publication Data
Hills, Alice, 1950–
  Policing Africa : internal security and the limits of
liberalization / Alice Hills.
     p. cm.
  Includes bibliographical references and index.
  ISBN 1-55587-715-X (hc : alk. paper)
  1. Law enforcement—Africa. 2. Law enforcement—Africa Case
studies. 3. Police—Africa. 4. Police—Africa Case studies.
5. Internal security—Africa. 6. Internal security—Africa Case
studies. I. Title.
HV8267.A3H55 2000
363.2'096—dc21   99-37488
                                                            CIP

British Cataloguing in Publication Data
A Cataloguing in Publication record for this book
is available from the British Library.

Printed and bound in the United States of America

∞ The paper used in this publication meets the requirements
   of the American National Standard for Permanence of
   Paper for Printed Library Materials Z39.48-1984.

  5 4 3 2 1

Contents

List of Tables and Figures vii
Preface ix

1 Toward a Critique of Policing and National Development
   in Sub-Saharan Africa Since 1990   1

2 Policing the Postcolonial State   27

3 The Police and Politics   55

4 Models of African Policing: Evolution and Conversion   89

5 Models of African Policing:
   Construction and Integration   115

6 Models of African Policing: Transition   139

7 Models of African Policing: Adaptation   161

8 Conclusion: Modalities of Policing Africa   185

List of Acronyms 193
Bibliography 195
Index 207
About the Book 213

Tables and Figures

Tables

3.1	Levels of Police Functions and Roles in Relation to State Development	80
6.1	State Policing Requirements	156

Figures

2.1	Policing in Africa: Thematic Diversity Since Independence	28
3.1	Layers of Policing in States	56
3.2	Role and Legitimacy in Police Systems	81
4.1	Ethiopia: Federal Police Structure	104
4.2	Ethiopia: Regional Police Structure	105
8.1	Enforcement Systems	189

Preface

This book aims to show that an investigation of policing in sub-Saharan Africa during the 1990s can improve our understanding of the broader issues associated with state-society relations and state behavior, especially with regard to security. I reconsider the significance of regime transitions during the first half of the 1990s in light of the police systems that, since independence, have evolved to mirror the states that justify them. The book is thus ultimately about the institutional incapacity of the African state to fulfill the expectations for liberal political development so prevalent in the early 1990s. It also explains why the turmoil of those years did not, indeed could not, fundamentally change either the nature of African institutional democratization or police forces.

The idea of a state's police acting as a general barometer for political development is not new. Indeed, in some cases policing has provided a test case for assertions that regime transition brings greater accountability. Yet the relationship, both in Africa and elsewhere, has received astonishingly little academic attention. African police may be a comparatively modern—and alien—invention, and police forces may be less influential and effective than the military, but police systems are, in Africa as elsewhere, tenacious. Police systems in Africa have survived most events since the 1950s, even in juridical states, and are likely to remain part of state coercive facilities for the foreseeable future. They deserve consideration in any discussion about liberalization because, as an expression of regime power, the police help to illuminate the character of a regime. It is too easy to forget that power is as central to liberalization and democratization as it is to restriction and authoritarianism.

It is not always clear why the police act as they do and, given the dearth of relevant material, it is probably unprofitable to try to identify the detailed emergence of the police function in contemporary Africa. Instead, it is better to search for the key areas of change and continuity, and political developments since 1990 present an ideal opportunity to do this. Moreover, policing is an excellent means for addressing the larger set of concerns related to the distinct but complementary political processes of liberalization and democratization. My working definition of the two is taken from Michael Bratton and Nicolas van de Walle:

> Whereas liberalization refers to the political process of reforming authoritarian rule, democratization refers to the construction of the institutions of divided power. . . . we define political liberalization as the relaxation of government controls on the political activities of citizens, with particular reference to civil liberties.[1]

Studies of the police in Africa have too often been divorced from such issues, and much of the wider Western academic police literature is inapplicable. Furthermore, though the professional concerns of policing in countries such as Ethiopia and South Africa have received attention from government-sponsored overseas advisers, the conceptual issues related to policing systems and national development have not.[2] Indeed, conceptual models of policing systems and national development in Africa since 1990, in terms of either police studies or development studies, are rare. A few notable exceptions to this generalization can be found in the recent work of the Centre d'Etudes d'Afrique Noire (CEAN) group of Bordeaux and that of several United Nations and U.S. security organizations, but in order to understand the effects of political change I consider a new paradigm of the role and function of policing in Africa. By drawing on events since 1990, I intend to place current policing into perspective by developing a typology specifically relating police systems to national development.

I have excluded the South African Police (SAP), though I do discuss the problems of policing South Africa. The theoretical utility of police studies on Africa in the 1990s has too often been limited by an overconcentration on South African issues. South African policing does, however, share many problems with its neighbors. It is a system in transition, whose central problem is that of political legitimacy in a violent society.[3] Its experience is of direct relevance to the viability of a liberalized political order in Africa, for the end of apartheid raised the question of the borders between criminality and political protest in a liberal regime, and the attendant rise in crime in southern Africa is of major regional concern.[4] I therefore address issues common to the region, specifically in relation to Namibia, as a more appropriate case of policing in a settler oligarchy, and in the context of topics such as self-policing.

To begin the book, I introduce policing in the 1990s and treat basic questions about what the police do and how this is related to political development. In Chapter 2 I explore the environment in which policing operates by identifying the evolution of contemporary police systems from those inherited by the postcolonial state, more particularly the postcolonial Anglophone state. Chapter 3 is a description of the six-stage typology of police systems that underpins my study. I define the phases of the paradigm model through the use of case studies in Chapters 4, 5, and 6. In Chapter 7 I look at some of the special policing problems of the 1990s that will affect typological development. Finally, in Chapter 8 I address two questions underlying the entire study: first, whether there are any changes discernible in current police systems that are directly attributable to the developments around 1990–1996; second, how the police evaluated the significance of recent political transitions. In other words, I ask, Has anything changed and, if not, why not? In this way, I bring critical rigor to bear on the investigation of policing in Africa and emphasize the wider applicability of the book.

Much of the supporting evidence is inevitably fragmentary and anecdotal. Networks of personal contacts support an analysis based on material gathered from primary journalistic sources, digests of political events, and secondary academic studies. I assembled details of police developments from interviews with British government advisers, consultants, and police officers and with senior African officers in person (in Britain) and by post and telephone. Many of my contacts asked that their comments be anonymous; I agree to this in light of current tensions and conflict. Some information was no doubt biased, but I have cross-checked with other sources wherever possible; I compared British views of Ethiopian and Nigerian policing, for instance, to those of nationals. I have allowed for political sensitivities, cultural norms, and the rank of informants.

I am especially grateful to an anonymous reviewer; to Sue King and Joe Frost at the British Police Staff College; and to Lionel Grundy, formerly at Britain's Overseas Development Administration (now the Department for International Development). I also benefited from a research grant from the University of Leicester.

The opinions expressed in this book are mine alone and should not be regarded as representing those of any British government department or institution.

Alice Hills

Notes

1. Michael Bratton and Nicolas van de Walle, *Democratic Experiments in Africa: Regime Transitions in Comparative Perspective* (Cambridge: Cambridge University Press, 1997), 108.

2. I use the word *professional* as a matter of convenience, but it should be understood that policing (especially in Africa) has more in common with a craft than a profession in the sense of law or medicine.

3. See Bill Tupman, "Policing in South Africa," *Intersec* 5: 2 (1995), 55–57; P. A. J. Waddington, "Policing South Africa: The View from Boipatong," *Policing and Society* 4: 1 (1994), 83–96; "Reinventing the South African Police," *Africa Confidential* 33: 17 (1992), 4; "South Africa: Partners in Policing," *Africa Confidential* 35: 1 (1994), 1–3; Mark Shaw, "South Africa: Crime in Transition," *Terrorism and Political Violence* 8: 4 (1996), 156–175.

4. I do not consider criminalization as such, but the criminalization of politics throughout sub-Saharan Africa is discussed in Jean-François Bayart, Stephen Ellis, and Béatrice Hibou, *The Criminalization of the State in Africa* (Oxford: James Currey, 1999). Their views should, however, be compared with those of Chabal and Daloz who describe such an understanding as "analytically dubious": "There has always existed in Africa a wide range of activities (such as corruption) which, although illicit from a strictly constitutional or legal point of view, have been regarded as patrimonially legitimate by the bulk of the population." See Patrick Chabal and Jean-Pascal Daloz, *Africa Works: Disorder as Political Instrument* (Oxford: James Currey, 1999), 79.

1

Toward a Critique of Policing and National Development in Sub-Saharan Africa Since 1990

One thing can be stated categorically. Very little is known about the police in Africa.
—Otwin Marenin[1]

In years to come, 1990 may be seen as a significant point in the development of African power structures. Just as 1960 was characterized by independence and 1966 by military coups, so 1990 was marked in many states by cautious moves toward a redistribution of political power by increased popular participation. The multiparty elections held or scheduled in countries as diverse as Gabon and Zaire, did not amount to a transition to democracy—indeed, they did not ultimately amount to anything positive in some countries—but they did suggest that a rebalancing of political power was possible. Optimists thought that most African states were moving away from the authoritarian political model they had followed since independence and thus were transforming the role of the state coercive agents responsible for regulating political life.

In 1960 the rebalancing of political power was based on the triumph of nationalism over external powers, but the upheavals of 1990 had more to do with the oppressiveness of the resulting internal structures and their inability to satisfy popular expectations in the face of international political change. The unrest derived from general beliefs that Africans should be able to criticize political appointments without being murdered or imprisoned. This belief resulted in pressure for change in the management of regime relations and the exercise of political authority, for citizens believed they should exercise a much greater influence over state institutions and officials and that these would demonstrate a degree of accountability to public demands. The institution of policing, intimately concerned with the day-to-day operation of state power and constantly encountering the public, offers an ideal opportunity to study this purported process. If the developments of the 1990s represent real change, then it should surely register in policing.

Much has changed since the 1960s, but the institutional pillars of the postcolonial state remain recognizable decades later. As Jackson wrote in 1990, "There is in most institutions to which individuals or states become attached a powerful conservatism."[2] This is particularly noticeable in internal security, broadly conceptualized, where there is evidence of both change and continuity. There was a clear shift in coercive systems during the 1960s, as events obscured the shape of the colonial inheritance. Indeed, it appears that the major milestone in policing probably lies in the 1960s, with the shift from colonial to postcolonial politics, as governments lost the institutional coherence previously provided by external support. The security establishment in Tanzania, for example, grew from 3,000 to 40,000–50,000 in the 1960s, and distinctions between policing and the military blurred still further. There was also a shift in the understanding of national security after independence, as protecting the state became a personalized concern for regimes. But force levels and the proliferation of security agencies in the intervening years also suggest a significant degree of continuity.

African regimes invariably include a substantial security establishment—the various institutions, groups, and actors who have a professional, or an informal interest in maintaining the regime and state. Ideally they are agents of the state that has defined their interests, but in practice they are more likely to be a distinct set of groups that perform certain functions for state officials while keeping a distinct set of interests. Moreover, the boundaries between the various police, paramilitary, military, and personal forces involved are often unclear. The Nigerian Internal Security Service is one such case. Formal distinctions among the various groups may not be readily apparent except for special units such as those belonging to a president. Those of Idi Amin, for instance, operated like the Haitian Tonton Macoutes, complete with garish shirts and sunglasses. Because the identity of the police is not self-evident, I give working definitions of such terms as *policing, paramilitary,* and *military* later in this chapter. Yet the need to delimit these terms in some way should not suggest a lack of recognizable if diverse internal security systems in existence in all of the forty-five or so states of sub-Saharan Africa.

The various aspects of state coercion have, with the exception of the military (which in Africa usually means the army) attracted little academic attention. Police studies, for instance, tend to concentrate on policing in democratic societies from the point of view of criminal justice, history, and sociology. Even in these cases, by the mid-1970s, there had been only three substantial and systematic attempts to analyze police activity in context of specific societies: Michael Banton's *Policeman in the Community*, James Q. Wilson's *Varieties of Police Behaviour,* and David H. Bayley's *Forces of Order.*[3] Banton and Wilson concentrated on American and British policing, whereas Bayley associated differences in Japanese and American policing with differences in national culture. Apart from work by authors such as Enloe, Lefever, and Baynham, studies of civil-military relations also ignored the police except in relation to the coups of the 1960s.[4] Baynham's impressive work on the police in Ghana, for example, was secondary to his interest in the role of the military.

It is not surprising that scholars have concentrated on the military. The military can dramatically affect state legitimation processes by the exercise of force. They frequently intervene in politics, usually have considerable resources, are largely isolated from the population, and tend to see themselves as a superior, highly specialized and self-sufficient caste. Public police forces—which may not be independent of military command, especially under military rule—are less elitist; they are neither well resourced, apolitical, nor respected. They are in daily contact with the civilian population, their status and educational level tend to be low, and they are more susceptible to political influence (though less likely to intervene in politics) than are the military. More surprising, given their paramilitary nature, the police in Africa have rarely been included in studies of the political influence of the military, perhaps because it remains difficult to discern the extent of their role. Theoretical distinctions can be made between the two, but in practice it is often hard to distinguish between the two in states with weak institutions. Indeed, empirical evidence suggests that tasks and categories of personnel are often blurred, except in wealthier countries such as Namibia. In practice this has meant that the police remain shadowy figures and are seen as merely adjuncts to the military.[5]

Otwin Marenin's judgment that "very little is known about the police in Africa" is generally as true now as it was in 1982. Perhaps this is not surprising given the difficulty of researching the police in the fragile political systems of Africa, but it does not satisfactorily explain why the police have received so little attention. The neglect is all the more remarkable because the police are a fundamental tool of state authority and power in most states. As Marenin says, "Police behaviour is state power; the police make real, by what they do or fail to do, the intentions and interests of the state."[6] It is therefore appropriate to use policing to test the claims of liberalization in the 1990s and engage with the broader theoretical challenges.

There are, however, more plausible reasons for such neglect by Western commentators. Western concerns such as crime prevention have never been high on the agenda of any African police force, and it is almost as if it is sufficient merely to acknowledge that most forces, if not all, are brutal, corrupt, and badly paid. Indeed, African police are usually mentioned in Western news reports only if their actions cause numerous casualties. Typical of such incidents was the occasion in Angola in 1997 when ten members of the National Union for the Total Independence of Angola (UNITA) died of suffocation in police custody in the central Malange town jail in what a UN observer called "an act of barbaric cruelty."[7] Some police units, such as the South African counterinsurgency Koevoet operating in Namibia, had an international reputation for brutality, but even the South African Police before the mid-1980s drew scant attention because the structures of apartheid required a relatively small police force.

Western Perspectives

Study of the relationship between policing and national development in the 1990s should include English-, French-, and Portugese-language sources, but relevant material is not yet available. Published work on policing Francophone Africa and the ex-Belgian colonies in English is almost nonexistent, and Lusophone Africa appears to have produced no papers or monographs known to British bibliographic sources.[8] Moreover, regimes regard policing as sensitive, and accessible material tends to be limited and anecdotal rather than statistical or organizational. The lack of support infrastructure and inadequate government support has meant a dearth of information about policing in countries such as Mozambique, where 1996 was characterized by a moratorium on recruitment and a complete absence of training. Suitable studies are conspicuous by their rarity.[9]

As Bayley commented in 1977, the idea that policing is directly affected by the environment in which it operates is neither novel nor profound, but "it is curious how often it is disregarded."[10] Since then it has become commonplace that the nature of policing is tightly linked to the nature of the state in which it operates. The clearest recognition of this link occurred around 1990, when attention focused on the South African Police as an archetypal politically partisan force and, to a lesser extent, on the new Namibian force as a symbol of a brave new postapartheid world.[11]

The related subject of overseas police aid has also been overlooked. Such aid (by means of consultation, training, or equipment) was offered by government-funded agencies in Cuba, France, Israel, Romania, the UK, the United States, and the USSR throughout the cold war.[12] Yet there are no open British studies, for instance, evaluating this aid. Indeed, there was little interest in international patterns of police aid until the role and function of the South African Police in support of apartheid attracted academic attention in the late 1980s, when funding became available for work on policing South Africa and Namibia.[13] Since then general issues of authority and political participation related to policing have tended to be confined to passing references in studies of demobilization, development, humanitarian relief, and security-sector reform.[14] The main exceptions to this generalization lie in the field of criminology, but the emphasis there is usually on crime prevention and victimology rather than the police, types of policing, or internal security.[15]

I present some fundamental characteristics of contemporary African police systems as reminders that the turbulence of the early 1990s has left many aspects of the African state unaltered. The resulting discussion runs the risk of presenting the truism that the police are a major force for repression, but this is a reflection of the reality of African politics. There has been no fundamental evolution of police systems since independence. The management and training of the police, as well as their relationship to the state, have changed little. There have been dramatic operational developments, but they may prove transitory because they depend on the expression of a political power that is itself essentially unchanged.

The central argument of this study is that certain characteristics remain consistent across all police systems. Police systems are, above all, tenacious and well placed to accommodate change. The police adapt to political and social developments at the same time they influence political participation by deciding whom to arrest or detain. They regulate many competitive processes, manipulate political groups, and defend (or abandon) regimes. Not only have police systems survived in both empirical and juridical states, but policing in the decades since independence is marked by cycles of progress and regression. This notion of alternating progress and regression is rooted within Western policing models and is a crude and artificial distinction, but it provides a useful tool for placing policing within the context of development.

Development is usually understood as a process of moving toward Western models of economic and consumerist societies, but its use here should not be taken as indicating the desirability of a unilinear model leading to a crime-detection style of policing. The transferability to Africa of the Anglo-American police concepts (such as autonomy and discretion) is in any case controversial. Moreover, African police forces are rarely judged in professional terms by their contemporaries. Despite this difference, Western notions are of analytic relevance to Africa for three reasons. First, there are no mature alternative conceptual models for understanding African policing. Second, Western models reflect the ideals of important past and present donors. Third, such models appear to be integral to the relationship (between ruler and ruled) necessary to make the institutional reform of the 1990s mean what many observers believe it means.

Three Fundamental Questions

There are three fundamental questions about African policing that need to be clarified before a formal critique can be developed:

- Who are the police?
- What is policing?
- What is a police system?

Who Are the Police?

Until the 1990s, when self-policing and private policing in postapartheid South Africa attracted attention, the police were rarely defined because theories of policing assumed that policing is essentially a statist function. Recent work related to township and commercial policing in South Africa has questioned the validity of this interpretation and indeed the relevance of policing based on Western models to Africa generally, both in terms of understanding and practice.[16] Such questioning is valuable, although, paradoxically, much of private policing, at least at the official level, operates through contracts or joint ventures with U.S., British, and South African companies. But the two are not necessarily contradictory, for private policing may be regarded as performing a state role if it is at the direction of state officials. The British company Saracen is, for instance, supposed to train Angolan police, and Nigerian "tax consultants" patrol opposition areas on behalf of state governors.

My concept of the police function is therefore based on two premises: first, that the national police forces are the formal conduit through which regime power or authority is normally channeled in most states and that they should therefore be treated as the primary statist policing agents; second, that policing in Africa nevertheless goes beyond formal civilian groups and that the focus should be on policing (as in the provision of order and enforcement) rather than on what organizations call themselves. How the police style themselves is less important than what they do or do not do, but for the sake of clarity, I use *police* to mean the public force unless I state otherwise. Whatever the changes of the 1990s, the police, however defined, continue to reflect the character of their regimes: Brutal regimes have brutal police. When states are fragile and lacking in institutional capacity, their police are likely to be undisciplined.

The rationale of the police remains maintaining the order that the regime sustaining them defines as appropriate. Further, national police forces cannot be defined only in terms of ends but must be understood also in terms of means. And the means common to all police is the use of coercion. So the police can be described as an institution usually (though not invariably) given the right to use coercive force by the state within the state's domestic territory.

I use the word *function* to indicate the formal requirements (such as regulatory activities and regime representation) placed on them as an organization; *role* describes the activities they perform. Function is thus the specific technical and officially required action, whereas the role may reflect different practical demands.

The police are part of but apart from society—not least because they supposedly serve the interests of the state or regime concerned rather than its citizens. They usually have low sociopolitical and economic status, particularly in the rank and file, and are often popularly regarded as no better than common thieves. Given the predilection of the various internal security and police elements for preying upon the citizens they are charged with protecting and their often negligible contribution to law and order, it is no wonder that this should be so. Yet although there have been many demonstrations and riots in the 1990s, police authority is rarely challenged directly, though officers (I use the term generically) may be physically attacked.

What Is Policing?

The formal primary functions of African policing remain as Potholm defined them in 1969: the maintenance of law and order, paramilitary operations, regulatory activities, and regime representation. It is reactive, repressive, and discretionary.

In practice, policing in Africa is much less clearly defined than in many Western countries, and its definition needs to be broadened beyond the activities of formal civilian groups. In Nigeria, for instance, policing must be understood in relation to the activities of the military, some eight or more paramilitary units, various palace guards, numerous quasi-official units in various states, and miscellaneous thugs associated with strongmen. And it is difficult to decide whether operations such as the Nigerian military's Operation Sweep in Lagos during 1996–1998, described as an anticrime measure, should be understood as a policing or a military action. Likewise, it often proved difficult to decide where policing ended and counterinsurgency began in states such as Rhodesia and Namibia.

The core of the definition I use is twofold. First, despite the ambiguities referred to above, policing concerns the enforcement of a state's (or regime's) definition of appropriate public order and behavior. Thus policing is internal as understood by most conventional definitions of sovereignty. This definition excludes the "action groups" employed by ambitious politicians and others to serve private interests, but it can include (Western) companies such as Wackenhut or Strategic Concepts that may be hired to assist in the imposition of order. This understanding of what the police really do highlights the essential feature of most postcolonial African states: The struggle of regimes to ensure their own survival in the face of competition from rival groups and a population that does not accept the regime's claims to legitimacy is a fundamental influence on the police. Second, policing refers to a de jure (if not de facto) exclusive monopoly on the use of force within a sovereign authority's territory.

Policing is usually a reactive activity dependent on the state for its existence and opportunity. Few if any African forces have any form of strategic or systematic implementation plan, with the (temporary) exceptions resulting from the presence of overseas advisers (as in Swaziland) or the influence of politics (in Namibia).[17] Policing is inherently political, for the police enforce decisions taken (or allowed) by political authorities, acting in support of specific regime concerns, such as survival. Policing may also affect public perceptions of a regime by its manner and means, by its manipulation of fears, norms, and symbols. Moreover, sustained repression may in turn legitimize regime rule itself: The "transformation of power into authority is accomplished by conditioning the great majority of people to accept power relationships as real, inevitable, unavoidable and perhaps even right."[18]

But even in states like South Africa under apartheid, it was simplistic to argue that the police automatically supported regime policies and interests. State institutions often have internal disputes that are reflected in political conflict, weakening the bond between the police and a regime as the police act on behalf of subordinate groups. And even close relationships between the police and a government can be strained if the police try to assert their independence through the manipulation of government priorities.[19] The police are agents of the state in an ideal sense, but they are also a separate societal group that effectively makes a deal with state officials and performs certain functions while keeping a distinct set of interests.

Africa's political traditions since 1960 suggest that the boundaries of policing have always been broad. Most states lack the institutional capacity required to systematically define and act on specific interests in a way that would constrain police actions. Yet certain generalizations about the police can be made. In any case policing tends to be recognizable as such regardless of its specific environment. The police are likely to be undisciplined, to pose a threat to regimes, and to pursue their own interests, often at the expense of formal rules. All these factors were present in the police mutiny in Lesotho in 1997, for example.[20] Policing is coercive and often repressive in the African context, especially in conditions where citizens do not widely accept the norms or customs proposed by a regime. It exacts compliance, and the onus of avoiding it is always on the civilian. This suggests that analyzing policing in terms of discipline (and the control of subordinate groups by dominant ones), as Foucault suggested,[21] is more relevant to African policing than any view of policing as crime-fighting or law enforcement as such.

Paramilitarism, reinforced by ethnic recruitment policies, is also often considered a defining characteristic of African policing, though (as mentioned) it is difficult to distinguish paramilitaries from the police and other specialist groups. There is no commonly agreed-upon definition of *paramilitarism*. It can describe a style of policing, a type of police structure, a series of relationships, or a force specially designed for operations thought to be beyond the scope of a civil police but not requiring the weaponry and training of an army. In British terms, paramilitary forces act in support of or in lieu of military forces, but the case is far less clear in Africa.

Paramilitarism in African policing may be symbolized by the willingness of, say, the Kenyan force to inflict civilian casualties and by the continuing importance of drill in many training schools. In Malawi, for example, drill represents 25 percent of the initial (and often only) police training. The police act in support of (or as a less expensive option to) the military in many states, whereas paramilitarism may be strengthened by the presence in a force of demobilized soldiers or fighters after civil conflict. In fact, even the "professional" identities of the police and military sometimes appear ambiguous, occasionally with violent results. In Togo, for instance, 500 army recruits were transferred to the police force on the orders of the military president in 1992. It is unclear why they were transferred, but the government's failure to pay up to eight months' benefits was probably instrumental in causing the heavily armed police to block streets and shoot when occupying key areas of the capital Lomé. They looted shops, occupied key ministries, and took over the international airport before the fighting was settled.[22]

The paramilitary nature of policing needs, however, to be seen in context. Although African policing has a hierarchical structure, it is generally characterized by bureaucracy and procedural red tape that leads to chronic inefficiency and dissatisfaction. There is also scope for the exercise of discretion, particularly by low-ranking officers. It is likely that discretion, which is exercised whenever the effective limits on his power leaves an officer free to make choices about possible causes of action or inaction, plays a far less important part in African policing than it does in Western policing. But its existence may offset some aspects of the militarized style of much of African policing. Paramilitarism is also counterbalanced by the inefficiency and dissatisfaction evident among many forces, which is in turn accentuated by the neglect of the physical infrastructure of policing. Training establishments are run-down, and vehicles (where they exist) are usually in need of repair, yet reports by overseas advisers suggest that in many cases the shabbiness exists because of apathy rather than insufficient funds, with the whole reinforced by low morale.[23]

The attributes that seem to legitimate such policing in the eyes of citizens (or, increasingly, international opinion) include sanction by law, regime recognition and recognition by other security forces—though moral authority has little to do with the compliance normally exacted by the police.[24] Legitimate policing, in the sense of adherence to a set of standards or customs, can be promoted in other ways, all of which are motivated by political considerations. The Namibian Ministry of Home Affairs sought to promote the legitimacy of the Nambian Police (NAMPOL) by a package of measures including a new weapons policy, new uniforms, and vehicles; the Eritrean police were able to capitalize on popular postwar support. Recruitment and ethnic composition can add or detract from acceptance, but such sensitive decisions are themselves shaped by politics. External support can play a role in bolstering legitimacy, too. British training aid, for example, has added to the aura of NAMPOL, though years of support to the forces of Nigeria and Uganda have not had a comparable effect. Indeed, it is more likely that the postcolonial loss of government command over security forces, combined with the willingness of the police to ignore formal rules, has led to a declining legitimacy as policing standards are widely repudiated by citizens.

None of these attributes is sufficient in isolation, but the legitimacy of a specific force (or its institutional setting) is usually lost or undermined as a result of political developments. Thus, the Rwandan gendarmerie fled (to a man, it seems) after the genocide of 1994 in which they were heavily implicated. But the barbarity of the Dergue police did not weaken their effectiveness or legitimacy, any more than it did for the South African Police. Neither have corruption and inefficiency impaired the de jure legitimacy of the Nigerian Police Force—popular acceptance of the "uniformed buzzards" is another matter. There have been no revolutions in policing, and even new forces (such as that of Eritrea) are usually recruited from an existing pool of ex-fighters and former officers.

What Is a Police System?

In the context of the state, the police sector forms a system that I define as an organization made up of groups and individuals, existing for a specific purpose, employing systems of relatively structured activity with an identifiable boundary, and driven by actors pursuing their own goals according to their own incentives and calculations.[25] The complexity of the internal security sector results from the interactions between the various parts of the system.

The general notion of a police system is a useful analytical tool for understanding policing. It indicates the overall type and shape of an existing national force. It also embodies a core of beliefs and practices about the legitimation of and limits to state or regime power (though there may be considerable disjunction between the perception of state officials and those of the populace). And it offers a sectional view of the police and political development. It is better suited for identifying continuities that persist over periods than explaining rapid change, but given the evolutionary nature of policing, this is appropriate.

There is, however, an important limitation to the system concept. It can offer only a partial explanation of the relationship of policing to the contemporary state because it does not indicate what happens to the system or its parts when a state fragments. Most if not all contemporary states have a police system, just as most if not all societies are policed in some way, both before fragmentation and afterward, when reconstruction usually takes place. There tends to be a blurring of police and military roles in such circumstances, with the military adopting a police role that reflects the increased focus on internal security. But it is not clear what happens to police systems in between these points. It is important to investigate this transition because the creation or conversion of a police force is always seen as a priority during reconstruction.

In the context of democratization in the 1990s, conversion implies a separation of the police from the military and a redefinition of a distinct function. But the resulting force will not be completely new because it will be a continuation of the past. No state creates a police force anew, and the civilianization or conversion of a previously militarized force is a stronger theme in "new" forces than revolution, if only because trained officers are always in short supply and suitable ex-fighters cannot be wasted or safely sidelined. The police (whether present or future) evolve from previous structures shaped by historical inheritance, political pressures, specific events, and professional concerns. The Namibian force, for example, was new in name, uniform, and weapons policy, but its leadership and structure were those of the old South West African Police Force. And even a force as notorious as that of Angola was described by the UN secretary-general's special representative in Angola in 1994 as being in need of improvement rather than destruction.[26]

The environment of the system is the state, and the key to African policing lies—with the above provisos—in its relationship to the state and the central concerns of regimes. It is for this reason that the maintenance of policing, as an aspect of internal security, can shed light on the overall institutional strength of African states.

The Police and the State

Although the African state appears to have failed as an administrative instrument and although there has been a gradual disintegration of many of the institutions that commonly make up the state, all states since independence have (or had, in the case of Somalia) a national police system. All states, both empirical and juridical, need coercive agents because politics since the 1950s has been for the most part a contest for survival and the control of resources.[27]

The concept of the state is, however, debated. Robert Jackson's judgment that "When we speak of 'the state' in sub-Saharan Africa, we are creating an illusion" is undoubtedly accurate.[28] It is also important because it introduces two fundamental paradoxes concerning the state and its police: Although police forces are tenacious, they need the state for their existence. And although African states are fragile constructs, they have survived because "their sovereignty is not contingent on their credibility as authoritative and capable political organisations. Instead, it is guaranteed by the international community, especially as embodied in the United Nations."[29] Police systems are likewise guaranteed, for there is an international consensus on the norms of state sovereignty: Insofar as the right to define the terms of internal order are ceded to states as a prerogative of sovereignty, states have police forces.[30]

Police and Regimes

The state can be pictured as a structure of domination and coordination that includes "a coercive apparatus and the means to administer a society and extract resources from it."[31] The police are part of that society even as they act on behalf of regimes; they are not neutral arbitrators but agents of the state, and at the same time they are a distinct societal group with a distinct set of interests. They are affected by political change, regime interests, and personal ambition. Furthermore, all three factors are linked because the term *regime* may refer to both procedures and individuals, as Bratton and van de Walle imply when they define political regimes as the sets of formal and informal political procedures determining the distribution of power.[32] I use *regime* here to refer as well to those (individuals and elite groups) who control state power; it is often a more accurate description than *government* because the latter suggests a degree of institutionalization—or international acknowledgment—that is frequently missing.

Despite the self-interest of police aims and objectives, it is not necessarily inaccurate to see these interests as usually (though not always) linked to those of regimes. Indeed, it is of value in this study, for just as regimes (primarily motivated by a desire to retain power and position) respond to changes in political moods (such as democratization) by assessing the best way to survive, so it is important to consider how police roles adapt to change. Likewise, the reality of specific changes should be questioned if the police remain fundamentally unchanged, for police elites are well positioned to judge the survival value of personalities and policies.

Policing can show us whether or not there are signs that states are becoming more responsive to the needs of Africans in the light of pressures for liberalization. The record of policing in the 1990s can indicate whether officials in new or reformed states (such as Eritrea, Ethiopia, and Namibia) have learned from the postcolonial experiences of other states and, if they have, whether they have the ability to avoid the dangers. The lack of real change could signal that many African states instead remain the type of state Jackson considered characteristic of the cold war era, externally secure but threatened by internal challenges. If this is so, then it is reasonable to expect policing to remain coercive, at odds with the interests of significant groups in society, and heavily involved with regime efforts to fight off internal threats.

Police and Politics

The police are tightly linked to the state, but they may withdraw their support from regimes. Such intervention is usually covert (as when senior officers instigated the 1966 coup in Ghana) rather than overt (as in Dar es Salaam in 1964). But an uneasy relationship may result in violent action. This is vividly illustrated by the Lesotho police mutiny of 1997, which lasted for eleven days before it was overcome by heavy gunfire from the army.[33] In fact the mutiny reflected the deep mistrust and competition between some elements of the police and the government and the strained institutional relationship between the police and the army.

The mutiny began when eight officers demanded amnesty for the murder of three fellow officers (killed in an exchange of gunfire at a police station) in 1995. This was in response to the government's only attempt to prosecute those it deemed guilty of extrajudicial killings or abuse committed during the conflicts of 1994–1996. The officers refused to appear in court, and the Lesotho high court dismissed, with costs, their application to have their indictment for murder withdrawn. The rebels then "dismissed" the police commissioner and took control of police headquarters in the capital of Maseru on 6 February, appointing a new commissioner and other senior staff. By 13 February the protest had spread until two-thirds of the 3,000-strong force was reportedly on strike. Ten of those arrested appeared briefly in court on 21 February, where they were remanded in custody on charges of sedition and contravening the internal security act. The prosecution politicized the case by arguing that the officers had unlawfully subverted state authority by resisting arrest and threatening to bring the government down if it did not negotiate with them. The prosecution also alleged that they fired at soldiers who had been told to restore the police force to normality—the army's lack of involvement in the mutiny is notable.

Internal and regional politics also played a part in the response. The South African foreign affairs director visited Maseru on 15–16 February, and local observers blamed South African involvement for the decision to confront the mutineers, an action judged to have created new dissent in both the police and the army. The newspaper *SouthScan* thought these events clouded the original reason for the mutiny: "While the confrontation seemed separate from the factionalising in the ruling party it is already apparent that connections have been made."[34] Thus, dissident police refused to do their duty, and the political dispute forming the background to the mutiny remained unresolved. In turn, a South African foreign ministry official said that South Africa could not accept an "unconstitutional challenge to the democratic order in Lesotho," and *Africa Analysis* reported that a South African rapid reaction force was poised for intervention, the move aborted only when the Lesotho army succeeded in putting down the mutiny. (South Africa had in fact used similar strong tactics during an attempted palace coup two years before.) South African military maneuvers then took place near the border, probably because instability in Lesotho posed a threat to a multibillion-dollar water project representing a key supply to South Africa.

The situation continued unsettled and inflammatory throughout the succeeding months. By early 1998, South African allegations of dirty tricks within the Lesotho police, combined with more personal and political concerns, resulted in discontent that spread well beyond the police. At the same time, unrest spilled over into the military, personal and constitutional disputes split the ruling Basutoland Congress Party, and the Lesotho Congress for Democracy (LCD) won seventy-nine of the eighty available seats in the (probably rigged) elections of May 1998. By September the situation deteriorated into a threatened mutiny by elements of the Lesotho army, a South African-led invasion, and the looting of Maseru by residents. The Lesotho Defence Force effectively allowed the center of the capital to be gutted by rioting mobs and mutinous soldiers; a few policemen were reported trying to halt the looting, but most were conspicuous by their absence.[35] Meanwhile, President Nelson Mandela of South Africa insisted that the South African National Defence Force (SANDF), which met no resistance from the police, would stay as long as it was necessary to restore stability and "create a safe environment." The showpiece military intervention was a fiasco. Apart from anything else, South African support of the unpopular LCD deepened the resentment many felt toward the LCD for having asked the SANDF to intervene. The symbolic importance of the police in such circumstances was acknowledged at the end of September, when a joint operations center was set up by SANDF, the Lesotho government, the Lesotho police, and South African and Botswana officials, specifically to get the police "going again."

Events in Lesotho serve to show that the police can become significant actors in their own right at a number of levels. Reality thus departs from the definitions of the police provided above, which should be seen as an ideal type in the Weberian sense of the word. There are situations in which the police behave as police and those in which they behave for themselves.

Policing in the 1990s

Policing, as generally understood, continues to be characteristically paramilitary, with the drill square often the best-maintained area in public training establishments; a high proportion of most basic training courses remains almost exclusively drill and associated military-related topics, with passing-out parades, marking the completion of a constable's initial training, usually considered a great strength. Discipline and protocol tend to be military in character, though there often appears to be an unwillingness among all ranks to accept personal responsibility for actions.[36]

Despite the paramilitary nature of so much African policing, the public police are generally headed by civilians and under the control of a minister of the interior, home affairs, internal affairs, or (as in Uganda) the president. They tend to wear special uniforms and shoes, but there is often a wide variation in the state and type of the uniforms even within a force.

Accommodation and wages are poor. Partly as a result (taken in conjunction with their power), the police are notoriously corrupt. Although much of the evidence for police corruption is anecdotal, it is so ubiquitous that it is difficult to dismiss.[37] In addition, allocated resources are usually inadequate, and governments rarely give the police priority. Most forces tend, however, to have special units available for rapid deployment that do receive special treatment; they deal with the serious crimes considered to threaten regime order. They may be called "mobile force patrols" (as in Malawi) or "operational support services units," and they invariably have better lodging, equipment, and uniforms than the operational police. Officers working in the intervention and protection section of the Angola Police (which provide protection of government strategic objectives and figures), for instance, earn three times the salaries of their public-order colleagues.[38]

Most aspects of public policing have not changed since the 1980s. The main formal roles of the police remain maintenance of law and order, national security operations, and traffic control.[39] As noted earlier, African police generally focus on the protection of regimes from domestic security threats to a greater extent than police in many other regions; crime prevention and the protection of life, cultural or religious values, and property continue to be much less important. Most forces do not in any case have skills, resources, or motivation needed to keep accurate criminal records. The main structural components of African forces remain headquarters, criminal investigation, accounts, special branch, central administration, and communications. Ranks and grade structures have stayed similar to those of the 1980s, too. Because they are centralized and available, the police still assume regulatory roles such as the supervision of trade, prison management, border patrol, currency enforcement, and refugee settlements.

Policing problems common throughout Africa have not changed dramatically. They continue to include the effects of high levels of urban growth (resulting in an imbalance between urban and rural areas in terms of economic development and health and education facilities), illegal immigration, smuggling, and the easy availability of weapons. The police role may not, however, be clear to either the police themselves or those with whom they work. The border police in Lesotho, for example, often seem to be interchangeable with customs and immigration officials.

Promotion opportunities vary enormously. There were none in some areas of Mozambique in the 1990s, whereas selection for promotion in Botswana was theoretically based on a written test and a closed system of reporting. It is possible to move from constable to commissioner with only the basic training provided in Botswana, but in practice many officers do not know why they have been given new ranks or responsibilities (for which there are in any case no training courses) or, conversely, why they have not been promoted. Training has a low priority throughout the continent and training officers have no status, so unfit or unwanted officers are all too often sent to training units "for medical reasons," by station commanders against their will. In an assessment of the Nigeria Police Force in 1988, for example, three British police advisers commented that there was a common belief that people were posted into training as a punishment. Not surprisingly they considered that "the worst recruits receive the worst training and become the worst policemen."[40] There are rare exceptions to this, especially in Zimbabwe, where visiting British officers in the mid-1990s described most provincial training as good.

Less is known about other characteristics of police work, such as social cohesion. African police culture may be similar to that described in many Western forces (that is, they feel isolated, defensive, and distrust other agencies), but there is little research to back up arguments about who the police are, where they come from, what work they do, or how well they do it. It is also unclear whether the mosaic of noninstitutional authority visible in other coercive organizations exists in policing.[41] Whatever the case, the attention the South African forces have received in recent years has not been paralleled by work on other forces and systems, and

Marenin's conclusion from 1982 remains valid: "Objective measurement[s] of how well the police do their job . . . are non-existent. There are simply no published, systematic studies of police performance by any possible measures."[42]

Liberalization and Democratization in the 1990s

Despite the evidence of declining legitimacy in the public police and challenges to it from private and informal civilian groups, the tenacious and evolutionary nature of police systems is striking. The effects of recent political changes on policing have not yet been assessed, but the 1990s provide a series of developments on which to judge the relationship between policing and politics, internal security and liberalization. Pressure for political change grew in the late 1980s, and by 1993 almost all of the forty-six countries of sub-Saharan Africa had implemented some form of political reform intended to accommodate the new demands.[43]

By the late 1980s, Western governments saw many of Africa's problems as essentially political in character. Political reform was thus added to the existing international program of economic structural adjustment, environmental conservation, and population control, and by early 1990 Western assistance was explicitly linked to political reform—in part, undoubtedly, because of a World Bank report of 1989, which called for loans to be contingent upon such change.

This in turn influenced police aid by European states. President François Mitterrand of Franch said that his country would link its future aid contributions to liberty and democracy. Douglas Hurd, the British foreign secretary, announced that Britain would encourage pluralism, public accountability, respect for the rule of law, human rights, and market principles, and in June 1991 Lynda Chalker, British overseas aid minister, tied these to "good government" (though none of these necessarily implied multiparty politics). In 1995 the Overseas Development Administration (ODA) further defined *good government* by dividing it into four main categories:

- Legitimacy, hinging on the consent of the governed and whether the government can be removed by elections or other forms of peaceful political process
- Accountability, which requires a network of checks and balances and defined performance standards for politicians and officials
- Competence, which involves the formulating policies and making and implementing timely decisions
- Respect for human rights and the rule of law

The third of these is particularly significant for this study because it refers to institutional capacity. All are, however, contested concepts, and none, least of all elections, is (as Patrick Chabal has pointed out) sufficient in themselves.[44]

International factors alone cannot explain the resulting transitions, and *Africa Confidential* is probably only partially correct in its assertion that the "principal cause of Africa's wind of change is the World Bank and the donor countries. They are explicitly demanding political change as a condition for further loans."[45] In a recent publication, Bratton and van de Walle propose instead that regime transitions are "most directly affected by domestic factors such as the relative strength and cohesion of incumbent and opposition forces. In particular, democratization requires a homegrown constituency for political reform."[46] It is clear, however, that it also requires a threat to cut off outside aid to regimes that rely on such support in the face of domestic unpopularity.

That the changes were turbulent is unquestionable, for most states were also confronting AIDS, economic decline or stagnation, environmental degradation, food shortages, population pressures, refugees, and war, as well as policy reforms related to structural adjustment, market liberalization and privatization. The changes have been heavily policed; regimes became more repressive as internal discontent grew during the late 1980s, and political protest was criminalized. This is an important paradox of reform in certain cases, though it is not necessarily so everywhere. Neither is it necessarily clear-cut.

Despite a competitive party system and regular fair elections, Botswana, for one, has since the 1960s been characterized by authoritarianism based on extensive presidential powers and a hierarchical and inequitable society. The early 1990s saw pressures for greater openness and participation, which resulted in some concessions (such as limiting presidential terms), but the political elite tended to classify demands in terms of lawlessness. Popular demands had become increasingly vocal by the time of the elections in October 1994, and serious public disorder resulting from student unrest followed in early 1995. President Ketumik Masire's state-of-the-nation address in November 1995 was pointedly devoted to crime and punishment, but it is unlikely that he was referring solely to crime that had spilled over from South Africa. Masire said that his government was worried by changing social trends but that student protests (which Good suggests had resulted from agitation against unresponsive authoritarianism) were illegal.[47] Certainly the response of the Botswana police was heavy-handed. They considered their public order training to be of a high standard in the region, though they evidently found it difficult to cope with the rioting (originating in the murder of a young girl) of early 1995. Armed police using live ammunition, tear gas, and batons, along with the Special Support Group and the Botswana Defence Force, clashed with student groups, commuters, and children on that occasion.

I do not consider the political developments of the early 1990s in detail here. My overall understanding of events is based on work by Bratton and van de Walle and Chabal because of their emphasis on pragmatic transformation, pragmatism being a key police trait. Bratton and van de Walle judge that the early 1990s represent a succession of transitional events (lasting for about five years) that precipitated a few key political trends. They suggest that political protest peaked in 1991 and liberalization in 1992, whereas most electoral activity occurred in 1993. The indicators of democracy continued to rise in 1994, though it was clear even then that the democracy movement had been unsuccessful in many cases: "Transitions away from one-party and military regimes started with political protest, evolved through liberalization reforms, often culminated in competitive elections, and usually ended with the installation of new forms of regimes."[48] Chabal's interpretation of how regimes attempt to keep themselves in power by force is linked to the definition of state policing I proposed. But as I show in Chapters 6 and 7, such an application of force is complicated by the nature of post–cold war states and the unwillingness or incapacity of insecure regimes to organize the police into efficient units. Thus, force is often applied in arbitrary and unpredictable ways at the hands of underpaid and undisciplined agents.

Liberalization involves potential operational changes in policing, especially in relation to the control of political activity, the release of political prisoners, and the removal of government censorship. But the advertised political liberalization has not been accompanied by fundamental changes in the organization or use of coercive power. Neither has there been institutionalization of the public accountability—or any other form of citizen oversight—of police agencies. There are few visible signs that African states are becoming more responsive to the needs of citizens. The police continue to be above the law, often using torture as a basic investigative technique when questioning criminal suspects, political prisoners, and opposition activists. Concern for human rights is considered to fetter police work. In 1993 President Daniel Arap Moi of Kenya, for one, empowered the police to avert the anarchy and civil war he claimed his opponents were prepared to unleash in their pursuit of political pluralism. He said that police commissioners must "use all the apparatus at their disposal to deal with the menace."[49]

That changes to policing have been superficial is unsurprising, for the degree of political change is debatable, with personal relationships between the "big man" and his followers remaining the core feature of African politics. Neopatrimonial politics, in which prevailing social norms make no distinction between public and private realms, penetrates all bureaucratic organizations. Political leaders fight for state prizes because they are a means to personal gain and the accumulation of the resources necessary to build a following.

Bratton and van de Walle identify three informal stable institutions resulting from this situation. The first they call presidentialism. This is the systematic concentration and personalization of political power in the hands of one individual, most vividly expressed by President Kamuzu Banda's comment in 1972 that "nothing is not my business in this country: everything is my business, everything."[50] Second, the fact that strongmen rely on the award of personal favors produces systematic clienteles, which encourage corruption and coercion. Third, and closely linked to clientelism, is the use of state resources for political legitimation. The consequence of these characteristics is that rulers survive through clientelism, compliance, and coercion. It is predictable that the formal institutions of internal security, especially policing, evolve and adapt to such pressures rather than undergo fundamental structural change.

The Broad View

There are naturally some limitations to my approach for understanding policing and national development. I have already mentioned the definitional problems associated with the police and policing in Africa; the networks requiring identification are processes as much as they are structures and as such are always difficult to identify. The collection of secondary data by government agencies and the production of police registers (from which information on the cases reported and the number of people taken to court are extracted) are often incomplete, especially in rural areas. Information may be haphazardly recorded in a mix of files, registers, and forms by semiliterate officers who receive little training in the filling out of dockets (which may, in any case, be in short supply). Criminal statistics are rarely available, and the scarcity and impenetrability of those that are may be compounded by poor documentation procedures, political instability, illiteracy, and conflict.[51]

Nevertheless, the notion of police systems' adapting over time is a useful tool because it not only indicates the overall type and shape of an existing force but also embodies a core of beliefs and practices about the legitimation of (and limits to) state and police power both in terms of the law and through adherence to widely accepted standards. It gives insight into the linkages among policing, internal security, civil order, political stability, and national development and produces a broad picture—even if it cannot answer specific questions about who controls the police or on whose behalf they act. That remains hidden. What is clear is that these links exist. There is thus a long way to go before the police arrive at the liberal democratic ideal that some observers of Africa propose.

Notes

1. Otwin Marenin, "Policing African States: Towards a Critique," *Comparative Politics* 15: 2 (July 1982), 385.

2. See Robert Jackson, *Quasi-states: Sovereignty, International Relations and the Third World* (Cambridge: Cambridge University Press, 1990), 195. Jackson also wrote that "once institutional arrangements become set they are difficult to change" (201) and that the institution providing independence could also be exploited to deny welfare: "International liberation could therefore be followed by domestic subjugation" (202).

There is a large literature on the nature of security from the perspective of African regimes, all of which are more concerned to preserve their own power than provide policing as a service. See, for example, Joel Migdal, *Strong Societies and Weak States: State-Society Relations and State Capabilities in the Third World* (Princeton, NJ: Princeton University Press, 1988); Mohammed Ayoob, *The Third World Security Predicament* (Boulder, CO: Lynne Rienner, 1995).

3. Michael Banton, *Policeman in the Community* (London: Tavistock Publications, 1964); James Q. Wilson, *Varieties of Police Behaviour* (Cambridge: Harvard University Press, 1968); David H. Bayley, *Forces of Order: Police Behavior in Japan and the United States* (Berkeley, CA: University of California Press, 1976).

4. See Cynthia H. Enloe, "Ethnicity and Militarization: Factors Shaping the Roles of Police in Third World Nations," *Studies in Comparative International Development* 11 (Fall 1976), 25–38; Cynthia H. Enloe, *Ethnic Soldiers: State Security in Divided Societies* (London: Penguin Books, 1980); Cynthia H. Enloe, *Police, Military and Ethnicity: Foundations of State Power* (London: Transaction Books, 1980); Ernest W. Lefever, *Spear and Scepter: Army, Police, and Politics in Tropical Africa* (Washington, DC: Brookings Institution, 1970); Simon Baynham, *The Military and Politics in Nkrumah's Ghana* (Boulder, CO: Westview, 1988).

5. This is true even of South African policing. For a survey of the literature on policing in South Africa, see John D. Brewer, *Black and Blue: Policing in South Africa*, (Oxford: Clarendon Press, 1994), 2–5. See also "South Africa" in John D. Brewer, Adrian Guelke, Ian Hume, Edward Moxon-Brown and Rick Wilford, *The Police, Public Order and the State* (London: Macmillan, 1988), 157–188. For South African Police crowd control methods and involvement in Namibian counterinsurgency campaigns, see Gavin Cawthra, *Policing South Africa: The SAP and the Transition from Apartheid* (London: Zed Books, 1993).

Preliminary work in articles such as Joab M. N. Wasikhongo, "The Role and Character of Police in Africa and Western Countries: A Comparative Approach to Police Isolation," *International Journal of Criminology and Penology* 4 (1976), 382–396; and Godpower O. Okereke, "Police Powers and Law Enforcement Tactics: The Case of Nigeria," *Police Studies* 15: 3 (Fall 1992), 110–117, remains undeveloped.

6. Marenin, "Policing African States," 385.

7. *Africa Research Bulletin* 34: 12 (1997), 12935. The archives of news services such as Reuters contain references only to episodes of extensive brutality or mass casualties caused by the police. Mentions of the opposite are rare. One such case occurred in Burundi (immediately after the UNITA deaths referred to earlier) when the UN special rapporteur on human rights noted that despite poverty and destruction in Burjumbura, a noticeable improvement in the security situation was mainly due to increased policing at the city's main intersections.

8. There are passing references to the gendarmerie in works such as J. S. La Fontaine, *City Politics: A Study of Leopoldville, 1962–63* (Cambridge: Cambridge University Press, 1970); Rene Lemarchand, *Rwanda and Burundi* (London: Pall Mall Press, 1970), 283, 356. I am grateful to the reviewer who drew my attention to Michael G. Schatzberg, *The Dialectics of Oppression in Zaire* (Bloomington: Indiana University Press, 1988), with its information on policing in Mobutu Sese Seko's Zaire. Full-length comparative studies of the organizational structure and operational techniques of a number of African forces do not exist.

9. The most consistently thought-provoking analyses of African policing since the 1960s have come from the United States, where comparative policing has aroused significant interest among scholars such Bayley, Lefever, Marenin, and Potholm. The pioneering article is that of Christian Potholm, "The Multiple Roles of the Police as Seen in the African Context," *Journal of Developing Areas* 3 (January 1969), 139–158. Lefever's 1970 study of the army, police, and politics in Ghana, the Congo, and Ethiopia from 1960 to 1970 is another significant development. The neglect is of course less marked among African commentators, and Nigerians in particular have produced many publications about policing and criminal justice in that country. See Philip Terdoo Ahire, *Imperial Policing: The Emergence and Role of the Police in Colonial Nigeria, 1860–1960* (Milton Keynes, UK: Open University Press, 1991); Clement Nwankwo, Bonny Ibhawoh, and Dulue Mbachu, *The Failure of Prosecution: A Report on the Prosecution of Criminal Suspects in Nigeria* (Lagos: Constitutional Rights Project, 1996); J. D. Ojo, "The Police Under the Nigerian Constitution," *African Notes* 17: 1 and 2 (1993), 13–31.

10. David Bayley, ed., *Police and Society* (London: Sage, 1977), 7. See also David Bayley, *Patterns of Policing: A Comparative International Analysis* (New Brunswick, NJ: Rutgers University Press, 1985).

11. The realities of policing were not always included in such calculations. In the neighboring southern state of Mozambique, the police were unrealistically expected to support the electoral process in a nonpartisan fashion even though their reputation for corruption and brutality was notorious. See Africa Watch, *Conspicuous Destruction: War, Famine and the Reform Process in Mozambique* (Washington, DC: Africa Watch, 1992); Chris Alden, "The UN and the Resolution of Conflict in Mozambique," *Journal of Modern African Studies* 33: 1 (1995), 124.

12. The U.S. Joint Coordinated Equipment and Training (JCET) program, for example, has provided training and supplies to "professionalize" policing in more than thirty African states in recent years. In contrast, more than 1,000 high-ranking officers from eighty-three countries worldwide attended the overseas command course at the British Police Staff College from 1970 to 1990. A low response rate to inquiries has made it difficult to chart their career progress since, but a 1991 evaluation exercise carried out on those who attended between 1985 and 1989 estimated that 82 percent had since been promoted, with 20 percent achieving the most senior ranks.

13. See Mike Brogden and Clifford Shearing, *Policing for a New South Africa* (London: Routledge, 1993). One exception to the general lack of interest shown in police aid was U.S. research on the activities of the U.S. Office of Public Safety established by President John F. Kennedy in 1961. See the Center for Research on Criminal Justice, "Policing the Empire," in the Center for Research on Criminal Justice, *The Iron Fist and The Velvet Glove: An Analysis of the U.S. Police,* 2nd ed. (Berkeley, CA: Center for Research on Criminal Justice, 1977), 160–174.

14. See World Bank, *Demobilization and Reintegration of Military Personnel in Africa: The Evidence from Seven Country Case Studies,* Report IDP-130 (New

York: World Bank, 1993); World Bank, *World Development Report 1997: The State in a Changing World* (Oxford: Oxford University Press for the World Bank, 1997); Mats R. Berdal, *Disarmament and Demobilisation After Civil Wars: Arms, Soldiers and the Termination of Armed Conflicts,* Adelphi Paper 303 (London: Oxford University Press for the International Institute for Strategic Studies [IISS], 1996); Mats Berdal and David Keen, "Violence and Economic Agendas in Civil Wars: Some Policy Implications," *Millennium* 26: 3 (1997), 795–818.

15. See Adedokun A. Adeyemi et al., "Ordinary Crime and Its Prevention Strategies in Metropolitan Lagos," in Hernando Gomez Buendia, ed., *Urban Crime, Global Trends and Policies* (Tokyo: UN University, 1989); Anna Alvazzi del Fratte, Ugljesa Zvekic, and Jan J. M. van Dijke, *Criminal Victimisation in the Developing World* (Rome: UN Interregional Crime and Justice Research Institute [UNICRI], 1995).

16. See Brogden and Shearing, *Policing for a New South Africa.* The notion of private policing also fits neatly into the neoclassical models fashionable in the West.

17. The same is true of governments. Consider an observation by Jackson and Rosberg: "In African countries governance is more a matter of seamanship and less one of navigation—that is, staying afloat rather than going somewhere." Robert H. Jackson and Carl G. Rosberg, *Personal Rule in Black Africa: Prince, Autocrat, Prophet, Tyrant* (Berkeley: University of California Press, 1982), 18.

18. J. Turk, "Policing in Political Context," in R. Donelan, ed., *The Maintenance of Order in Society* (Ottawa: Canadian Police College, 1982), quoted in Otwin Marenin, "The Police and the Coercive Nature of the State," in Edward S. Greenberg and Thomas F. Mayer, eds., *Changes in the State: Causes and Consequences* (London: Sage, 1990), 127.

19. John D. Brewer expands on this understanding in "Some Observations on Policing and Politics—A South African Case Study," *Policing and Society* 4: 1 (1994), 175–189.

20. The opposite was true when Zimbabwe sent 1,500 military police to Democratic Republic of Congo in November 1998 because it was thought that troops there were on the verge of a mutiny. The military police were used for routine duties such as guarding prisoners, traffic control, and routine discipline.

Zaire became known as the Democratic Republic of the Congo in May 1997, following the success of Laurent Kabila's rebel alliance in removing President Mobutu from power. Before 1971 there were two states in Africa called Congo. The former Belgian Congo changed its name to Zaire at independence in 1971, while the former French Congo (sited north of the Congo, or Zaire River), with its capital at Brazzaville, kept its old name. The two states were often distinguished by the addition of their capitals: Congo-Brazzaville and Congo-Kinshasha.

21. Michel Foucault, trans. Alan Sheridan, *Discipline and Punish* (London: Penguin, 1991).

22. The airport was kept open by regular soldiers. *Africa Research Bulletin* 29: 3 (1992), 10515.

23. This should be seen in perspective. African police may live in miserable circumstances, but seven years after the and of the cold war the Hungarian police, to name a European force, were reported to be in a state of crisis. Many officers in the capital were effectively homeless or lodged in industrial accommodations unfit for human habitation, yet money was lavished on extravagant building projects for new headquarters. *International Police Review* (January/February 1998).

24. Legitimacy implies that the activity is in some way acceptable. See Seymour M. Lipset, "Social Conflict, Legitimacy, and Democracy," in W. Connolly, ed., *Legitimacy and the State* (Oxford: Basil Blackwell, 1984), 88. In policing terms, the appropriateness of a force is generally taken to mean acceptance or compliance by the majority of a population, though Reiner argues that it is not necessary for police work to be accepted or condoned by all because policing is always against the interests of someone or some group. Robert Reiner, *The Politics of the Police,* 2nd ed. (Brighton, UK: Harvester, 1992), 4.

25. R. Daft, *Organization Theory and Design* (St Paul, MN: West, 1992), 9. See also P. Terrence Hopman, "Complexity and Uncertainty in International Systems," *Mershon International Studies Review* 42: 2 (November 1998), 313–316.

26. *Africa Research Bulletin* 31: 2 (1994), 11338.

27. This may provide the key to the tenacity of repressive regimes and their police systems. In Schatzberg's words, "Insecurity and scarcity are the twin motors powering a dialectic of oppression." *Dialectics of Oppression,* 135.

28. Robert H. Jackson, "Juridical Statehood in Sub-Saharan Africa," *Journal of International Affairs* 46: 1 (1992), 1.

29. Ibid., 2.

30. See Jackson, *Quasi-states,* 193. Jackson suggests that securing a "less corrupt and more humane" government depends on those in control of government.

31. Robert Fishman, "Rethinking State and Regime: Southern Europe's Transition to Democracy," *World Politics* 42 (1990), 428. Schatzberg's analysis of Zaire is guided by definitions of states as "administrative and coercive organizations," reinforced by ideological mechanisms. See Schatzberg, *Dialectics of Oppression,* 4–5.

32. Michael Bratton and Nicholas van de Walle, *Democratic Experiments in Africa: Regime Transitions in Comparative Perspective* (Cambridge: Cambridge University Press, 1977), 9.

33. See *Africa Research Bulletin* 34: 2 (1997), 12580; *Africa Confidential* 38: 11 (1997), 8; *Keesing's Record of World Events* 43: 2 (1997), 41479.

34. The following account is based on material in *Africa Research Bulletin* 34: 2 (1997), 12580; 34: 3 (1997), 12626; *Africa Confidential* 38: 11 (1997), 8; *Keesing's Record of World Events* 43: 2 (1997), 41479.

35. Many of the Basotho work in South African mines, but thousands have lost their jobs as mining has been modernized in recent years.

36. Okereke discusses discipline in Nigeria, pointing out that the rules and regulations handbook (1976) defines discipline as obedience and respect to senior government and police officials. Accordingly, the average officer sees his job as "serving and protecting the interests of those in power." Okereke, "Police Powers and Law Enforcement Tactics."

A markedly military style of policing may be considered most appropriate. This appears to have been the case in Mauritius, where a new police commissioner (one of the most important state posts under the Mauritian constitution) introduced a number of projects considered to be in keeping with this approach. They included collaboration between the regional police and the Special Mobile Force to combat drug trafficking; the banning of the police motorcycle squad from controlling taxi drivers (because of a number of suspected cases of ransom demands); and the creation of eight squads authorized to search motor vehicles. See *Indian Ocean Newsletter* 645 (5 November 1994), 4.

37. Corruption can be defined as a particular public reaction to political or administrative behavior rather than an illegitimate act as such. The low wages are

an undoubted invitation to corruption. Zairian police, for instance, were reported to earn about $6 a month in the late 1980s. See Adedokun A. Adeyemi, "Corruption in Africa: A Case Study of Nigeria," in Tibamanya mwene Mushanga, ed., *Criminology in Africa* (Rome: UNICRI, 1992), 83–103; Alberto Ades and Rafael Di Tella, "The Causes and Consequences of Corruption: A Review of Recent Empirical Contributions," *Liberalization and the New Corruption, IDS Bulletin* 27: 2 (1996), 6–11; Mushtaq H. Khan, "A Typology of Corrupt Transactions in Developing Countries," *Liberalization and the New Corruption, IDS Bulletin* 27: 2 (1996), 12–21.

According to Transparency International, a nongovernment pressure group, Nigeria (along with Colombia) is commonly reported by international surveys as the most corrupt country in the world. See *Transparency International: The Coalition Against Corruption in International Business Transactions* (Berlin: Transparency International, 1997).

38. Swaziland's units, attached to each region, are unusual in that they also undertake operational roles such as border patrols and some crime prevention patrols.

39. None of these is clear-cut, least of all national security. Take the case of Lesotho: At no time since independence have any of Lesotho's rulers provided a coherent definition of *national security*. In practice, at least until the overthrow of Leabu Jonathan by the Lesotho Para-Military Force in early 1986, national security meant defeating the opposition Basutoland Congress Party's Lesotho Liberation Army insurgency (which was trained and supported by South Africa). Jonathan was replaced by a military regime. This consolidated military rule at the same time it maintained internal stability by focusing on internal national security, in which police action reflected the regime's survival concerns and the maintenance of the status quo. See Francis K. Makoa, "National Security with Reference to the Lesotho Ruler's Conception," *Strategic Review for Southern Africa* 19: 2 (November 1997), 111–121.

40. A. H. Pacey, T. B. Davey, D. C. Blakey, "The Nigeria Police, Future Training Needs. Report on Reconnaissance Visit, January 1988." Unpublished typescript, 7.

41. The Zimbabwe National Army is an example of a coercive agent in which authority is increasingly based on patron-client relationships in addition to organizational structures. There is a trend, for example, toward a clientalistic relationship among officers, chiefs, and other ranks. See Eric T. Young, "Chiefs and Worried Soldiers: Authority and Power in the Zimbabwe National Army," *Armed Forces and Society* 24: 1 (1997), 133–149.

42. Marenin, "Policing African States," 389.

43. In his continent-wide survey of governments elected in multiparty elections, Wiseman estimates that the proportion of African countries with competitive party systems increased from 10 percent to 75 percent between 1989 and 1995. John Wiseman, *The New Struggle for Democracy in Africa* (Aldershot, UK: Avebury, 1996).

44. Lynda Chalker, "Good Government and the Aid Programme," speech to the Overseas Development Institute, Chatham House, London, June 1991; Sammy Adelman, "Accountability and Administrative Law in South Africa's Transition to Democracy," *Journal of Law and Society* 21: 3 (1994), 317–328; Patrick Chabal, "A few Considerations on Democracy in Africa," *International Affairs* 74: 2 (1998), 289–303.

45. *Africa Confidential* 31: 15 (July 1990), 3.

46. Bratton and van de Walle, *Democratic Experiments,* 33; Patrick Chabal, *Power in Africa: An Essay in Political Interpretation,* 2nd ed. (Basingstoke, UK: Macmillan, 1994), 33.

47. See Kenneth Good, "Towards Popular Participation in Botswana," *Journal of Modern African Studies* 34: 1 (1996), 53–77.

48. Bratton and van de Walle, *Democratic Experiments,* 3.

49. *Africa Research Bulletin* 30: 1 (1993), 11238. Bratton and van de Walle state that regimes in Francophone Africa worked through their ministry of the interior or its equivalent in order to maintain direct control over the appointment of electoral personnel and the implementation of campaign and polling procedures during the early 1990s. They also note that opposition forces were often able to penetrate the state apparatus, and some public employees openly allowed their preferences to be known; some judicial and police officers (in unnamed countries) are described as refusing to implement orders to quash opposite rallies. Bratton and van de Walle, *Democratic Experiments,* 114.

50. Bratton and van de Walle, *Democratic Experiments,* p. 63. Quoting from Jackson and Rosberg, *Personal Rule,* p. 165.

51. Adewale Rotimi and Olufunmilayo Oloruntimehin, "Teaching and Research Network in Africa in the Field of Criminology," in Tibamanya mwene Mushanga, *Criminology in Africa* (Rome: UNICRI, 1992), 233–248. The authors refer to the continuing validity of Clifford's observation of 1965 that criminologists in Africa lack adequate data. Crime statistics can be reliably collated only for the period since 1991 in Uganda. See Paul Collier, "Demobilisation and Insecurity in Ethiopia and Uganda: A Study in the Economics of the Transition from War to Peace," in Jackie Cilliers, ed., *Dismissed* (Midrand, South Africa: Institute for Security Studies, 1995), 104–111.

In the same context, discussion about the police-state nexus should ideally employ structural variables such as specialization, hierarchy, and personnel ratios, and equipment and environment should provide specific variables. But this degree of information is also lacking for Africa.

2

Policing the Postcolonial State

Contemporary African police systems have evolved directly from those inherited at independence. There have been no revolutionary and few unprecedented developments in policing since the 1950s, and the distinctive features of national organization remain much the same as at independence (see Figure 2.1). This characteristic is important for two reasons. First, it emphasizes two fundamental attributes of police systems that provide a key to understanding the relationship between policing and national development—that they are evolutionary and superbly positioned to accommodate political change. And second, it shaped the environment in which the events of the 1990s took place.

The police forces of all colonial states played a major role during the transfer of power, though I focus mainly on the situation in Anglophone Africa. The administrative and operational control of such forces was politically significant because they were in closer proximity to nationalist and anticolonial politics than were any other government agents. The centralized bureaucratic nature of their organization was tempered during independence because whereas the colonial state represented a body of law, the postcolonial state was effectively controlled by an elite that had captured the organization of the state and established their own governmental priorities.[1] But this was not a clear-cut process, for although British colonial rule imposed a body of law, it also displayed an institutional bifurcation of regime law and popular authority; British common law was used for some classes of offenses and "native law" for others. This may also be understood as presaging subsequent problems of legitimacy, when states attempted to impose uniform legal codes.

Such points do not, however, in themselves explain why the policing systems inherited on independence should prove to be so easily turned into instruments of regime interest. Nor do they explain why, if they were not

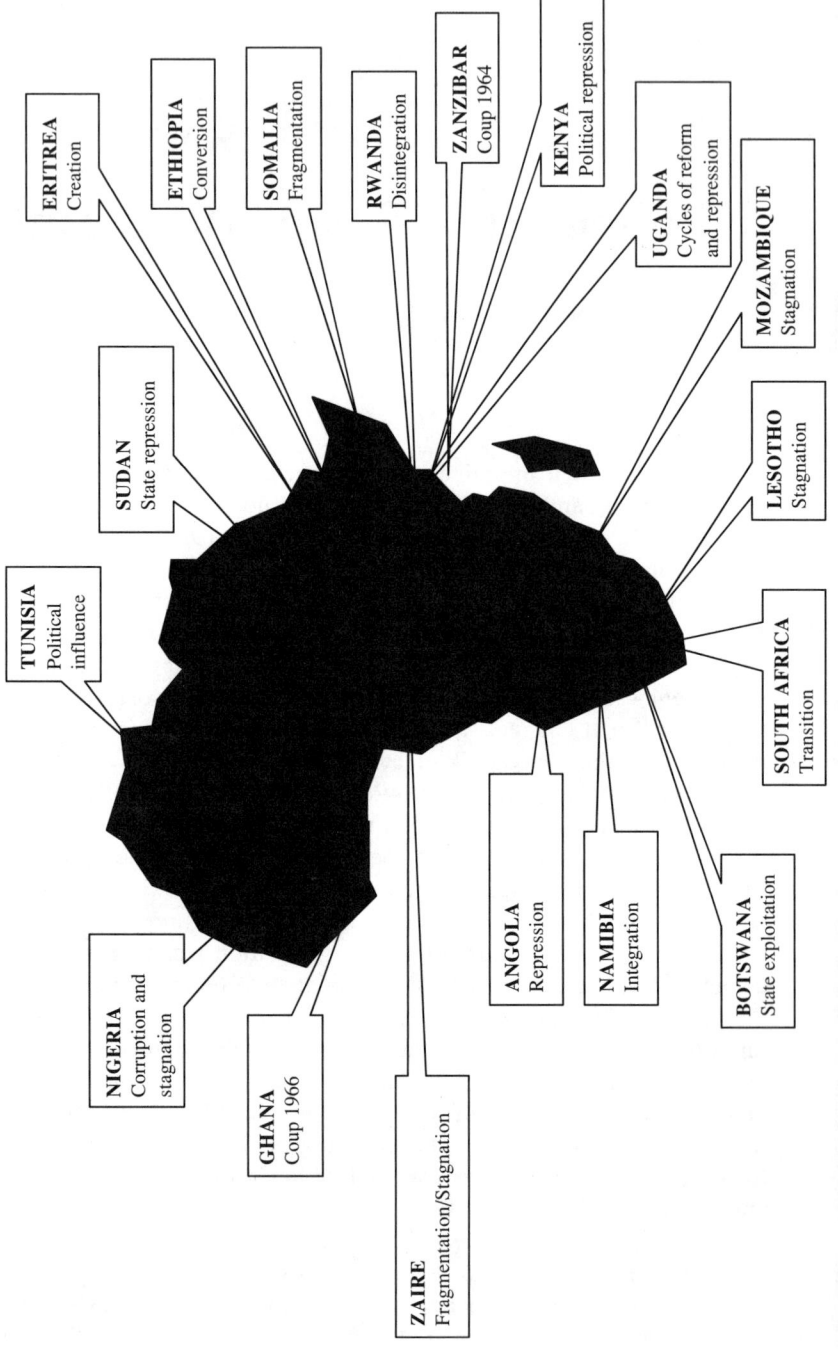

Figure 2.1 Policing in Africa: Thematic Diversity Since Independence

inherently inadequate, they so easily lost the European concept of the police as agents of the law. Nevertheless, the legacy of postcolonial policing provides a key to the nature of the police and the state in Africa, which is relevant to the debate over liberalization in the 1990s.

Colonial Policing

No accurate account of policing before the arrival of the British in Africa can be given because there are few records. It is likely, though, that many of the most powerful traditional rulers maintained bodies of men whose roles could be likened to those of the police.[2] But whether policing as a permanent, rule-based institution was an alien Western imposition had become for all practical purposes an irrelevant issue by 1960 because it was an accepted attribute of states in the same way that lawmaking and prisons were. That colonial law, for example, was radically different from precolonial customs in terms of the scope of jurisdiction and procedures is undisputed: "But whether one looks at pre-colonial custom romantically and nostalgically or tries to look at it dispassionately, it is quite irretrievably past. It may be important as a myth of national identification but it cannot be regained."[3]

It is typical that customary law in postindependence Africa is actually a mix of traditional and modern law infected with alien values. And the same is true of penal systems, as was acknowledged by the Ugandan minister of justice at a Pan-African seminar on prison conditions in 1996. He said that prisons may not be indigenous to Africa but they have proved a useful means of controlling criminals and opponents.[4] In other words, African criminal justice systems may be a colonial invention, but they soon became entrenched as part of the independent state's coercive apparatus.

British colonial policy had kept the institutions of policing as British as possible.[5] The guiding forces—before direct nationalist challenges—were that policing was essentially concerned with the preservation of order and (only then) the prevention of crime and that the police were agents of the law rather than of specific governments.[6] It was accepted that the institutions of British policing had to be modified to fit local conditions and that the constabulary concept needed to be strengthened in order to contain unrest. There was a consequent blurring of the distinctions between policing and the military as provision was made for police deployment in gendarmerie and frontier military roles (such as the British West African Frontier Force and the King's African Rifles of British East Africa), with the forces concerned under the control of a central rather than local authority. That such needs led to the superimposition of the traditions of the prepartition Royal Irish Constabulary, which had received a military training, is documented by authors such as Ahire, Clayton and Killingray, and Jeffries.[7] A consequence of this was that direct coercion, or at least the threat of it (through the adoption of special powers and emergency provisions), in place of the rule of law was a feature Ireland shared with states such as Nigeria.

As nationalist fervor increased in the 1940s and 1950s, it became clear that such styles of policing were more suited to public order situations than to politically sensitive protests. After 1945, therefore, the constabulary concept was strengthened as far as educational and political conditions allowed, and military techniques were kept for emergencies. This represented a crucial if short-term break in policing because it provided clear institutional boundaries between the police and the military, at least in urban areas.

As decolonization progressed, the role of the police increased in importance. They managed the transitional process as it affected the mass of the population, for they controlled anticolonial protests in towns such as Accra in 1948. The result was that policing in the 1950s was dominated by issues such as "the impact of nationalist politics, the difficulties of policing communal conflicts, the militarisation of police forces and their use in counter-insurgency measures, political intelligence-gathering and its use, and the reform, development and shifting ideologies of policing."[8]

Effective police forces were vital during transition, particularly as their role changed from principal agent of colonial control to servant to inexperienced governments. But to the extent that nationalist politics was salient in individual colonies, the police often came out on the wrong side politically in the run-up to independence. The problems confronting policing during this period are well covered by Anderson and Killingray, whose studies of Ghana, Kenya, and Malawi show that the police were in fact "weak, ill-organised and poorly funded, unsuited to effective civilian policing or to combat potential threats to internal security."[9] At the same time, police faced unprecedented pressure from demands for expansion, Africanization, new responsibilities, and rapid political change.

Independence

The postcolonial state was to be constructed on the foundations of the colonial state, but this resulted in a situation in which neither the political systems created at independence nor the police systems that were to regulate them had roots in the societies they were to order. Police forces were alien organizations, but their inappropriateness was mitigated by three factors. First, all fully fledged states were understood to have police forces; indeed, it is noticeable that all the new states had police forces even though not all had armies. Second, unlike colonial rulers, new African regimes needed some form of police because they had no higher authority to draw on if their authority or position was threatened. And third, the police adapted to the changed situation. These factors were reinforced by the essentially coercive and bureaucratic nature of colonial states, which had similar devices to enforce their administrations. Consensus may have been sought, but coercion and compliance remained fundamental and were usually translated into practice through policing. Vulnerable rulers, particularly after the coups of 1963 (in Togo and Benin) and 1966 (Nigeria, Ghana, and Benin again), quickly found that colonial emergency provisions and paramilitary police could serve their security interests, too. The essential characteristics of African policing were thus derived from both European systems and the Africanization policies marking the adaption of colonial patterns of thought and organization to African realities.

This process of adaptation was furthered by the rapid changes in the organization of national and district-level government after independence. In Uganda, for instance, a political compromise resulted in a mix of federal, semifederal and district areas with variable status, and President Milton Obote's political priority was to form the various units into a cohesive state. Accordingly, the relationship between the districts and the central government was transformed so that the center exerted greater control. The reform of the judiciary, creating a uniform system of courts and law for the whole of Uganda, was part of this process and was accompanied by a similar process in the police. Similar developments took place in most colonies.

The result was that the first ten years of independence saw a sweeping transformation of authority patterns at the local level, most marked in the replacement of the all-purpose authority of the chief with a multiplicity of government agents whose work was not directly coordinated with that of the chiefs. The new patterns of authority highlighted the lack of effective groupings capable of protecting individuals or acting as a check on interpersonal violence. In a real sense, the state had become more remote in rural areas, leaving individuals to deal with a distant police force, an alien judicial system, and chiefs whose powers had been dramatically weakened.[10]

The state police were initially tied to colonial rule more closely than the military because any redefinition of crime and its supporting judicial processes was more complex than the redirection of an army task (though unwanted procedures or inheritances were rapidly ignored or replaced). But it was not long before the military became the regime in a number of states, taking direct control in Ghana and Nigeria in 1966, for example, and in Sierra Leone the following year. Both security forces represented significant pressure groups and could act almost as trade unions; it was clearly in their interest to adjust their demands and position so as to gain as much profit as possible from the new state system.

In retrospect the policing systems inherited on independence appear inadequate and exploitable. But it is unclear what could have taken their place, given that the new states expected to have police. The reasons the European concept of the police as agents of the law was lost so easily is a reflection on African politics and the tight relationship betwen policing and political developments. It is less a matter of dysfunctional policing than a result of the attempt by state officials to maintain order in ways that did not undermine their own hold on power. Serious moves to strengthen professional standards were made in British colonies in the 1950s, partly in response to political pressures, but the actions were far too late.[11] The attempts were not seriously disrupted by nationalist politics, which unintentionally accelerated reform by bringing more resources to policing. But the transfer of power and independence raised serious issues about the operational and administrative management of forces because the new governments needed to control "their" police, who, with the army, underpinned their newly acquired authority. It was often rational for the new government to deprive the police of resources in these circumstances, since they might be used against the regime itself or its interests.

Policing was inevitably modified to suit the new political environment in which the nature of sovereign authority changed from that of officeholders (whose powers were specified by an imperial authority and who could ultimately rely on the protection of an imperial army against internal threats) to those where new rulers were limited by either a new national constitution or personal domination. In the first decade of independence, this usually resulted in deterioration of the reliability and capability of the police, the political results of which soon became clear in countries such as Ghana, where President Kwame Nkrumah purged the police hierarchy and subordinated the security services to his personal control following an assassination attempt against him by a constable in 1964. Such events emphasize that the critical break in policing in Africa occurred during the shift from colonial to postcolonial politics. The disjunction formed part of the loss of institutional coherence experienced by many governments when the external support of imperial armies was removed, for it had not been possible for native constabularies or military forces to seize power against a colonial regime.

Nkrumah's relations with his police provide a well-documented illustration of the relationship between power and authority on policing in the early years of a postcolonial state. The Gold Coast Police Force of the 1940s had been a disciplined body. The transition to independence passed smoothly, according to the British officers interviewed by Clayton and Killingray, because of the following factors: ten years' careful preparation for the Africanization of senior ranks, the absence of settlers and a color bar, Ghanaian respect for traditional authorities, and the existence of a large middle class that had property to protect.[12] In addition, the Ghana Police Force had good relations with the judiciary and the military. Not only did the police remain loyal to the concept of upholding the law immediately after independence, but they also accepted being organized into one national police force—which provided a safeguard against the influence of local politicians.

National politicians were another matter, as the events of the early 1960s made clear. Ghana did not suffer from class conflict so much as competition between elites, each trying to gain control of resources associated with state power. As Simon Baynham (whose study of the 1966 coup I follow) makes clear, power and patronage were overwhelmingly concentrated in the state apparatus as personified by Nkrumah, whose authority was dramatically challenged by bomb explosions and a number of assassination attempts in the early 1960s, including one by an armed police constable who may have been in the pay of senior police officers. The result of the last incident was a purge of the police command and the reallocation of security responsibilities at the officers' expense. A major reorganization of the force was enforced, and the head of the Criminal Investigation Department (CID), J. W. K. Harlley, was promoted to commissioner of police. Two years later Harlley inspired and organized the coup against Nkrumah by the army and the police after Harlley's own position was threatened.

Two points of particular interest emerge. The first is that the police were identified with Nkrumah's repressive regime at the same time many policemen were more concerned with increasing their salaries (either through corruption or as compensation for falling salaries) than upholding the law. The second is that by early 1966 police grievances resembled those of the army, and the insecurity, political interference, and economic depression to which they were subject appeared to be underscored by existing (British) norms on non-interference and promotion policies. According to Harlley, Nkrumah's actions after the failed assassination attempt by the constable humiliated the service; they were designed to punish and control the police. The insecurity was then increased by the Police Service Act of April 1965, which made the president the sole appointing and dismissing authority. That the two most senior officers doubted their own security of tenure must have affected the timing of the coup.

It appears that although the coup could not have succeeded without the support of the army, the police played a decisive role in Nkrumah's downfall:

> Not only did the seeds of the plot spring from the top two police officials, but in the execution of the rebellion the police also performed a leading role. It was Harlley who was responsible for the detailed co-ordination of police operations with those of the army. . . . As Nkrumah himself admitted, "the police alone possessed the necessary vital information needed for . . . success."[13]

As commissioner, Harlley had a national force comparable to the army, a sophisticated communications system, an independent intelligence network, and close personal involvement in Nkrumah's security machine. The coup itself was a military affair, but Harlley's influence continued to be felt because he set the style of the postcoup rule when he joined the National Liberation Council (NLC). Under NLC rule, national and local leadership passed into the hands of the old elite of chiefs, professionals, senior civil servants, and wealthy traders. This solved the problem of the internal legitimization of the new order (though externally it was challenged for almost a year by several radical regimes). The police kept a low profile throughout the life of the junta because of the low esteem in which the military held them.

It would be inaccurate to say that the police gained no special favors from the coup. Lefever's assertions to this effect are called "misleading" by Baynham, who notes that the privileges and favors awarded included cash bonuses, calculated on a sliding scale according to rank; improvements in pay and conditions were financed by an increase in capital expenditure by the NLC. The police had gained new equipment when Nkrumah played them off against the military in the early 1960s, and the coup resulted in higher salaries, new uniforms, foreign visits, chauffeured Mercedes and Peugeots, and women for the senior officers. After 24 February 1966, they were at the core of top government, social, and diplomatic functions. They diverted scarce public resources for their own purposes and acquired considerable fortunes, building large houses in Accra and establishing friends and relatives in profitable commercial enterprises. The number of senior posts in the police force was expanded and Harlley was promoted to the new rank of inspector general of police. The Ghana coup was unusual, but it demonstrated that the police may themselves form part of a regime or elite.[14]

Characteristics of Postcolonial Policing

Postcolonial police systems proved enduring no matter what their status. Regimes had little room for maneuver in fundamentally redesigning the organization of their security forces, whereas senior or specialist police officers were well placed to judge events and the survivability of political figures; they had intelligence and communication networks that facilitated adaptation. Significantly, most police forces accommodated change without needing either overtly to intervene or to adopt foreign ideals. The rule of law, for example, may be understood by the West as representing impartial policing, but in Africa impartiality was (and remains) a novel concept—intelligence systems invariably became personalized and politicians expected to bend the rules for appointments and prosecutions. State security became defined in terms of regime security and was expressed in terms of the dominant type of political competition; state organizations such as the police become significant weapons. The police were inevitably entangled in the reorientation of political authority because they had to enforce law and order (and maintain their own interests) just as intimidation became an important political weapon.

Traditional systems of control do not appear to have been significantly exploited by the new forces, and the main characteristics of policing across most states remained paramilitary and coercive.

Paramilitarized Policing

There is no agreed definition of *paramilitarism,* but it seems reasonable to understand paramilitary forces, as I suggested earlier, as those "whose training, organization, equipment and control suggest they may be usable in support, or in lieu, of regular military forces."[15] It also helps to understand African policing if paramilitarism is defined in terms of relationships—the police to the military, the state and the dominant style of political power, and regime security as the enforcement of regulations—rather than solely in terms of command, special groupings, or operational styles. The prominence of paramilitary police in Africa is then more directly attributable to the fragility of civil order, the nature of political power, and the ambiguity surrounding the professional identities of various state coercive agents, some of which (such as the Nigerian National Guard set up in 1989 directly under the president) cover both conventional police and military roles.[16] The paramilitary nature of the police meant that they were potentially too powerful an instrument not to be centrally organized. As events in Ghana proved in 1966, there was always the danger that local strongmen or presidential associates could exploit the coercive powers of the police unless they were kept under central control.

The Nigeria Police Force (NPF) provides an instructive case. The NPF was the descendant of commercial and militarized forces such as the Royal Niger Company Constabulary (created in 1888) and the paramilitary Hausa Constabulary (founded in 1879). Although the police forces of northern and southern Nigeria were merged to form the NPF, headquartered in Lagos, in 1930, most police remained associated with local governments (native authorities) until the 1960s, under the First Republic, when their scattered units were first regionalized and then nationalized.

The NPF performed conventional police functions and was responsible for internal security generally and for military duties as necessary. Although officers were not usually armed, they were more adept at paramilitary operations than any form of crime prevention, detection, or investigation. Their performance record in the mid-1960s was much the same as in the mid-1980s, when the federal police minister acknowledged that they had recovered less than 14 percent of the $900 million worth of property reported stolen in the preceding six months.[17] Police collusion with criminals was common, as were official appeals to officers to change their attitude toward the public and become more honest.

Nigeria in fact had the worst reputation for corruption of any state from the 1950s onward. Tignor says that by independence in 1960, "many Nigerians regarded corruption as the main issue by which they and the outside world would judge the country's capacity for self rule."[18] The military seizure of power in 1966, for example, was publicly justified by accusations of civilian gross malfeasance. But corruption was only one of many issues in the 1950s. Thuggery in politics, lack of commitment to democracy, ethnicity, and bureaucratic incompetence and inexperience all were causes for concern, even though corruption dominated and became Nigeria's symbolic fault. By the 1960s and 1970s, "the personal deficiencies of the politicians, the dictatorial and anti-democratic impulses of the parties, and the penchant to use violence to accomplish their ends, were steady themes."[19]

In such a context, paramilitarism is unlikely to imply military skill. And NPF claims to paramilitarism should be seen in the light of a senior British officer's comments that although it was necessary to maintain such a stance in accordance with police regulations, both drill and musketry left much to be desired. Many constables carried weapons, even though they had no experience in firing them, and some of the guns in police stations or in operational use were dirty and rusty.[20]

The Kenyan police shared similar characteristics. They operated under the office of the president through a commissioner in Nairobi, a city that grew from the site of the principal railway workshops in 1896 to the center of government administration and the main industrial base of the country, as well as a major communications and business center for East Africa. The force was administratively controlled from police headquarters through provincial and divisional commands down to station level. Further, most Kenyan police stations were established during colonial times, when location was determined by race, not by size of population, so most remained in low-density, white areas. It is unlikely, however, that this differentiated the Kenyan police from those in other colonies that lacked such a police-settler relationship.

Such policing cannot be considered centralized. It became so in the sense that statehouses, in Ghana under Nkrumah, for instance, imposed a tighter control over the police, but the process was accompanied by the proliferation of armed units in Ghana and elsewhere. During the thirty years after 1965, Zaire saw the creation of the following agencies charged with maintaining order and enforcing regime directives: Centre Nationale du Documentation, Division Spéciale Présidentielle, Service d'Action et Renseignements, Conseil National de Sécurité, Garde Civile, Forces d'Intervention Spéciales, Forces d'Action Spéciales, Centre National de Recherches et d'Investigations, and Service Nationale d'Intelligence.[21] There were also many informal units, such as the Hiboux, often acting as death squads. This appears to represent strong institutional centralization, but in practice it meant fragmentation and incapacity. Mobutu probably feared an efficient force, so almost all the agents were strong enough to enforce some order and fear each other, while at the same time they were poorly paid, badly armed, and required Mobutu's patronage.

Coercion and Legitimacy

State policing was, when sanctioned by law or adherence to widely accepted standards or customs, legitimate. But policing also had a more subtle potential in that coercion itself legitimized certain state activities through the medium of repression or protection. Both affected the degree of political participation in a state, though they used different mechanisms. As Marenin comments, "Repression functions largely in a directly instrumentalist way for the state, but ultimately also can have legitimating or delegitimating consequences. Protection mainly affects the ideological processes through which states become legitimized."[22] The balance of repression to protection in African policing is always in favor of the former, and sustained repression eventually legitimized state rule as power was transformed into authority in states such as Ghana and Uganda. From a consideration of these processes, Marenin develops a concept of coercive legitimation that can be used to increase understanding of the nature of postcolonial (and contemporary) policing.

Marenin's argument can be applied to postcolonial policing here because he suggests that the police affect modes of legitimization in that they are important symbols of dominant political and legal norms. That Western-inspired norms of impartiality and service by the police proved so weak supports the argument that policing reflects the nature of the state in which it operates. Marenin closely links the two by suggesting that the police influence legitimation processes in specific ways and that control of the processes thus becomes a key aspect of governance, though he does not distinguish between legitimacy in the eyes of the population and legitimacy in the eyes of the state. According to his argument, the police can have an impact on state development by their semi-independent use of coercion and "specifically, through the effects of their coercive acts on the capacity of states to sustain existing legitimations or create new ones."[23] This may in turn be balanced by the fact (as Marenin notes) that repression can undermine legitimacy if repression is unsuccessful or overused and that appeals to (popular) legitimacy are a more effective way to achieve compliance.

The concept of coercive legitimation (in relation to the state rather than the population) does not address why the police act as they do, nor does it indicate on whose behalf they operate. It does not explain how legitimacy is promoted or lost, nor why policing, as an activity and organization, is recognizable as such. But it does stress that institutions such as the public police are endowed with their authoritative and legitimating purposes by the attribution of stateness. Used in this sense, *stateness* "refers to the functional ability of institutions to organise constraints and effect compliance to orient human action towards certain expectations and rules of procedure."[24] Stateness is thus the way in which the institutions of the state provide for the legitimation and exercise of police power—and a warning sign of failing legitimacy will occur when a regime loses control of its agents. There is a further relevant paradox: A popularly acknowledged legitimate police may become more effective and therefore a greater threat to a regime.

The argument runs the risk of circularity, but the notion of coercive legitimation is valuable because it emphasizes the lack of institutionalized means of change and the highly personalized and comparatively unrestrained nature of African politics. Power in the postcolonial state was regulated by personalized politics. The police may have accordingly carried out political (order) functions, but such politics is now less likely to be considered an acceptable system of "*public* governance or *rationalist* decision-making."[25] Yet coercive legitimation remains a useful concept because it stresses the distinction between observed and ideal relations to the state and throws light on the more general issue of the degree of institutionalization of state authority in Africa.

Politics and Policing in Malawi

Policing is often a more reactive—or submissive—activity than the concept of coercive legitimacy suggests, for it also operates in response to specific political requirements, taking its operational cues from regimes. The close relationship between policing and politics (and the slippage from British traditions this symbolizes) is illustrated by events in Malawi in the years after the replacement of the Nyasaland Police Force by the Malawi Police Force in 1964.

Originally a military organization with imported Indian soldiers, the Nyasaland police developed into a civil force during the early years of the twentieth century. By 1964 it had three divisional headquarters, each responsible for a number of districts, and four locally based inspectors attending the Metropolitan Police Training School at Hendon under the auspices of Britain's Department of Technical Cooperation. Civilianized uniforms symbolized the independence and legitimacy of the force; junior ranks were equipped with Terylene shorts instead of khaki drill, and drill bush shirts were replaced by gray wool shirts; headgear changed from a shako to a blue peaked cap.

Policing and politics were tightly linked from the beginning of the new state. There was a cabinet crisis when several ministers resigned or were dismissed in late 1964, but the force continued to carry out its duties under expatriate leadership. Crime increased during the first year of independence by about 26 percent, partly in consequence of political considerations. The drastic reduction in the police establishment also played a part, as did the release (to celebrate independence) of some 920 convicted criminals, of whom 103 were identified by crime scene fingerprints to have committed further offences immediately after their release.[26] Then, on 13 February 1965, armed rebels attacked the Fort Johnson police station and government communications center, seizing arms and destroying radios and telephones as part of an attempted coup. The attempt was foiled, however, when the police officer in charge escaped and notified Zomba (the former capital) of events, and other police seized the communication routes out of the area. The police and army then began rounding up known rebels, the police mobile force aided by Banda's personal militia, the Malawi Young Pioneers. The Young Pioneers' position was regularized during 1965, and they were given legal authority to act as an integral part of the government security services.

After Malawi became a republic in 1966 the training of locally based officers to replace expatriates accelerated, with a number completing British courses, and by the beginning of 1969 the first local officers reached the rank of supernumerary senior superintendent. During 1970 two Malawian officers were promoted to the rank of assistant commissioner of police for the first time, and in September of that year a Malawian who had joined the Nyasaland Police Force as a general-duties constable at the age of eighteen and risen steadily through the ranks was appointed deputy commissioner of police and commissioner designate for the force at the age of thirty-five. By 1971 the majority of the nonspecialist posts were filled by Malawians, leaving twenty-six European officers (down from a peak of 227 in 1962), of whom eleven were specialists.

It is difficult to judge whether this evolutionary transition resulted in a more professional police, because the political limitations Banda's Malawi imposed on the public police were sharp. Much police work was done by party organizations, and political developments meant that Malawi appeared to be free of many crimes during these years. The police were undoubtedly a low priority, and recruitment stagnated—many of the current staff in the establishment of about 5,300 for a population of 11 million are now near retirement age. There is still a regionally based Police Mobile Force of 600 that deals with public disorder and border patrols and is available to reinforce police stations, but serious shortages of equipment have limited tactical options for many years. There is no forensic laboratory and no equipment for ballistics training even though armed crime has increased dramatically. By 1995, criminals were exploiting the new system when they were bailed out or brought to court in accordance with the law, and it was popularly thought that the crime wave was connected to the activities of armed members of the Young Pioneers and the presence of many Mozambican refugees, as both groups have been heavily involved in crime.[27] In other words, the Malawi police were, like most forces, underresourced for political reasons; they were underpaid and underequipped, with inadequate transport and accommodation, and too few in number to control the population. This ensured that they could not become a political threat to the regime.

One incident vividly illustrates the regime's appropriation of the police and the courts as a means of enforcing order. In 1983 the police, acting on instructions from the authorities (that is, Banda), used hammers and clubs to murder four cabinet ministers who had refused to carry out Banda's orders. Three of those involved were known to be members of the Police Mobile Force in the special operations squad of the Malawi Police Force. The commission of inquiry set up to investigate the deaths was not established until after Malawi's first democratic elections had ousted Banda in mid-1994 in favor of Bakili Muluzi. That it was established, and reported six months later, is directly related to the new president's use of the deaths as a campaign issue. An unrelated shooting incident had provided the government with evidence to prosecute once powerful figures such as John Tembo, the heir apparent and then treasurer general of the ruling Malawi Congress Party.

Senior police appointments in the 1980s also reflect political concerns. There were, for instance, four police chiefs in eighteen months at the end of the 1980s. In October 1989, E. F. Mbedza retired on health grounds. He had taken over the post in early 1988 from L. G. Ngwata, who had himself held the post only a year, having succeeded the John Tembo stalwart Mac Kamwana. Ngwata's early replacement was attributed to his dislike of Tembo, which had aligned him with the army chief, who was seen as Tembo's rival for succession to Banda. Mbedza did not support Tembo and was soon replaced by his deputy.[28]

The Legacy of Postcolonial Policing

What, then, is the policing legacy of the postcolonial years? Many of the important characteristics of contemporary state policing were laid down in the 1960s and 1970s, and the environment of policing today is not fundamentally different from that of the 1980s because the political and social trends of the 1990s appear to have been superimposed on existing patterns of thought and behavior; corruption, (neo)patrimonialism, and poverty remain as strong as ever.

At present African police systems, like those of criminal justice, remain linked to their past, with methods of crime control and detection remaining substantially the same as in the 1960s.[29] The organization of most public forces remains similar, with units for both general policing responsibilities and special duties, the most significant of which include the CID, special branch, and general service units for riot control. Their formal duties remain the prevention and detection of crime, the general maintenance of law and order, and the protection of life and property, although these functions are consistently downplayed. For if the police do their job well, they could threaten their regime. They might launch their own coup or, if they were truly independent, they would investigate regime officials suspected of violating the law. It is thus not in regime interests that the police should become efficient, effective, or provide citizen protection. In general, regime concerns ensure that African police forces remain urban, underresourced, brutal, and stagnant.

Further discussion of these themes is best rooted in specific cases. I introduce the defining characteristics of urbanization, underresourcing, and stagnation by reference to the Anglophone states of Nigeria and Uganda, which I then compared with policing in the Lusophone state of Angola.

Policing in Nigeria

Though a number of organizational changes have occurred over the years, the NPF remains, for the moment, an archetypal, urban force, inferior in status and resources to the military. It was reaffirmed as the national police with sole jurisdiction throughout Nigeria by the 1979 constitution. (Constitutional provision also existed for the establishment of separate NPF branches "forming part of the armed forces of the Federation or for their protection of harbours, waterways, railways and airfields.") The NPF was under the general operational and administrative control of an inspector general responsible for the maintenance of law and order, but he was appointed by the president and was obliged to comply with any presidential directives.

Further reorganizations appear to have been prompted by military needs or perceptions, as in 1986, when reorganization, prompted by tensions between the police and army, was announced by the armed forces chief of staff. The police complained that the army had usurped their functions and kept their pay low. Fights over jurisdiction ensued, and in late

1986 the NPF was restructured nationwide into seven area commands in place of a command structure based on the states. Each command was under a commissioner of police and was further divided into police provinces and divisions under local officers. Five directorates (criminal investigations, logistics, supplies, training, and operations) under deputy inspectors general were formed. NPF headquarters, which was also an area command, supervised and coordinated the other area commands. About 2,000 constables and 400 senior police officers were then dismissed, but none of these moves changed the focus of policing.

If anything, the militarized character of the NPF was reinforced by another reorganization in 1989 when a Quick Intervention Force (separate from the mobile police units) was set up in each state. Each state unit (of between 160 and 400 police) was commanded by an assistant superintendent and equipped with vehicles, communications gear, weapons, and crowd-control equipment, including cane shields, batons, and tear gas. They were established specifically to monitor political events and control unrest during the transition from military to civil rule.

The proliferation of different units has, however, undermined the reorganization of policing. It appears that two things happened in the 1990s. First, Presidents Ibrahim Babangida and Sani Abacha feared effective policing for its potential, as an organization, to side with political rivals. They therefore created counterbalancing organizations (such as Babangida's National Guard) and deliberately blurred distinctions among policing, paramilitary, and counterinsurgency roles in order to deal with internal security threats yet ensure that armed forces could not endanger the regime. Second (and this is an especially strong trend), military rulers and local strongmen alike increasingly use irregular forces, such as the River State Task Force or "tax consultants," to enforce decrees. Studying the activity of policing thus offers greater insights than trying to determine who the police are. As I suggested earlier, it is reasonable to consider such activities as policing, even though the units concerned are tied to the agendas of individual politicians or factions.

Urbanization. The centralization of influence in the state and policing, combined with the presence of leading politicians and shortages of transport and communications, has meant that public policing is overwhelmingly an urban phenomenon in Africa. Rapid urbanization is also a problem in itself, compounding policing challenges, for it provides opportunities for corruption and predatory crime. In the big cities, rapid population growth has led to high rates of migration from other parts of the country, unplanned settlements, and pressure on the infrastructure of housing, transport, water, power, and drainage, which leads to slum development. The result is increased crime, which further highlights the inefficiency and corruption of police forces. The ratio of police to population in Lagos was 1:337 in the late 1980s; this was high for a developing country, but it existed because the elite were there, rather than because Lagos had the highest crime density in the country.[30]

Crime. Urbanization cannot be considered in isolation from the conflict, insecurity, and high crime levels endemic in Nigeria since the 1960s. Such factors cannot but shape policing. During the five years immediately before the Nigerian civil war of 1967–1970 (which resulted in about 2 million deaths), for example, mass violence was frequent, and the twenty years after independence in 1960 saw a number of coups and attempted coups that were exploited by various interest groups. The resulting insecurity was then aggravated by other fears, such as those concerning the illegal aliens attracted by the oil wealth of the 1970s.[31]

Ordinary crime (or the common crimes or offenses handled by the criminal justice system that are used to indicate trends) remained predatory. In Lagos in the late 1980s, it included murder, manslaughter, attempted murder, assault, stealing, burglary, housebreaking, robbery, and wounding rape. Kenya provides a useful comparison, for Nairobi had similar patterns but included infanticide, prostitution, abortion, and kidnapping as well.[32] Such categorizations result from social norms that appear consistent since the 1960s: After examining crime trends in Lagos, Buendia and his colleagues came to the conclusion that levels of crime were in fact related to major national political or economic events. For example, crime levels peaked in 1980, the first year of civilian government after an extended military interregnum, and again during the 1982 recession. In the same way, robbery levels remained high regardless. Violent crime seemed to decline when a new government took over or improvements in social conditions appeared possible; fraud peaked during prosperity.

Policing had little effect on any crime. Police (or soldiers) caught selling arms were threatened with execution in 1988 by President Babangida, but such a combination of partial enforcement and official corruption effectively *managed* crime because it punished only petty offenders, allowing most types of white-collar crime to flourish. Serious crime was popularly thought to reach epidemic proportions in the 1980s, exacerbated by worsening economic conditions and police corruption, but it is difficult to do more than generalize about crime levels because most of the countryside (where 75 percent of the population lived) was unpoliced.[33] The situation probably became much worse in the 1990s, as rogue soldiers also became heavily involved in criminal activities. An indication of the seriousness of the policing problem is that the major anticrime initiative of 1996–1998, Operation Sweep, used military units for police work. The significance of military involvement, especially when taken in conjunction with the organizational developments referred to earlier and the fact that the operation was driven by political concerns about dissidents, is unlikely to have been lost on the regular police.

Rural Policing in Postcolonial Uganda

Accounts of police systems in Africa are inevitably weighted toward the urban environment, but a useful counterweight to such views is provided by Suzette Heald's anthropological study of the Bugisu district in Uganda during the mid-1960s. She records how the weakening of state authority left the Gisu people using violence to control their fear. The Gisu organized themselves into vigilante groups and drinking companies, initiatives they saw as establishing a distinctive form of Gisu government with new and effective sanctions to control violence and to police and eradicate thieves and witches in their areas. Heald describes lynch mobs in pursuit of thieves as a "common sight in Bugisu."[34] Indeed, killings by mobs of this kind formed a significant percentage of the court cases she sampled.

Heald found the Gisu pessimistic when she started fieldwork there in 1965–1966. Villagers did not know what to do about problems with thieving neighbors, for their chief's powers were severely limited by the new government. The Magistrates' Courts Act of 1964 had significantly reduced the chief's authority by separating the judiciary from the administration, whereas previously chiefs had acted as judges, trying cases under the jurisdiction of the Native Courts Act. The chiefs were to some extent rivals of the police in that they performed functions the new state justice system took over. They adjudicated in dispute settlement and tax avoidance cases in rural areas, and they retained wide powers through their overall responsibility for the maintenance of law and order in their area, which allowed them to arrest persistent offenders of bylaws.

Gisu attitudes toward the police were ambivalent. The police saw vigilantes as a direct threat to public order and tried to suppress them. Government, however, did not provide the means to police rural areas on a regular basis. Even where the police were active, cases that were registered often remained unprosecuted. There were several reasons for this. Dealing with the high murder and violent crime rates would present a tremendous amount of work to the police. In addition, they were almost completely reliant on eyewitness statements to achieve a prosecution, since circumstantial evidence without forensic proof was unacceptable in the courts, and the only forensic evidence usually available was that of postmortem reports. Moreover, the police were not used to working in the villages and indeed could operate effectively only if the chiefs (who were local men) cooperated. But the chiefs tended to hold the same opinions as their villagers and so would press for prosecution only in response to local demand.

The result was that the police investigated just the serious crimes in rural areas and even then usually delegated their powers to local chiefs. Occasionally, in times of unrest, a few would be stationed in rural areas, but with little effect. In the face of this withdrawal, Heald considers vigilante groups to have operated in the spirit of rather than in direct opposition to the police. She refers to the people of one subcounty who drew up a list of twenty-five witches and thieves and issued an ultimatum to the police to the effect that the community would take its own steps if the police did not act within a month. Vigilantism was an attempt by people "to supply their own remedies for what they conceived as essentially local problems."[35] Policing was thus broadened beyond the activities of formal civilian groups.

Underresourcing

Deliberate underresourcing is a key factor in African policing. It has been the result of rational considerations by Nigerian regimes, for example, since such resources might be used against the regime concerned. The NPF's operating budget between 1984 and 1988 remained at an average of 370 million naira. This figure is not adjusted to inflation, but during a period of double-digit inflation it clearly represents a dramatic decrease in funding in real terms. The force did receive additional sums of N206 million in 1986 and N300 million in 1988, which represented between 2.5 percent and 3.5 percent of the total federal capital expenditure for the years concerned. The money was used to buy new communications equipment, transport (such as 100 British LeylandDAF Comet trucks), and weapons, but the NPF still thought its budget would have to double to meet its needs. The situation was not easily remedied because it seems that inefficiency, indifference, and entrenched corruption were also involved in the apparent lack of resources.[36] Forces such as the NPF appear to have stagnated rather than evolved.

Stagnation. Many of the reports written by visiting senior British officers to countries such as Nigeria during the 1970s and 1980s, identifying weaknesses and suggesting remedies (few of which have been acted upon), imply stagnation and a waste of existing resources. An example is provided by two reports concerning the NPF in the 1980s.

In 1982 the British government, under British aid arrangements, commissioned a report on the future training needs of the Nigerian force. The report identified a number of weaknesses relating to recruitment and training, clustered around the fact that "the police service does not attract applicants of the right quality for several reasons, the main ones being poor pay and conditions of service."[37] Recruits were paid a national minimum wage, with no overtime, and they had to buy their own mattresses and lecture notes and spend one-third of their monthly pay on food.[38] The minimum age had been lowered to seventeen, but this meant too many recruits were immature. Many were also barely literate, and 70 percent were unemployed before joining: "The worst recruits receive the worst training and become the worst policemen," the report noted.[39]

Training facilities left much to be desired. Some dormitories had no ventilation, electricity, or windows; the lavatories had broken down a year before the report's author, Albert Pacey, visited the Police College Maiduguri, but no repairs had been attempted, and Police College Ikeja had not had piped water since 1975. There were classes of 126 and 140 at Police College Ikeja, and, not surprisingly, "There is a belief in the Force that people are posted into training as a punishment."[40] Pacey concluded that NPF training was at least twenty years behind what it should have been.

Pacey returned to Nigeria in 1988 and reported that although his recommendations had either been accepted or noted, little had been done to implement many of them.[41] Nigeria's severe economic decline and fiscal problems in the years since 1982 had less to do with the NPF's failure to act than entrenched habits. By then the British government had stopped offering scholarships (because of Nigerian oil wealth even in the face of fiscal problems), so the Nigerians asked for the secondment of British officers to establish a central planning unit at Jos and a detective training school at Enugu. They also wanted scholarships for command courses and courses for trainers, drugs dogs and their handlers, antiambush security escorts, detectives, public order managers, advanced drivers, and drug intelligence officers.

In spite of Pacey's damning report, the stated objectives of the NPF remained unrealistically ambitious. President Babangida laid the foundation stone of Nigeria Police Academy (NPA) in the state of Kano a few months later. The NPA was to be modeled on the Nigerian Military University in Kaduna and would offer a five-year academic and professional degree programs. Grandiose ambitions and repeated requests for assistance effectively replaced basic reform, as Babangida also disclosed plans to obtain British technical assistance to create a central planning and training program to modernize and upgrade police training at the same time. Negotiations were also taking place with other donor countries; shortly before this, for example, the NPF inspector general had visited Algeria and was considering new training practices as a result. Nigerian requests bore little relation to the realities of NPF training. Apart from the addition of information technology, interests—and resources and skills—remain much the same now.

Aid. Postcolonial policing in Uganda and Nigeria emphasizes that aid alone has never been the answer to policing inadequacies, even though requests for and receipt of overseas aid have been a consistent theme since the 1950s. The value and significance of such aid is open to debate, for it may well have fueled the cycles of progress and regression exhibited by many forces, at the same time as it has satisfied donor politics and consciences during and after the cold war.

The form that overseas aid has taken over the years has varied according to the donor. British aid tends to be in the form of management expertise, whereas some other Western European states provide equipment but no training. In either case, the provision of aid is a political and, increasingly, commercial concern. In 1995, for instance, the British Home Office (prompted by the market philosophy of the Conservative government) embarked on an attempt to sell British policing techniques. The initiative followed a directive from Prime Minister Margaret Thatcher in late 1994 that each Whitehall department should examine its potential for overseas trade. At the time, the forensic science service, DNA testing methods, and database technology were singled out. An official was appointed, directly linked with the Department of Trade and Industry, and a Home Office minister of state led the first such trade mission to South Africa in early 1995.[42] The relevance of such initiatives to African policing is questionable. For example, Lesotho has a forensic science laboratory (under)-staffed by graduates who have received specialist skills training provided by Britain, but its facilities are seriously limited; fingerprints are filed manually, and exhibits are filed on shelves in the laboratory, thus creating a risk of contamination. There is no ability to undertake sophisticated procedures such as DNA typing.

A Comparison: Policing in Angola

In this chapter I have proposed that African policing is urban, under-resourced, and stagnant. A comparison of policing in Uganda and Nigeria with that in the Lusophone state of Angola raises interesting points of comparison that support this assertion, not least in terms of politics and overseas aid.

The national Angolan People's Police of the 1990s evolved from the Portuguese colonial police and the People's Police Corps of Angola, which had been established under the Ministry of Defense in 1976. The force had changed its name from that of "security police" to the "police" of Angola in 1975, but it remained centralized and militarized. Its three levels of command (national, provincial, and municipal) were centered on a national headquarters in the capital, Luanda, and it numbered about 8,000 men and women, supposedly supported by a paramilitary force of 10,000, in the late 1970s. The police were subject to ideological and institutional controls and were heavily influenced by Soviet, East German, and Cuban doctrines and practices that flowed through the advisers from these countries positioned in the security ministries. Cuban advisers provided most recruit training in Luanda, but some training was also given in Cuba and Nigeria. Indeed, the presence of and reliance on so many foreign advisers was eventually seen by the Angolan government as a potential security problem. There was never any doubt that the police should respond to political direction.

The police role in policing was supplemented by that of the People's Vigilance Brigades (Brigadas Populares de Vigilância, or BPV), a vigilante force created in 1983 as a mass public order, law enforcement, political and ideological public service force for urban areas. The brigades were also closely linked to the military (for whom they may have recruited), and expanded rapidly in areas affected by UNITA insurgency. A large number of soldiers from the People's Armed Forces of Liberty of Angola (Forças Armadas Populares de Libertação de Angola, or FAPLA) were integrated into the BVP to strengthen its numbers and technical military skills in 1984, and by 1987 the BVP was 800,000–1.5 million strong. Such a force was neither police nor military in the conventional sense and raises the definitional problems I described in Chapter 1.

It is difficult to generalize, but it is likely that in Angola as in other states experiencing rapid social change and the dislocation accelerated by conflict, migration from rural areas to cities and the growth of slums were exacerbated by warfare and serious economic problems, leading to a rise in urban crime and a black market. Illegal currency dealing and smuggling, especially of diamonds and timber, were frequently reported as major criminal offenses (often involving senior government and party officials). They were also political offenses in that they were strategies used by insurgents to finance their activities. The police were reckoned to be heavily involved in embezzlement, pilfering, and property theft. The enormous extent of this problem was indicated by an official estimate in 1988 that 40 percent of imported goods did not reach their intended customers because of the organized parallel market system. Criminalization was clearly not straightforward, and the government's characterization of UNITA and other insurgent groups as bandits, gangsters, criminals, puppet gangs, rebels, counterrevolutionaries, and the like suggests a political criterion. Whatever the case, criminal violence became indistinguishable from political violence, and fighting among members of the police, military, and bandits in a large, open-air market on the outskirts of Luanda regularly resulted in fatalities.[43]

By the late 1980s, years of neglect and war meant that the Angolan state infrastructure had fragmented or broken down, with inevitable repercussions for the police. The repercussions fell unequally: Some senior officers had well-equipped offices even as others suffered the effects of power strikes, broken equipment, and rising crime.

Conclusion

The police systems inherited on independence in Africa were not inadequate in themselves, though they were tied to the institutional coherence of colonial government. In retrospect they were inappropriate and easily exploited, but given the political imperatives of the time and the nature of both policing and the processes of state collapse, this was probably inevitable.

The fundamentals of contemporary police systems were laid down by the early 1970s, though the evidence I present in this chapter shows that the institution has become more fragmented since then. Political authority and policing authority were inextricably entangled by the 1960s and 1970s because the police had to enforce order and maintain their own interests at the same time intimidation (by and on behalf of regimes) became an important political weapon. Given the reactive nature of the policing, it is no surprise that the alien (and rarely understood) concept of impartiality was rapidly abandoned.

Thus, African policing has changed in various ways since independence, and a key element has been the interplay between politics and the police. There is consequently a need to identify the modalities initiated by political change. I develop a conceptual framework for this in the following chapters.

Notes

1. Corruption was not absent from colonial policing, especially at lower levels, such as that of court messengers. The role of the police and corruption in colonial Sierra Leone is covered in Martin Kilson, *Political Change in a West African State: A Study of the Modernization Process in Sierra Leone* (Cambridge: Harvard University Press, 1966).

2. Goody provides a salutary reminder that although the police and colonization have become identified with European expansion, "What rarely receives a mention is the fact that colonisation has also been a continuing aspect of the interaction of African societies, at least the centralising ones. Most traditional states arose by conquest." Colonization "had various indigenous counterparts in the form of invading dynasties and the like, and it can usefully be seen as a particular case of the many systems in which power was held by an elite, and order was combined with domination." Jack Goody, "Decolonisation in Africa: National Politics and Village Politics," *Cambridge Anthropology* 7: 2 (1982), 2.

3. Michael Reisman, "Towards a General theory About African Law, Social Change and Development," in P. N. Takirambudde, *The Individual under African Laws,* proceedings of the First All-Africa Law Conference, 1981 (Swaziland: Kwaluseni Swaziland Printing and Publishing, 1982), 186.

4. *African Topics* (15 November/December 1996), 13. When Banda informed the Malawi parliament of the establishment of a new prison for political offenders

in 1965, he said: "I will keep them there and they will rot . . . and they will rot and I am going to make sure that in addition to the regular prison officers we have additional warders . . . who . . . will know what to do with these fools. . . . They will knock some sense into their heads." See also Cyril D. Robinson and Richard Scaglion, with J. Michael Olivero, *Police in Contradiction: The Evolution of the Police Function in Society* (Westport, CT: Greenwood Press, 1994), 47–58.

5. In the same way, the main characteristics of the police in Algeria, Cameroon, Chad, Congo–Brazzaville, Guinea, and the Ivory Coast can be traced to French policies and practice. The police of the former French colonies were organized along French lines and were trained to French standards. See P. E. Igbinovia, "Patterns of Policing in Africa: The French and British Connection," *Police Journal* 54: 2 (April 1981), 127.

6. This may be contrasted with the police belonging to the Christian King Andereya of Bunyoro in the Northern Provinces of the Ugandan Protectorate in the 1910s. The missionary Albert B. Lloyd provides a description of the king's police in 1910 in *Uganda to Khartoum: Life and Adventure on the Upper Nile* (London: Collins' Clear-Type Press, n.d., [probably early 1910s]): "The King's police are always in attendance and are supposed to maintain order. Personally, I think they often make more noise themselves than the whole crowd combined. . . . The hippohide whip is the usual accompaniment of the native policeman when on duty, and he does not forget to use it freely" (57).

The police were much disliked because of their heavy-handedness, arrogance, and drunkenness. Some guilty policemen had been flogged and forcibly retired, but Lloyd did not think it made much difference to the quality of the force. The paramilitary theme emerges clearly in his account. During a later visit to the Acholi country to the north of Bunyoro, he commented that although the chiefs and richer men who visited the European settlement aspired to soldier's coats, the police bought up all the old putties of the government troops. The usual police dress included a black frock coat and linen knickers, though a photograph in Lloyd (opposite p. 72) shows seventeen policemen saluting while wearing miscellaneous jackets, baggy breeches, putties, and fezlike hats. Three in the front row wear shoes and one is wearing trousers. Two carry canes.

7. Philip Terdoo Ahire, *Imperial Policing: The Emergence and Role of the Police in Colonial Nigeria, 1860–1960* (Milton Keynes, UK: Open University Press, 1991), 55; Anthony Clayton and David Killingray, *Khaki and Blue: Military and Police in British Colonial Africa* (Athens: Ohio University Center for International Studies, 1989); Charles Jeffries, *The Colonial Police* (London: Allen & Unwin, 1952), 30. Jeffries judged that "the really effective influence on the development of colonial police forces during the nineteenth century was . . . the Royal Irish Constabulary" (30). By the late nineteenth century, the success of the British police in maintaining order in Britain had less to do with operational techniques than with the success of political institutions in providing class conflict with an institutional expression.

8. David M. Anderson and David Killingray, *Policing and Decolonisation: Nationalism, Politics and the Police, 1917–1965* (Manchester, UK: Manchester University Press, 1992), 4.

9. Ibid., 6.

10. For a well-written account of the state becoming remote in rural areas, see Suzette Heald, *Controlling Anger: The Sociology of Gisu Violence* (Manchester, UK: Manchester University Press, 1989).

11. The concept of professionalism is usual in this context but is in fact un-

helpful, for policing is not an occupation requiring advanced training in a specialized field in the way that law is. It is more accurate to see policing—in both liberal democracies and Africa—as a craft in which skills are acquired through experiences limited to those in the same occupation.

12. Clayton and Killingray, *Khaki and Blue*, 22.

13. Simon Baynham, *The Military and Politics is Nkrumah's Ghana* (Boulder, CO: Westview, 1988), 200.

14. That police interests may dominate calculations is also indicated by the visit of a new inspector general of the Malawi Police to London in 1988. He was looking for British aid in training and technology, but he also met representatives of security companies (such as International Military Services) in an attempt to strengthen the role of the police as Malawi's main internal security body and an important political counterweight to the army. *Africa Confidential* 29: 24 (1988), 8.

15. International Institute for Strategic Studies, *The Military Balance, 1993–1994* (London: Brassey's for the IISS, 1994), 5. See also Alice Hills, "Militant Tendencies: 'Paramilitarism' in the British Police," *British Journal of Criminology* 35:3 (1995), 450–458.

16. Ambiguity between police and army roles may lead to violent clashes such as those in São Tomé in 1992, when announcements that the police were due for a pay rise whereas the army was to be reorganized resulted in violent clashes between the two. About forty soldiers broke into a police station to free arrested colleagues. The police then fled, leaving soldiers to patrol the streets. *Africa Research Bulletin* 29: 8 (1992), 10691.

17. See, for example, P. E. Igbinovia, "Police Misconduct in Nigeria," *Police Studies* 8: 2 (1985), 110–122.

18. Robert L. Tignor, "Political Corruption in Nigeria Before Independence," *Journal of Modern African Studies* 31: 2 (1993), 175–202.

19. Ibid., 182. See also P. E. Igbinovia, "The Police in Trouble: Administrative and Organizational Problems in the Nigeria Police Force," *Indian Journal of Public Administration* 28: 2 (1980), 334–372.

20. A. H. Pacey, T. B. Davey, and D. C. Blakey, "White Paper on Future Training Needs of the Nigeria Police Force," Lagos, 1982.

21. I am grateful to the reviewer who provided this information.

22. Otwin Marenin, "The Police and the Coercive Nature of the State," in Edward S. Greenberg and Thomas F. Mayer, eds., *Changes in the State: Causes and Consequences* (London: Sage, 1990), 125.

23. Ibid., 129.

24. Gilbert M. Khadiagala, "State Collapse and Reconstruction in Uganda," in I. William Zartman, ed., *Collapsed States: The Disintegration and Restoration of Legitimate Authority* (Boulder, CO: Lynne Rienner, 1995), 34. Khadiagala is speaking of statist functions, but his words are applicable to policing.

25. Robert H. Jackson and Carl G. Rosberg, *Personal Rule in Black Africa: Prince, Autocrat, Prophet, Tyrant* (Berkeley: University of California Press, 1982), 18.

26. C. Marlow, *A History of the Malawi Police Force* (Zomba, Malawi: Government Printer, 1971).

27. *Africa Research Bulletin* 32: 5 (1995), 11859.

28. *Africa Confidential* 29: 24 (1988), 8. There is nothing unusual about such developments in the region, as the justice minister of Zimbabwe made clear in 1996. When accused of amending the constitution and eroding judicial independence, he said, "We make changes that are necessary to us." As lawyers pointed

out, since 1991 the Zimbabwean constitution had been amended four times to reverse decisions made by the supreme court, notably in cases where the government had previously lost in court. *Africa Research Bulletin* 33: 9 (1996), 12398.

29. See Hernando Gomez Buendia, ed., *Urban Crime, Global Trends and Policies* (Tokyo: UN University, 1989). A recent development that may influence future policing is that of drug-related organized crime, not because of its impact on policing so much as its interest to Western governments. Nigerians, for example, are notorious participants in international drug trafficking, with Nigeria a major transit point for heroin from Afghanistan, the Indian subcontinent, and the Far East, and for South American cocaine. It has good flight connections and an inexhaustible supply of couriers and entrepreneurial talent. According to the director general of the UK's National Criminal Intelligence Service, West Africa is now part of the mainstream of organized crime, and conservative police intelligence estimates suggest that fraud by West African criminals in the UK alone in 1997 represented a total of about £3.5 billion ($9.8 billion).

30. The size of a force bears little relation to its reputation. Compare the 40,000 officers dealing with Angola's population of 12 million in 1996, with Malawi's 5,500 for 11 million, or the Tanzania Police Force of 26,400 for a population of approximately 27 million.

31. There were also two big expulsions of illegal aliens in the 1980s. At least 1.3 million West Africans (mainly from Ghana, Niger, Chad, and Cameroon) were expelled in early 1983, and another 700,000 illegal aliens were ordered out two years later.

32. Subsequent details are from Buendia, *Urban Crime,* 413ff.

33. The per capita income fell from about $1,000 a year to approximately $300 in the 1980s. The relationship between the two is debatable, but police involvement in crime is not. In July 1987, for instance, soldiers had to disperse market traders after a six-hour fight prompted by anger at police harassment and extortion. And shopkeepers in Katsina market raised the alarm when police raided suspect stores in 1989—they thought it was a police robbery. The examples could be repeated for any number of forces.

The situation in Nairobi was similar. Police officers were probably behind a wave of armed robberies in Nairobi in daylight in 1996, which the police appeared to be unable to do anything about even though the government unit set up to respond to it included the police commissioner, CID chief, intelligence services head, and several other security officers.

34. Heald, *Controlling Anger,* 41.

35. Ibid., 249. Vigilantes also made up the core of the people's militia formed in the 1980s in Bugisu to protect the rural areas against the incursions of the civil war (254). I further consider vigilantism in Chapter 6.

36. President (General) Muhammuda Buhari had relied on his military for policing during campaigns such as the War Against Indiscipline (WAI) in the early 1980s.

37. Pacey et al., White Paper, 6.

38. The division between ideals and reality is evident here. Nigeria's 1974 Labour Decree established a forty-hour workweek, prescribed two to four weeks of annual leave, and set a minimum wage. The last government review of the minimum wage, undertaken in 1991, raised the monthly minimum wage from 250 naira ($11.36) to 450 naira ($20.45). See "Trade Compass," *Economic Policy and Trade Practices: Nigeria* (http://www. tradecompass.com/library/dos/ecopol/nigeria.html, 11 Aug. 1998).

39. Heald, *Controlling Anger,* 6.
40. Ibid.
41. Albert Pacey, T. B. Davey, D. C. Blakey, "The Nigeria Police, Future Training Needs." Report on reconnaissance visit. January 1988.
42. For British aid generally, see *Britain and Africa* (London: HMSO); *British Aid Statistics* (London: HMSO); *British Overseas Aid: Annual Review* (London: HMSO). Forty-five percent of the overall 1991/1992 figure of £1.8 million ($5.4 million) in aid went to Africa.
43. U.S. Department of State, Bureau of Democracy, Human Rights, and Labour, *Angola Human Rights Practices 1993* (Washington, DC: U.S. Department of State, 1994).

3

The Police and Politics

Police systems show remarkable powers of survival. It may be inaccurate to suggest that "police organisations do not adapt to the work they must do. Rather, the work they must do is adapted to the police," and much is left undone, as the evidence cited in Chapter 2 (especially from Nigeria) suggests.[1] But police systems exist across a spectrum of states—those where experiments with democratic governance have been a feature since the 1960s; those where they are a recent experiment; those where a regime is populist but military or where it is made up of elements from one party; and those where the social infrastructure is in the process of postwar reconstruction. Police forces are often inefficient or unreliable, and (as I noted in Chapter 2) their effectiveness and institutional coherence may be positively correlated with a country's economic performance. But whatever the case, they are evidently too useful (or potentially dangerous) for regimes to dispense with their services. It does not seem too extreme to predict that for the immediate future most states will continue to be run for the benefit of regimes that impose some form of coercive system in which policing plays a significant part.

Political Relationships

The emphasis of this study is on policing at a national level, but there are at least five levels at which relationships operate between the police and the political society in which they exist:

1. police and international concerns (expressed through Interpol and the concerns of the European Union, or EU, about organized crime, for example)

2. regional concerns (as in initiatives such as the Southern Africa Regional Police Chiefs Cooperative Organization [SARPCCO])
3. national concerns (Nkrumah and Harlley in Ghana in the 1960s, for instance)
4. provincial concerns (such as kickbacks from local councillors or promotion depending on politics)
5. local concerns (low-level bribery, for instance, or roadblocks).

They can be expressed diagramatically as a series of intersecting layers, as in Figure 3.1.

International and Regional Policing

Although African policing is in many respects specific to the continent, it needs to be discussed using the vocabulary of international policing.[2] One reason for using Western concepts (such as discretion) is that their absence may be as instructive as their presence because our understanding of policing is built on their use. There are in any case no internationally recognized policing qualifications, and ranks vary from country to country, though the lowest ranks in the different countries often have more in common than they do with their own chief officers, even though the latter may

Figure 3.1 Layers of Policing in States

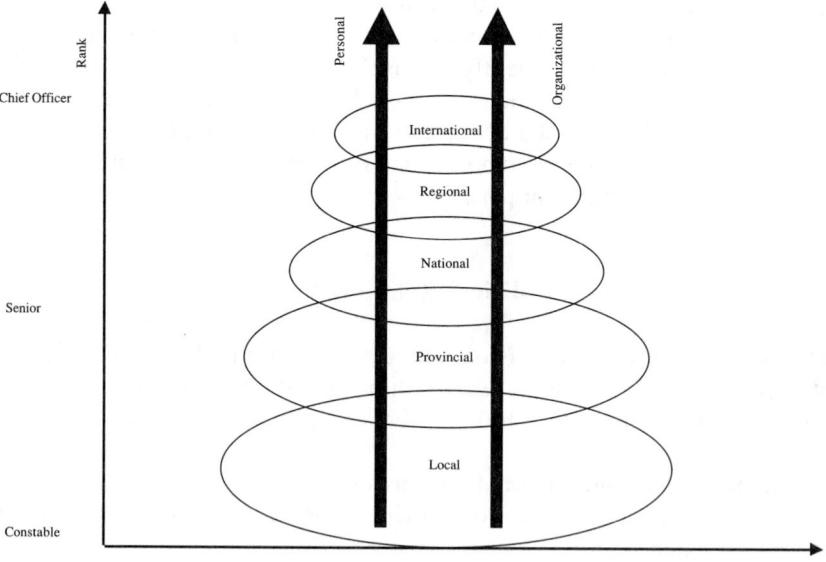

have risen through the ranks. Senior officers tend to belong to an international occupational culture through attendance at national staff colleges and connections with foreign forces or intragovernmental organizations such as Interpol and regional organizations such as SARPCCO. For this reason, I consider the idea (and limitations) of a regional layer of policing, particularly as certain problems (such as transnational organized crime) are increasingly acknowedged in many regions of sub-Saharan Africa.

SARPCCO. SARPCCO illustrates both the relevance and limitations of using the concept of regional policing. The organization was formally inaugurated in 1995 and consists of Angola, Botswana, Lesotho, Malawi, Mozambique, Namibia, South Africa, Swaziland, Tanzania, Zambia, and Zimbabwe. Its general aim is to strengthen cooperation among member countries in all aspects of operational policing, and it assumes the existence of an international police culture. The declared principles of SARPCCO are presented in a language derived from Western policing. They specifically include equality of forces, nonpolitical professionalism, mutual benefit, observance of human rights, respect for national sovereignty and bilateral agreements, and the amicable settling of differences.

These aims are ideals rather than descriptions of reality. There is, however, a recognition of the need to coexist and the cross-border nature of many policing problems. Recent regional efforts to combat crime, for example, include agreements among the interior ministers from Mali, Mauritania, and Senegal to combine efforts to combat drugs and arms trafficking and cattle thefts on their joint borders and to organize "simultaneous" patrols.[3] Cooperative efforts can also be illustrated by the Malawi-Mozambique Joint Security and Defence Commission, created to step up patrols and address crimes such as armed robbery, drug trafficking, and cattle and vehicle theft. In 1995 it was agreed that each security force could enter the other's country to capture thieves, and the two countries signed an extradition treaty to facilitate legal repatriation and the investigation of crime.[4]

The understanding such high-level, strategic agreements represent is limited to senior officers, as even those who have attended overseas command or training courses rarely transfer their experience or knowledge to others in their force on their return home. Although it might be expected that additional training would influence the way they do business, such courses are essentially a perk for senior officers, who come back to an environment in which conventional management skills may play little part.[5] Some senior officers, such as a Royal Swaziland Police commissioner trained in Zambia, may have experience of policing elsewhere on the continent, but this would be exceptional. The failure to pass on skills and experience is a problem common to many ranks across all forces.

A shared understanding undoubtedly exists concerning certain skills at the operational level, however, and is facilitated by such means as the sharing of training methods and programs. President Joaquim Chissano of Mozambique was so impressed by the effectiveness of Angola's notorious Spanish-trained riot police that he personally asked the Spanish prime minister for assistance in training Mozambique's newly created paramilitary police in late 1992.[6] And a number of Mozambican CID officers in regional headquarters were trained in either Cuba or East Germany before the mid-1980s (though there has been no training since). Other specialized facilities that have been operationally influential in the region include the impressive SAP dog training school, which has run training programs in patrol, tracking, narcotics, explosives, and other techniques for dogs and personnel from Kenya, Tanzania, Uganda, and Zambia. In this limited sense, certain foreign and regional training programs have had a practical impact.

The real limitations to regional policing are shown by recent developments in cross-border cooperation. A common understanding among chief police officers is, for example, facilitated by a round of conferences, such as that organized by Interpol in Harare in 1993, which proposed greater cooperation among forces dealing with drug smuggling, car theft, and other common types of organized crime. In addition, an Interpol subregional bureau in Harare has recently been created so as to enable the countries in SARPCCO to exchange criminal intelligence more promptly. Zimbabwe's senior assistant commissioner, Frank Msutu, head of the Interpol bureau, described this as consistent with the SARPCCO objective "to promote, strengthen and perpetuate co-operation and foster joint strategies for the management of cross-border crimes with regional implications."[7]

Despite such good intentions, however, regional policing is hampered by the environment in which it is expected to work. Cross-border crime along Nigeria's frontier with Benin, to take one serious problem, has no obvious solutions, for the boundary is over 1,000 kilometers long, highly porous, thickly forested in parts, and very difficult to police. Officials in both countries are complicit in the clandestine trade. And the creation of special units or battalions to deal with similar problems of controlling the frontiers with South Africa—and the smuggling of arms and so on from South Africa by the Mozambican police—has been intensely controversial. The deputy chief of staff of the Mozambican army (and former head of Mozambique National Resistance Movement's [RENAMO] intelligence services), for one, claimed that the police were unable to control such areas, adding that they increased the insecurity of the region. In fact, they are partly responsible for the problem.

Regional policing thus falls far short of the language of regional agreements. According to recent publicity, such deals should translate into instant cooperation: "Following a request the Interpol office in Madagascar will get, within seconds, a response similar to someone either at CID headquarters in Harare or someone from Tanzania."[8] The spokesman said that the extradition of criminals needs further attention because criminals take advantage of the absence of treaties. He is not, however, quoted as mentioning that such techniques will require not only language expertise in French, English, Portuguese, and possibly local languages but also fluency in police jargon. In reality personnel (especially on borders) lack common languages, procedures, skills, training, and report forms. Most forces cannot successfully prosecute serious crime even if they want to, because they have neither the necessary experience nor the capacity to deal with forensic analysis or crime scene examinations. Although some SARPCCO countries have units to tackle fraud, money laundering, and the identification of stolen vehicles, they rarely have the equipment, personnel, and training needed to do so effectively or indeed efficiently. The investigation of fraud, for instance, may take a knowledge of banking procedures and company law, whereas dealing with organized crime will always be an area in which only the most able detectives are competent.[9] To state that a force such as the Mozambique Police should train investigators to deal with drugs and money laundering is laudable but unrealistic for a number of reasons, not least of which are entrenched corruption (in both regime and police), low pay, low skills, shortage of resources, and cultural norms. The accommodation, training, and resources such staff need are usually lacking; there is rarely any means of analyzing or disseminating intelligence; and few countries have the expertise or resources to deal with sophisticated criminals operating at national and international levels.

Transnational crime. The scale of the problems facing SARPCCO members becomes clear in looking at transnational organized crime. Policing in southern Africa has been confronted by the tremendous rise in crime attending the end of apartheid. This is not a variable in many other cases, but it is a major regional concern—not least because, as the African National Congress (ANC) government now acknowledges, crime poses a significant threat to the existing political order in South Africa.[10]

According to the organized crime unit of the South African Police, there were seven major crime syndicates operating in the gold and diamond sectors in 1996.[11] The picture is complicated by the fact that the traffic in gold (valued at about $34 million) involves middle-management personnel who are familiar with the security measures in place. The crime syndicates that control the traffic can have the gold refined, licensed, and exported because they have access to the legal and illegal international sales markets. Diamond smuggling, also registered in billions of rands, often forms part of the overall money-laundering operation. According to the organized crime unit, much of the contraband gold is purchased using cash from drug trafficking before being sold to regular buyers in Britain, Germany, and Switzerland in order to acquire foreign currency.

The most common crimes in SARPCCO countries include armed robbery, money laundering, hijacking, illegal immigration, and rape. The most prevalent cross-border crimes involve armed gangs who run a profitable trade in stolen luxury cars from South Africa; cattle rustling from Swaziland and South Africa; and gun smuggling and the illegal drug trade to South Africa.[12]

Factors such as these emphasize that policing is no longer of purely national concern. Although it would be wrong to exaggerate it, the trend toward transborder and regional negotiations at the most senior levels adds another strand to the relationship between policing and politics, for what were regional concerns in 1990 are now of international interest. The European Union (EU) and Southern African Development Community (SADC), for instance, have scheduled conferences on drug smuggling in southern Africa, and antidrug programs are an EU priority in aid to SADC, along with regional integration and mine disposal. The measures the EU proposes include reinforcing frontier controls, judicial cooperation, and legislation to combat money laundering and the illegal acquisition of certain chemical products. The practical effects of such plans on the problem are likely to be small, but they are indicative of a strong Western interest in transnational crime in the region.[13]

Reference to EU aid indicates that the external, diplomatic, political element in policing is reinforced by issues related to aid and foreign involvement. As an example, a German federal police officer arrived in Dar es Salaam as part of a cooperation program in 1995 because Tanzania was by then regarded as a major crossroads for international drug trafficking, recent drug seizures having suggested that Tanzania was no longer just a consumer society with a domestic problem. In such cases, the drugs arrive from India and Pakistan, transit through Dar es Salaam, and are reexported to Europe, the United States, or countries in Africa—hence the cooperation between German federal police authorities and Tanzanian police. Such policing policies are well established, with cooperation between these two states in sectors other than drugs going back to 1985, when Germany supplied equipment. Germany also provided new vehicles and communications equipment to the Tanzanians in 1995, in addition to training and technical assistance.

Among the other European states that offered expertise or equipment in 1995 to southern African countries was France, which sent security advisers (including officers from the intelligence-gathering Renseignements Généraux, CID, and antiriot units) to help train a 10,000-strong multiparty National Peacekeeping Force (NPKF) originally proposed by the ANC during the 1993 multiparty negotiations. The NPKF, a public order force considered to have the necessary legitimacy to replace the discredited Internal Stability Unit, the riot-control arm of the SAP, was to be made up of soldiers and policemen from thirteen forces.[14] France was chosen because of its experience in public order policing and in particular its system of two public order bodies, one army controlled and the other under the police. The military force, the Gendarmerie Mobile, has both military and police duties (including civil unrest in rural areas) and is reputed to be better trained and disciplined than the Compagnies Républicaines de Sécurité (CRS), two of whose officers also visited South Africa to hold talks with the police and the military.

There are two important caveats to this picture of regional cooperation in the face of transnational crime in southern Africa that are applicable to all regions. The first is the continuing influence of context and cultural mores across the spectrum of police activity. Witchcraft is still an integral part of many community systems of belief. In the Northern Provinces of South Africa, at least 300 witchcraft-related murders have been recorded since 1990—200 of which occurred in 1994, a time of great social and political upheaval, which suggests that witch finding is used to settle jealousies and rivalries. The horrific deaths of seven elderly women in one night in 1995 as a result of the earlier death of a schoolgirl by lightning is one such case. Details were recounted by an inspector in the Gilead district police in January 1998. The province has the highest incidence of lightning strikes in the world, but following the death of a school girl, villagers paid a traditional healer £200 to "sniff out" the evil causing the death. The inspector said he did not believe in witchcraft or zombies, but "more typically, the sergeant manning the front desk does: 'They admitted they were witches when we brought them in.'"[15]

The second caveat regarding regional cooperation concerns the regimes involved, who are unlikely to have ignored the increased regional cooperation and effective policing. As Good points out in a discussion of corruption in southern Africa, it is important to consider who might gain and who might lose from the institutional erosion and resource dissipation the present situation represents. His answer is that "an élite of politicians, bureaucrats, and businessmen appear to have made significant material gains."[16] Indeed, he alleges that the ANC leadership and government are unconcerned by corruption, preferring to keep performance and standards low in the police service and the ministries of justice and safety and security. The many anticorruption and good-governance campaigns of recent years are in practice of little relevance to the reality of crime in the region and elsewhere, since the trade in drugs, gems, weapons, and so on is either tremendously profitable for many politicians or is quite outside state and police control anyway.

National, Provincial, and Local Policing

Although the boundaries between the police and military are ambiguous in Africa, the police generally operate within society in a way that the military (with their barracks and separate status) do not. Policing cannot be divorced from social and political concerns. Indeed, the police were specifically designed to penetrate society in a way impossible for the military, and their fundamental task has been described as "the creation and maintenance of, and their participation in, external relationships."[17]

One result of this integration of policing and politics is vividly illustrated by events in southern Africa, where policing has had to deal with the significant political shift consequent on the dismantling of apartheid control. The resulting political struggles, especially in South Africa, exposed serious communal and political rifts at all levels, not least in the police themselves. In July 1994, for example, officers in almost every police station in the kwaZulu homeland went on strike. The strike was originally led by policemen keen to break away from Chief Buthelezi's Inkatha Freedom Party, long seen as an ally of President De Klerk's government, and speed up amalgamation of the eleven existing police agencies into a single national structure, but it was hijacked by those supporting the kwaZulu deputy commissioner, Sipho Mathe. The strike then focused on complaints against "racist" white officers rather than Inkatha connections, which helped Mathe's own bid for the post of commissioner. Furthermore, the weapons that had fallen into civilian hands during the struggle against apartheid and the justification of violence so common at the time have resulted in a particularly violent society in which crime is generally agreed to be "out of control" as President Mandela acknowledged in August 1996. One effect of this is the high casualty rate among serving officers in the South African Police Services (SAPs), as the police are now known.[18]

There are also more subtle issues involved that have wider implications for policing. The precise location of the borders between criminality and political protest in liberalized regimes is one. In Namibia, for instance, where there is significant criticism of a political settlement that allowed the beneficiaries of apartheid to keep their wealth, it is not necessarily clear whether theft is an expression of protest or the violation of a societal norm. As in other countries, the Namibian and South African governments respond to public fears about crime by promoting measures that their opponents perceive as politically motivated. Such moves reinforce the involvement of the police in society.

It is all the more important to understand the police within the context of the society because there is not a police caste as such, nor a police equivalent of the military college (such as Britain's Royal Military Academy, Sandhurst) network, and clientalism may be as true of the police as of society in general. A system of patron-client ties may bind relationships and provide forms of mutual assistance and support within forces. Peer-group solidarity will certainly be significant—every member of the inner police circle involved in the Ghanaian coup in 1966 was a Ewe who had received only the most basic education (only commissioner Harlley had attended secondary school).

Police involvement in politics may also be highly individual, and a number of African leaders (such as Mohammed Siad Barre of Somalia) have been policemen at some time in their careers. President Zine El Abidine Ben Ali, the Tunisian president, to name a comparable example from north Africa, learned his politics as a policeman specializing in intelligence and security. This experience formed the power base from which he became prime minister and then president in 1987, and it was the main instrument he used to crush the Hizb Ennahda (Renaissance Party) Islamist movement. His understanding of and connections with foreign police forces and the Interpol system also helped him to handle personal problems such as a drug-smuggling scandal in which his brother was convicted of drug trafficking in France in 1992.[19]

Such direct links between political and police power are unusual, and it is probable that indirect links are even more influential in states experiencing economic crisis, political turmoil, or endemic conflict, such as Nigeria and South Africa. The same applies to political interference in policing itself. Attempts have periodically been made to address this. Thus, the framers of the 1963 constitution in Nigeria tried to include checks and balances that would stop any misuse of the police by the federal government. But the gesture was without substance and was followed by two coups in 1966, civil war in 1967, and blatant abuse of the system under the second republic, when the police became tools of the ruling party, the National Party of Nigeria. As soon as it came to power in 1966, the army ordered all local and native police forces to be placed under the inspector general of police. By 1971 the various forces were abolished and there was just a single force, the Nigeria Police Force (in which some of the local and native police were absorbed and retrained to meet the national standards). But this could not ameliorate the problem of political interference because, as with the case of the constitution drafting committee of 1975–1976, it "did not address itself to the problems that could arise if the Police were used as pawns by the Government in power. The Drafting Committee was more interested in curbing the powers of the federal Government in taking over the government of a State if the machinery of government should break down in a State."[20]

There are exceptions to the incremental politicization of policing, but they tend to involve individuals. A British deputy chief constable visiting Ghana in 1971, for instance, recorded that a regional executive put great pressure on the local assistant commissioner of police in charge of Sekondi to open fire on demonstrators. This was when police interests were under great pressure and the Ghanaian parliament had recently conferred policing powers (such as crime detection) on all members of the armed forces above the rank of sergeant. In this case the officer refused to be intimidated, reminding the politician that the Police Service Act of 1970 expressly provided that he should take orders only from senior members of the Ghana Police Service.[21] The British officer reported many examples of interference in promotion and transfer cases, but the instances were more noticeable to him than to the Ghanaians he interviewed. African officers were rarely judged by their contemporaries in terms of professionalism, so there was no pressure to promote or enforce Western notions of impartiality.

Events in Ghana in 1966 and 1972 suggest, however, that career police officers were prepared to intervene through alignment with the military, justifying their actions by an appeal to the preservation of law and order—sometimes at the risk of damaging their own standards of professionalism. John Cobbina, inspector general of police and commissioner for internal affairs in the national redemption council of 1972, for example, justified the role of the police with the words, "We did not help to overthrow Dr Busia. There was a change of government and we came in to preserve law and order. That is our job."

The police rarely intervene as an extralegal pressure group in the way the military have. The best-documented instance of such intervention remains that of the 1966 coup in Ghana (though there have been other examples in Sierra Leone and Togo), but overt intervention is rare. The only regime to have been successfully overthrown by its own police remains the Arab Zanzibar Nationalist Party (ZNP) in Zanzibar in January 1964, though it is significant that Zanzibar had no troops. Although colonial officers in Zanzibar had relied on mainland police officers rather than the army, the new regime in Zanzibar sent the officers home because police support lay with their chief opponents. They failed to manage this effectively, and revolutionaries in Zanzibar under the self-styled field marshal John Okello soon recruited supporters among the dismissed officers, who quickly provided him with details of the armories of key police stations. The British police commissioner, who left the island with the deposed sultan once the last police station surrendered to the revolutionaries, was then replaced with a commissioner from Tanganyika. Tanganyika also sent about 130 armed policemen to Zanzibar to help maintain order until the Zanzibar police force had been reconstituted.[22]

The rarity of overt intervention must be seen in the light of the evidence that a lack of resources, deprofessionalization, and deinstitutionalization of the police seriously weakens their group identity and capabilities. It reinforces Potholm's observation that the police, as an institution, are "more consistently involved in the output side of the political process. It tends to enforce decisions taken by the political authorities rather than make them."[23] It is partly for this reason that "political systems get the law enforcement agencies which they create. The responsibility for their quality lies with the political authority."[24]

In 1969 Potholm (whose work represents the first attempt to understand postcolonial African policing as a whole) categorized the resulting police functions as:

- the maintenance of law and order
- paramilitary operations
- regulatory activities
- regime representation.

These functions are then affected by variables such as:

- the ratio of police to population
- patterns of recruitment and promotion
- organization and styles of training
- the social and political orientation of police personnel.

Potholm's variables are ideal analytic tools, particularly for the identification of political orientation, but patterns of recruitment and advancement, for instance, are clearly significant because they are political decisions in themselves. His expansion of regime representation to include political socialization in the sense of the police as a socially integrating factor, as a modernizing agent and a channel of upward mobility, is less convincing in the 1990s: "A well-run police force exhibits the organizing norms and value clusters associated with modernization. It may also promote values such as punctuality, neatness, and record keeping. A policeman in . . . Ghana stands out as a prototype of what modernity is all about."[25] Indeed, it was unconvincing even in the 1970s, when the force virtually collapsed as Ghanaian state institutions in general experienced a serious recession.

The police may, however, be agents for change because they may be one of the means by which theories of development are translated into practice, as has happened in Sudan. The regime of Khojali Osman in Khartoum claims to be introducing "participatory democracy," but the opposition has been broken, the appointed assembly overruled, political parties banned, and professional organizations destroyed. Lacking popular support, the regime appears to rest on ruthless security. Indeed, the activity of policing was expanded in 1992 when General Omar Hassan al-Bashir announced the establishment of a new force called the People's Police. It was aimed at entrenching Islamic values and mutual assistance, in addition to filling gaps in regular police operations and preserving security activities such as patrols in residential areas and markets. Radio Omdurman reported him as saying that the new police were not a substitute for the regular police, but even so the general stressed the need to combat "negative aspects which characterized the police in the past until it was possible to establish a police of the Islamic society." In other words, policing was politicized at the expense of professionalization. Later Western reports speak of the establishment of 120 stations in Khartoum, with many further bases in suburbs and camps, to supplement two other existing forces and military and paramilitary groups.[26]

The police are usually subservient to the politics of other groups in the state in a way that the military are not. This emerges as a constant theme. This is probably so because the police, unlike the military, rarely have access to resources they can themselves control. Thus, they do not build power bases to rival military or civilian rulers. Unable to operate as independent political actors, the police more often attach themselves to other groups, hoping to attract favors and the resources necessary to sustain themselves.

Unlike senior military officers, the police are far less likely to consider themselves the guardians of national security; they are adjuncts to other groups that control resources directly. This is so even when policing is militarized, as in Gabon in the late 1980s, when at least ten senior officers held the rank of police general. Although the police may intervene to uphold the law, they rarely claim to be in charge of or to restore security in the way the military do. It is difficult to imagine the gendarmerie of Burundi, for instance, justifying intervention in the terms used by the Tutsi-dominated army when it launched a coup against the incumbent Hutu president in July 1996: "We are in charge of security, we believe that our responsibility is to prevent political action and possibly some actions likely to jeopardise the security of the people and their property, which we are supposed to protect."[27]

Politics is a key variable in policing, yet police systems are in general remarkably tenacious, outwardly adapting to political change even while remaining fundamentally unaltered by it. Some changes, such as those involving increased repression in Sudan, are easier to accommodate than others (such as democratization) that highlight accountability or protection. But the roles of the police in Africa include the regulation of politics on behalf of other groups, in one form or another. Regimes or local military leaders determine who can participate in politics, but the police (with varying degrees of discretion over whom to arrest and detain) execute the decisions. They regulate public conduct during meetings and demonstrations. They may decide issues by standing aside at significant moments or by allowing the stronger side to win. Their special branch or its equivalent may also manipulate political processes, particularly if the existing social order is threatened.

In summary, police systems are deeply enmeshed in political developments, reflecting the concerns of many interest groups or individuals in addition to their own and that of the regime. Although the vocabulary of international policing is strong at the level of chief officers, it stops there, and neither the resources nor the willingness to extend it down exist. All states were touched by Africa's new winds of change in the 1990s, and brutality may now be less systematized in some states.[28] But national, provincial, and local policing has changed little because the nature of political power and regime concerns are essentially the same as they were in the 1960s. Civil order continues as politicized and fragile as ever.

The Political Environment: Key Concepts

Just as African leaders identified the need for civil order as a priority in 1960 (prompted, perhaps, by events in the Belgian Congo, which collapsed within days), so civil order remains key to understanding the political environment in which African police systems operated in the 1990s. Indeed, discussion about increased political participation or representation, for instance, cannot realistically take place in isolation from calculations about order and internal security. But civil order does not provide a sufficient explanation on its own, so in this study I link order to security and governance. A fourth factor, reconstruction, must also be taken into account in the 1990s. And at a secondary level, I introduce additional concepts relating to contemporary police systems and the problem of politicized police forces. These center on law, justice and human rights, and civil-military relations. Applying the resulting model developed in the following chapters to a continent as complex as Africa may appear somewhat simplistic, but it is necessary if the subject is to progress beyond the anecdotal level.

Civil Order

Conceptual models of African policing systems need to incorporate two major elements: the universal nature and function of policing and the specific environment. The key concept underpinning both is order, which is usually seen as both the most widely acknowledged function of policing agencies and as essential to the preservation of states, regimes, and societies.

Order, understood in terms of the preservation of an essentially political system of norms, participation, and distribution of power, is invariably more important than law in fragile states. That law cannot exist in the absence of order is made explicit by the endemic conflict in much of Africa.[29] There is no effective judicial system to which anyone in a state such as Chad can appeal, as irregular armies control territory and the military appears to be fragmented but uncontrollable. Not surprisingly, Chad's policy for cutting crime is to shoot presumed criminals. An order signed by the head of the national gendarmerie says, "No thief must be the object of any [legal] procedure whatsoever. In a case of *flagrante delicto,* proceed immediately to his/her physical elimination." Failure to do so will lead to "very severe penalties, even demotion and dismissal from the army."[30] Chad's policy "is working," according to the foreign affairs minister. "We no longer experience the previous levels of violence."

Order is an elusive concept but refers to a situation where a certain respect for the limits of violence as an instrument of policy has developed. Order implies regularity even if it reflects special interests. It also implies the existence of a degree of crime management and social stability when it is identified in a state-organized society.[31]

The relativity of order is seen in a report in the *Economist* of 12 November 1994, four months after a new government took power in Rwanda: "Ministries have no staff, no files, no paper, no running water. The state has no tax officials, so no revenue; no judges, police or prison officers, so no law. Order depends on the Tutsi army that won the civil war. . . . Its soldiers, 30,000 ragged and unpaid youths, hang about hungrily at road-blocks."

It is a function of policing generally to provide one of the mechanisms by which both general and specific order operate. This remains so even if the more usual role of the police at the local level of substations and district headquarters is tax collection or social mobilization, as for the police in Tanzania in the early 1970s. The role of the local police in rural areas of Tanzania was to promote rural change, and the maintenance of local order was shared with the youth wing of the Tanganyika African National Union (TANU). Serious internal disorder, however, resulted in the rapid deployment of a contingent of the national police Mobile Field Force Unit, which was usually stationed in district headquarters. Twenty-five years later, Tanzanian politics had changed significantly, but the force had no plans for dramatic change in the way policing was delivered. There remained a stated intention that the public should be involved as much as possible in the policing of local areas through schemes such as auxiliary police and crime-stopper systems, as well as weekly radio programs. Policing clearly extended beyond the formal group.

Order thus serves different purposes. In Chad and Rwanda, the emphasis on order followed episodes of severe violence, whereas in Tanzania order is better characterized as efforts to intervene in political power struggles. The key factor is that order is not neutral. Yet this understanding was more typical of the 1990s than the 1960s, when civil order in Africa was first considered in an influential analysis of national development after independence by J. M. Lee. Lee took as his 1969 field of study thirty African nations in order to trace the relationship between armies and civil order, the latter having been identified as a necessary condition for national development. His conclusion was unambiguous: Common features in African societies "make it possible to explain the problems of government and military rule in Africa by reference to a single basic idea—the absence of civil order."[32]

Lee did not, however, explain what held society together in the absence of order or, indeed, the absence of central as opposed to local order. Nor did he clarify how coercion and consent mingle in some states, and it is not clear that he deals adequately with the issue of legitimacy—states without coercive power may collapse, but this does not mean that coercion is the only effective prop of a regime. In any case, the norms associated with government operations and the institutions of government associated with independence suggest that different levels of legitimacy may be involved. He did not deal with the subsequent problem of patrimonial rule and institutional collapse.

Lee underestimated the role of violence and purely coercive concepts of civil order in situations such as those of contemporary Somalia, where factional leaders impose local order by guns and militiamen. As Bienen noted, "We speak of a collapse or breakdown of order when we really mean the failure of central rule."[33] Lee may have underestimated the comparative nature of civil order, and he probably underestimated civilian forces for stability because he concentrated on the military as the most resilient force in society. This reflects the concerns of the 1960s, when the military and order attracted more attention than did associational life. Nevertheless, his analysis remains valid to Africa in the 1990s:

> The "peaceful transfer of power" in tropical Africa created new states in which the state apparatus itself was the only major expression of political convention. "Civil order" is the acceptance of certain norms within a broader definition of the state than that provided by the formal institutions of government, which help to remove the high degree of uncertainty that might otherwise prevail in political negotiations. The attempt to create order in Africa is really a fight to define the limits of political action.[34]

Thus, political dissent was a matter for the police. But civil order is not synonymous with public order, though the two may appear so, because public order is usually derived from a specific, often narrow (or at least official) understanding of political order. Neither is civil order necessarily related to stability, especially when it is not accompanied by legitimacy, though both are about agreed sets of rules. Both civil order and stability accommodate blood feuds and concomitant murder, for example, as an accepted way of settling disputes in Somalia. The three concepts are, however, entwined. They are specific to their environment, a matter of perception and political judgment. Regimes tend to focus on public order because it implies control, whereas external judges (such as donor countries) prefer to concentrate on the less emotive issue of civil order, with its implications of institution building. Contradictions can emerge in that the authorities may see the latter as threatening to the former, a matter that will entail a very different use of the police. Public order is thus closely related to internal security matters, whereas civil order is understood, by the West at least, as linked to human rights, law, and acceptable forms of order enforcement.

Security

The second key to understanding the environment of African police systems is security, for the police are usually expected to play a part in the enforcement and maintenance of internal security.

The redefinition of security after the ending of the cold war may have extended the police role in some states:

> For countries suffering from economic and infrastructure under development, unstable political systems . . . and ethnic and other social cleavages, a wide variety of problems pose security threats because they undermine the autonomy and survival of the state from within. Indeed, these various internal dilemmas form the main security challenge to most developing countries.[35]

The Sudanese undersecretary of state for justice, Shawgi Hussein, accordingly defined security as "national unity and safety." He described how the requirements of security, as expressed in a new emergency law, allowed the president to declare a state of emergency throughout the country if Sudan were threatened by a foreign invasion or siege or crises that jeopardized the country's economy, such as rebellion, illegal fighting, insurrection, rioting, and natural upheavals.[36]

The multifaceted concept of security is as elusive as that of order, especially in the 1990s. There may be distinctions between internal and external security—internal security has to be defined in terms of the type of internal political competition, whereas external security will depend on the international environment—but they tend to have less relevance for African police systems, which reactively enforce internal order. Moreover, the security of the state and regime often cannot be separated because the main weapon in a state armory is the state organization itself. The state is associated with the group running it and is regarded as primarily an organization whose component parts are subject to competition. Accordingly, control of the economy and government appointments provides regimes with the means of defeating political opponents. Parts of the state organization may then develop their own rules, and (as Lee pointed out) the discipline organizations such as the police can impose on their members assumes a new significance when there are few agreed norms.

Security is, ultimately, a perceptual matter about when an individual or group feels safe and able to maintain independent identity.

Stability is both a function of, but distinct from, security in that tight security can bring about temporary stability. This was illustrated by General Sani Abacha of Nigeria, who personally acted in at least three coups. Security was more important than stability as such to General Abacha because security and coercion—or illegitimate stability—kept him in power long after the precariousness of the stability he tried to impose was clear. Abacha attempted to legitimize stability when he took power following the army's annulment of the 1993 elections, at a time when it seemed that the ethnically divided nation could fragment. It was the army that tried to enforce this promise when it put down riots the following year. Less serious street violence was repressed by police with tear gas and clubs.

Abacha created a degree of macroeconomic stability initially by controlling expenditure, but this soon slowed, and political and economic instability intensified in 1998 as the price of Nigeria's crude oil fell on the world markets, capital flight increased, protest at Abacha's wish to stand for president grew, and Western countries pressed for the release of political prisoners and a genuine democracy. The direct relationship between stability and security can be seen in the belief of many in Lagos that Abacha should stay because he was the one man with the security (coercive) powers necessary to keep an unstable situation under control.[37]

Governance

The third key concept is governance. The term *governance* attracted significant attention in the 1990s because of its association with the good-governance proposals of the World Bank and donor countries and with the good government (which is not necessarily democratic) judged essential for the delivery of development. The World Bank, for example, identifies good governance with liberal democracy: Governance "entails the development of legitimate authority based on a generalised normative consensus that fosters and regulates a communitarian web of reciprocal relations between rulers and ruled."[38] Douglas Hurd, the British foreign secretary, effectively defined Britain's understanding of the comparable concept of good government in 1990 when he said that "countries tending towards pluralism, public accountability, respect for the rule of law, human rights, and market principles should be encouraged. Governments who persist with repressive policies with corrupt management . . . should not expect us to support their folly with some aid resources."[39] Hurd's understanding of good governance is explicitly linked to repression and coercion and thus, by implication, coercive agents such as the police.

In practice it is difficult to define *good governance* precisely because even donors have not done so. The EU has not, for instance, whereas the United States conflates it with democracy, and Britain and Sweden focus on public administration efficiency and effectiveness. In contrast, good government may be a more accessible concept, for it suggests ideals that even colonial governors would recognize; that is, fair taxation, parsimonious spending on public works and administration, and the avoidance of bribery and corruption.[40] The colonial understanding of good government showed a high regard for the rule of law and market principles, though it also excluded pluralism and human rights. It belongs to a past age, yet such an understanding may yet be closer to that of many Africans than Hurd's. The heart of good government may still lie in fair taxation and rulers who eschew corruption.[41]

Governance has traditionally been seen in terms of the interaction between government and society, and so I use the concept in the sense developed by Hyden, for whom governance is the management of regime relations and structures.[42] I understand *regime* as

> the arrangement of authority, power, and political interests in a state. This arrangement may be constitutionally or institutionally governed or it may be informal, as it is in personal systems. If informal, it is likely to change when rulers change, in response to a new ruler's desires and aversions, interests and indifferences, strengths and weaknesses, and political formulae—that is, his ideas, procedures, and manner of ruling.[43]

The concept of governance is of relevance to policing because it refers to the set of fundamental rules that establish "the framework for the conduct of politics."[44] It has two dimensions, here defined in terms of structural factors and human agency, in which the police form an essential element because they are the extension of regime and state authority with which the rest of society has the most contact. The governance of a state will affect the police because they must manage its expression. Pressure for liberalization in the 1990s did not affect this fact, though it can be argued that the question remains whether reforms actually change the manner of governance (that is, the basis for how police behave). For as Hyden observes, "Commonly, incumbent elites regard political liberalization as an unpalatable but unavoidable step to salvage central political control within a destabilised state. And contenders for power often perceive multiparty competition as a chance for access to rent-seeking opportunities so long denied to them as political outsiders."[45]

Reconstruction

A fourth factor is that of reconstruction after conflict. Conflict has had a formative effect on many police systems in recent decades. The police often find themselves fragmented or superseded in conditions of social disintegration and fighting, as in Angola, though their role expands once conflict is ended or frozen. This is particularly so once demobilization and disarmament take place because of the economic and political costs of keeping conflict structures in place. In states where international opinion has influence (such as Namibia) or where there has been a violent reaction to previous security practices (as in Ethiopia), military forces have been placed under civilian control and police forces retrained or replaced.

The provision of physical security after war is essential, but it is complicated by the usual inability of the police to enforce existing laws; they are frequently disorganized, invariably underresourced, underarmed, and regarded with fear or contempt by the populace. At the same time, there is usually poor gun control and a large arms market, to say nothing of porous borders. In Angola, Chad, Mozambique, and the Sudan, for example, general security was sought through three means: police enforcement of a prohibition against openly carrying weapons, of offering benefits in exchange for guns, and seizure of weapons by an armed force. But a common problem for all such programs was that the value of weapons remained high because of insecurity and the lack of an effective police force. At best, such actions resulted in some improvement in local security. There is anecdotal evidence of an increased crime rate, but this is more likely to have been the result of the conditions to which the policies responded than that the policies themselves led to a higher crime rate.[46]

Ethiopia illustrates the potential size of the problem, for approximately 350,000 combatants were demobilized by 1995, with a significant potential effect on urban unemployment and the crime rate. Absorption of ex-fighters into the police is one option for states facing such a problem. Disarmed and demobilized combatants have, for example, been absorbed into existing police forces in Zimbabwe, where 5 percent of former guerrillas were in the police force in 1993, and in Namibia, where even the notorious paramilitary Koevoet force was initially absorbed as a counterinsurgency force.[47] These cases are in stark contrast to that of Angola. In Zimbabwe and Namibia, opposing armed forces were integrated into a single institution, whereas in Angola the process formed part of preparations for continued war. The Movement for the People's Liberation of Angola (MPLA) allegedly shifted military units to paramilitary units in the police force, which fell outside the UN mandate. Events in Angola also demonstrate that parties that do not wish to give up their military often claim they are police. UNITA refused to give up its army of more than 30,000 in August 1997, insisting that it merely had up to 5,000 "police."

The problems associated with reconstructing a police force are also affected by the expectations, resources, and demands of intergovernmental organizations and national aid departments, as a report in the *Daily Telegraph* of 25 March 1994 made clear. The United States earmarked $437 million to equip and train a police force of 8,000 in Somalia, even though there was no government to create or direct it. The force was to receive 500 M-16 assault rifles, 5,000 .45-caliber pistols, 5,000 pairs of handcuffs, 358 vehicles, and 2.3 million rounds of ammunition. The policing problems presented in the 1990s were thus very different from those of the 1960s, though new forces were still likely to be initially influenced by Francophone or the Anglophone models of policing, and training aid or assistance remained likely to come from countries such as Belgium, Germany, Israel, and the United States.

Law and Human Rights

Law and order are generally coupled together in Western policing, but law (and related concepts such as justice and human rights) can never be more than secondary in African policing because the overriding problems remain the enforcement of public order and the maintenance of political order.[48]

It is pertinent to note here the dominant historical sequence that shaped the character of policing in many British territories after decolonization. There was initially intense emphasis on coercion and control, when order as defined by the new rulers was the prime object. At the same time, police training was similar to that of the military in countries such as Ghana, for the military role was designed for internal (rather than external) security, whereas the police in turn displayed paramilitary characteristics. To Western visitors in the late 1960s, the Ghanaian police's use of armored cars and guards at police stations, for example, appeared strongly militaristic. Soldiers controlled traffic, and traffic control points were usually outside military establishments on busy roads. Indeed, visiting British officers in 1971 called the police an imitation military organization. Earlier, the National Liberation Council had given the military some police powers in that the functions conferred on the police by enactments in relation to crime prevention and detection, the apprehension of offenders, and the maintenance of public order could be performed by any soldiers acting on the instructions of a sergeant or higher-ranking officer.[49] Statute and case law were built up only after this, with the police becoming (marginally) more concerned with crime and reflecting differences between urban and rural provisions. This was often, however, followed by a breakdown in order due to the strains of internal conflict.

The relationship between policing and law in Africa is never self-evident. Because the state is understood as at best a framework for government rather than a system of law, regimes usually appropriate state organizations and the resources they represent. The control of key resources, such as judicial systems, patronage, and the media, are then given to privileged individuals as a political reward. The resulting enforcement of law is likely to be partial, and rule is more likely to be *by* law (which may permit manipulation of the courts) than *of* law.[50] Moreover, routine police work is never just the enforcement of (criminal) law, and the invocation of law is more likely to be the result of expediency than a static notion of legality as such. In other words, the law is always a resource for solving practical problems because all policing is a matter of negotiation—or, in practice, the coercion of enemies.

Justice will also be filtered through various ethical or cultural systems, as will policing concepts based on the individual, such as human rights. This applies to donor nations as much as to African states, for discussion of police systems and styles has tended to be understood—in intergovernmental organizations, at least—in relation to ideal liberal models, in which accountability and human rights dominate. This has resulted in discussions of political—and policing—change in Africa invariably involving the word *democratization*. But it may be more accurate to talk of development (or of democratization as an aspect of development) in which references to accountability may be laudable, or even desirable, but also partial. This is not, however, to imply that order should take precedence over other ideals.

No Western discussion of contemporary African policing takes place without reference to the themes of accountability and human rights, though it is often forgotten that, as Hyden commented in 1992, liberalization and democratization are autonomous as well as complementary processes. The former requires the dismantling of authoritarian regimes, whereas the latter demands the construction of specific institutions for a different purpose. But the underlying structural constraints imposed on existing economic crises can act against both democratization and liberalization, thus creating additional tensions in the short term. This will inevitably affect policing. Also, the continuing importance of coercion, along with other strong characteristics, such as neopatrimonialism, ensures that elites continue to employ the coercive resources of the state for as long as they can, no matter how weak their political legitimacy and economic base. For a tendency to personalize power is at the heart of neopatrimonialism, making no distinction between the private and public realms; all government powers and their corresponding economic advantages tend to be treated as private rights. In other words, the concepts of liberalization and democratization do not necessarily progress understanding of African policing or, indeed, of humane standards of policing as such.

Human rights also remain controversial. Certainly the majority of African writers on the subject in the 1970s considered individual rights to be a Western issue; in Africa rights were seen as communitarian or group based. The issue of human rights was not a prominent or politicized concern in Nigeria, for example, until the late 1970s, even though military rulers routinely assaulted, harassed, and tortured opponents.[51]

Human rights is inevitably a relative concept in practice. Prisoners in a Nigerian jail, for instance, may not be given water every day, yet Nigeria is party to several international human rights treaties, including the 1949 Geneva Conventions, the Convention Relating to the Status of Refugees (1967), the International Convention on the Elimination of All Forms of Discrimination Against Women (1977), and the African Charter on Human and Peoples' Rights (1981). Nigeria has not, however, signed the International Covenant on Civil and Political Rights of 1966 or the Convention Against Torture and Other Cruel, Inhuman, or Degrading Treatment or Punishment. The concept of human rights does not in practice aid understanding of existing policing because it exerts so little influence.

Civil-Military Relations

I refer to civil-military relations not in terms of a concept so much as an approach which should be applied to police-state relations in Africa. Though the study of the police is normally approached through analytic tools taken from criminal justice, history, and sociology, an examination of civil-military relations provides several useful tools and insights as the police are a hierarchic and disciplined force and the military perform many policing activities. Yet this facet is often ignored.[52] Specific concepts include the suppression facility (or the ease with which masses can be constrained in cases of internal threat), the military participation ratio, and the way in which the political values of a state are shaped by its military experience.

To a certain extent, civil-military relations establish the environment in which most if not all policing systems in Africa work because so much policing is paramilitary. As I have already stressed, paramilitary units are integral parts of many police systems (which are themselves militarized and operating in turbulent or fragile environments). Paramilitary units are usually better resourced than operational ones, and they tend to have smarter uniforms, better vehicles, and newer equipment and premises. But the ideas of civil-military relations may also be helpful for more practical purposes; paramilitary police may make pragmatic sense because they are cheaper than the military, they can be targeted more narrowly, and their use is often less controversial. They may be more loyal to key individuals or factions and more reliable in fractured political environments. The special force created to ensure the security of people and goods before, during, and after elections in Togo in 1993 is a case in point. It was composed of gendarmes, police, and prefecture guards but did not include the military.

Societies that have been militarized by acute internal instability may use the army to maintain order, but in many countries the government does not trust the army to refrain from coups or plotting. In some states neither the military nor the government wants the army closely identified with domestic security operations, so the government tries to blur the issue by building up paramilitary forces as an alternative to the army. It is not possible to suggest one definition to contain all such forces, but it must be the relationship of the police to the military that defines whether or not a police organization is paramilitary, not its willingness to use force.

Police Structures and Linkages:
The Primacy of Political Order

Order is the most important of the concepts I introduce here; internal security may underpin or flow from it, and its imposition may form part of governance, but neither is sufficient in itself to reveal the police purpose. They need to be superimposed on the fundamental attributes of police systems, and the totality must then be placed within a specific political and historical context.

The precise relationship between the elements varies according to context, and links will be shaped by factors such as the changing boundaries of public and official tolerance or momentous political shifts. Crime, for instance, becomes a socially acceptable survival strategy and a quick mechanism for resolving difficulties during times of great insecurity, with the result an increased incidence of robbery and rape. There also appears to be a visible relationship between continued high levels of crime (in areas such as the western Cape) and the acceptance of significantly higher levels of violence, at least in certain specific circumstances such as the end of apartheid.[53] But it is difficult to judge whether there is more crime in, say, Gaudeng or Johannesburg, because its use is widely accepted or because a high crime rate is related to the nature of the political order. There are also more subtle issues involved with fundamental political changes. The precise location of the borders between criminality and political protest in liberalized regimes is one. In Namibia, for instance, where there is significant criticism of a political settlement that allowed the beneficiaries of apartheid to keep their wealth, it is not necessarily clear whether theft is an expression of protest or the violation of a societal norm. As in other countries, the Namibian and South African governments respond to public fears about crime by promoting measures that are then perceived by their opponents to be politically motivated.

The relativity of political circumstances will in turn be reflected in policing priorities. Crime prevention will not be a priority outside an overcrowded jail in Angola, but it will be in an affluent suburb of Windhoek. Criminalization may also be a means by which governments enforce order, especially if order enforcement addresses criminalized behavior such as the inability of illegal migrants to buy residence permits. This appeared to be the case in the expulsion program initiated in 1992 and 1995 by Gabon in an attempt to control "criminal types"—particularly those from Nigeria, popularly regarded as the main source of armed robbers and hard drugs.

The institutional vacuum that encourages crime and insecurity affects police systems, too, because their organizational structures are shaped also by political turmoil, internal insecurities, and regime strategies. But police structures are most influenced not by crime or law and order issues but by a special kind of crime—by offenses seen to threaten the political order. And the more frequently such offenses take place and the more serious they are perceived to be, the more likely police resources will be controlled centrally and the more repressive the response. At the same time, it is also more likely that policing will be institutionally fragmented, as rulers rely increasingly on paramilitary and special units that act alongside or in place of the less reliable police. The current organization of a police system may therefore provide a key to a regime's perception of security or liberalization.

Linked to this emphasis on order is the unquantifiable but overwhelming anecdotal evidence that the existing order in most African states effectively permits—or even encourages—the key institutions of state to reward ruthlessness, nepotism, and plunder. Building a liberalized society will not necessarily dovetail with this situation or with the practical concerns of elite security, as the disastrous impact of Idi Amin's attempts to secure sufficient political authority to maintain order and security made clear in earlier years.[54] The potential for undesirable consequences to result from changes accompanying liberalization remains high. Amin's obsessive fear of challenges, which caused him to arm many different agencies in the hope that they would compete among themselves rather than plot against him, is typical of any number of leaders. The legacy of such regime security concerns is underlined by Wiseman's conclusion that between half and two-thirds of all major politicians in Africa since independence have been imprisoned, exiled, or killed. He describes political competition as having taken on the character of a zero-sum game, though other authors judge that one-third of all leaders are still in office after eight years.[55] In either case it remains unclear which dimensions of regime management are important for understanding how either order or political systems can be sustained or developed. The only clear conclusion to be drawn is that internal security will remain key and states will continue to include police systems.

Models of Police Systems

There is no ideal model of policing appropriate to specific types of national development in Africa because of the number of counties involved and the fragility of the African state and because the meaning of policing is not self-evident. There is, rather, a range of types that reflects the spectrum of state institutional capacity evident in the 1990s.

The policing systems that could be identified in the late 1990s did not spring fully formed from independence in the 1960s or from conditions of conflict in the 1980s. Rather, they emerged as the elements of statehood were built, developed, and rearranged over forty or more years. They are unlikely to have been changed as a result of the political events of four or five years. In Africa the development of the police function reflects and depends on the development of the state, which (with the exception of Somalia and states such as the Central African Republic, Chad, Congo [Zaire], and Sierra Leone) remains definable in terms of authority and territory (see Table 3.1). The reflection exists partly because the police play a crucial role in the relationship between the central political authority (or regime) and the population at large, and partly because they are agents of both state and society—the very definition and management of civil order is in part shaped by their interests, yet their actions are linked to patterns of regime action. A schematic indication of the links is shown in Figure 3.2.

The political changes in Africa since 1990 serve only to underline the difficulty of establishing paradigms analyzing these relationships. In addition, conflict in countries such as Rwanda and Somalia has sharply limited opportunities to research what remains of previous systems, let alone how they function (if at all) in extreme situations. Yet all is not lost, for such countries offer other new categories of policing that, in the case of Somalia, certain authorities, such as those in the United States, are convinced are viable propositions. Policing in Rwanda is also of active interest to donors. There are undoubtedly formal and informal networks between policing systems, there are "international" standards concerning humanitarian methods of policing, and there is comparative work on crime. But there is currently no methodical comparative research on police systems across the continent or on core areas of policing, such as the use of force and the detention of suspects.

Despite these considerations, some generalizations about police systems can be made, for (as I have stressed) police systems show great powers of

Table 3.1 Levels of Police Functions and Roles in Relation to State Development

Phase	Police System			
	Police (organization)	Policing (activity)	Function	Role
Postcolonial	National force derived from colonial models	Africanization Rural-urban split Recruitment ethnicized	Law and order enforcement Paramilitary support Regime representation	Regulatory (e.g., border and traffic control) and maintain political order (internal role)
Fragile	Visible coercive agent	Rural-urban split Recruitment ethnicized	Order enforcement Paramilitary support Regime representation	Inconsistent patterns of activity
Fragmenting	Loss of central control and formal infrastructure	Selfish/survival activities only	Repression	Roles may be maintained by small units
Fragmented	Numerous overlapping agencies	Security privatized	No formal functions	Security provided by range of armed groups
Conflict	State policing militarized	Civilian activities suspended	Subsumed under war fighting	Subsumed under fighting war
Collapsed	Power vacuum; privatized freelancing		Support of a faction	Regulation and security provided by private suppliers
Reconstruction	New civilian national force	Bureaucratic practices (e.g., criminal records) Training provided by overseas aid	Law and order enforcement Paramilitary operations Regime representation	Regulatory activities

Figure 3.2 Role and Legitimacy in Police Systems

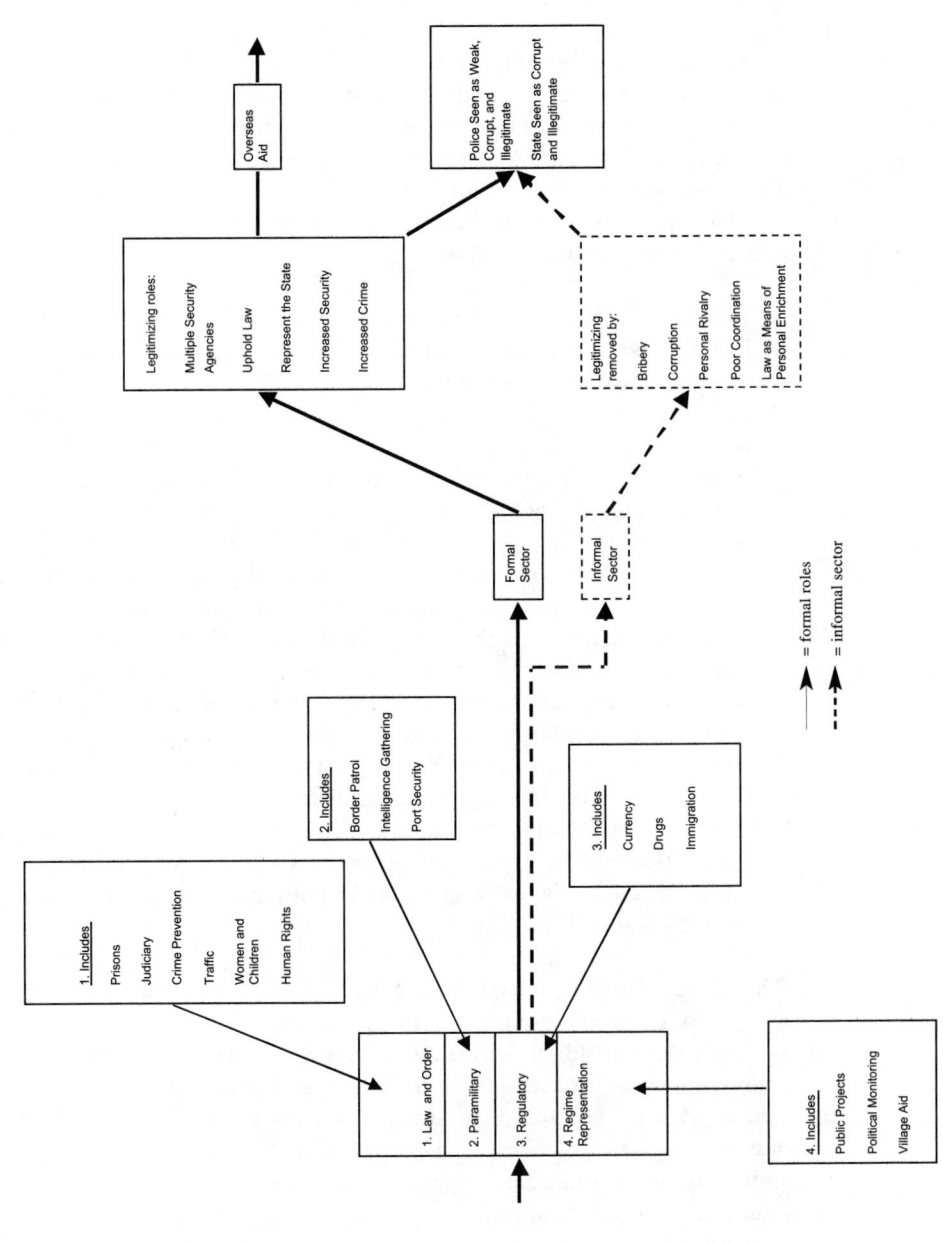

survival. With the exception of the political changes involved in the end of apartheid, wars, liberalization, and international aid probably left most existing systems fundamentally unchanged in the 1990s simply because the essential nature, expression, and problems of public policing remained the same as in the 1980s. It is unlikely that this situation will change dramatically in the near future, for police systems are notoriously conservative. Where change may come is on the periphery of policing, where private security is increasingly able to exploit existing relationships between state structures and the maintenance of order.

On this basis, six main processes in the development of African police systems could be identified in the 1990s:

1. *Evolution:* a mature system in states (such as Uganda) where there is a high degree of institutional capacity developed from structures existing since independence.
2. *Conversion:* a system created by a new regime emerging from an insurgency, which is presented with special opportunities to legitimize itself as a reformist alternative to an old, corrupt government. This involves the deliberate conversion of an existing police force, as in Ethiopia.
3. *Construction:* a system created by a new regime, formed out of a successful reformist insurgency, which incorporates the insurgent's own organization into the new government, as in Eritrea.
4. *Integration:* a system in which existing forces are integrated into a new security force after a negotiated settlement in a state with a high degree of institutional capacity, as in Namibia.
5. *Transition:* policing in a fragile transitional environment where there is a low or nonexistent state institutional capacity, as in Somalia, the self-proclaimed republic of Somaliland, and Congo (Zaire).
6. *Adaptation:* where public police forces are in the process of adapting to specific new developments in policing, such as commercial security and self-policing.

This simple model is a first move toward a critique of policing and national development. The classification is of necessity artificial, but the simplicity of the sixfold model makes it sufficiently flexible to incorporate the wide range of approaches to the rationale and organization of policing adopted in Africa. The type of regime and the circumstances under which it came to power are, of course, critical, but such variables are offset by the similarity of the inherent properties that give policing its characteristic nature in all forces, though cultural, religious, and environmental differences must be acknowledged. This is proving the case even in a state, such as Eritrea, heavily influenced by its insurgent organization. The internal dynamics of hierarchies and cliques, as well as corporate and personal ambitions and traditions—to say nothing of political judgments and regime concerns—will shape the resultant systems but cannot be factored into the initial model.

The categories presented are ideal; the countries chosen to illustrate them focus attention on a specific trait, although at the expense of complex reality. They indicate dominant aspects of police systems and the range of state institutional capacity. This results in artificial delimitation, as some of the countries demonstrate several themes. Uganda and Nigeria are prime examples of the (dominant) evolutionary nature of police systems, but Ethiopia may also be placed in this category. In many respects the real distinction between Ethiopia and Eritrea versus Namibia is that the Ethiopian and Eritrean regimes came to power as a result of an insurgency that developed along the periphery of the state before fighting its way into power. (Uganda also fits into this category.) In contrast, Namibia's regime did not win a war militarily and was subject to a negotiated settlement. In Ethiopia and Eritrea, the new regime incorporated the insurgents' own organization into the new government. Each regime had a strong leader, and (unlike in Angola, Mozambique, and Namibia) each took power without facing continued war from rival insurgents financed by external powers.

The regimes in all three states also claimed to be the postcolonial successors to colonial rule. Yet Eritrea had a new regime that created a police system in its own organizational image in a way that Namibia could not. Namibia's rulers (who did not win a war) were subject to a negotiated settlement in which they were forced to integrate an old paramilitary organization into their security forces. In a sense, Namibia more closely resembles some of the postcolonial nationalist regimes in Africa (such as Congo) that inherited security forces staffed with personnel who were hostile to the new regime. In contrast, the regime of Meles Zenawi in Ethiopia inherited a hated police system, which it rejected, and a long-established culture that it found much more difficult to discard. It can be argued that both Ethiopia and Namibia represent countries with a high degree of state institutional capacity. In terms of such a capacity, Uganda, Ethiopia, and Eritrea were offered the special, perhaps transient, opportunities presented to successful insurgencies. They suffered from serious resource problems, but they were able to benefit from their legitimacy as reformist alternatives to corrupt governments (though this was less so for Ethiopia).

These facts do not, however, invalidate the importance of the overall themes of the model. The model is simple and does not require explicit identification of the place the various case studies occupy on the spectrum of state institutional capacity. Its uncomplicated nature means that it provides clear insight into the dominant trends and linkages between the various elements of internal policing and regime type.

Notes

1. David Bayley, *Police for the Future* (Oxford: Oxford University Press, 1994), 12.

2. Mawby has argued that an international comparative element to specific policing practices is inevitable because of one or more of the four processes: emigration, conquest, joining, and borrowing. See R. I. Mawby, *Comparative Policing Issues: The British and American Experience in International Perspective* (London: Routledge/Unwin, 1990).

3. *Africa Research Bulletin* 34: 11 (1997), 12886. SARPCCO can be usefully compared to other regional initiatives such as the Association of Southeast Asian National Police (ASEANPOL). ASEANPOL meets periodically to discuss common concerns (such as organized crime), but it has had little impact on operational policing. The infrequent meetings are restricted and concentrate on the most basic issues permitted by political guidance.

4. *Africa Research Bulletin* 31: 8 (1995), 11939. Many such agreements now involve South Africa. The lack of contact between South Africa and its neighboring states previously made transborder investigations impossible.

5. Overseas officers visiting the UK are usually more impressed by the independence of a British chief constable and his information technology resources than by the need for financial planning or efficient criminal records systems.

6. The Rapid Intervention Police (RIP, known as Ninjas because of their dark uniforms) were created with Spanish assistance in 1992, in contradiction of the 1991 Bicesse Peace Accords. At the time the government claimed they numbered about 5,850, but the Washington-based *Angola Update* newsletter refers to the minister of the interior's figure of 30,000 as accurate for 1994 (*Angola Update* 4: 6 [10 July 1996]). The RIP are, however, police in name only. They receive special forces training and have tanks and helicopters.

7. *International Police Review,* November/December 1997.

8. Ibid.

9. Even SAPS is particularly weak in its detective services.

10. The phrase *war against crime* is commonplace, but the language and resources used in South Africa are more meaningfully military, with troops from the Angolan war (such as the Thirty-second Battalion) being deployed in the Johannesburg area. See *Financial Times*, 31 August 1996.

11. *Indian Ocean Newsletter* 724 (2 June 1996), 5.

12. *Africa Confidential* 36: 8 (1995), 7. Traders in Mozambique were not worried about being caught: "If you do get caught, you can buy these guys off."

13. Special antidrug programs by SADC member countries can be financed by funds from the Lomé Convention. *Indian Ocean Newsletter* 691 (28 October 1995), 3. External resources may be provided to promote such goals, but their probable effectiveness is debatable, even when they represent a significant element in the relevant budget.

14. *Africa Confidential* 36: 2 (1995), 2.

15. *Independent on Sunday,* 18 January 1998.

16. Kenneth Good, "Accountable to Themselves: Predominance in Southern Africa," *Journal of Modern African Studies* 35: 4 (1997), 554. In contrast, the deputy president, Thabo Mbeki, politicized the situation by arguing that action by former and current security force members loyal to the apartheid regime was the key factor in the crisis.

17. Albert J. Reiss and David J. Bordua, "Environment and Organization: A Perspective on the Police," in David J. Bordua, ed., *The Police: Six Sociological Essays* (New York: John Wiley & Sons, 1967), 25.

18. In the last six months of 1997, 119 officers were murdered, forty-three on duty and seventy-six off. This represented a rise of 29.3 percent over the figure for the same period in the previous year. The prime motive for the murders is the theft of officers' firearms. Drug-related crime is becoming increasingly prevalent. The casualty rate is not unconnected to the automatic carbines from Mozambique in many of the incidents. The price of a new AK-47 in Maputo in 1998 (still in its factory grease) was about $50. *International Police Review*, November/December 1998, 16.

Although the South African force is seriously understaffed, there is no shortage of applicants. A constable earns 35,000 rand (about $3,000), whereas a sergeant earns 49,000 rand (about $4,000). These figures are supplemented by 880 rand a month housing allowance and in some areas 200 rand danger money and 300 rand high-risk money. A senior superintendent earns about $12,500 a year. See *Police Review*, 28 November 1997, 22–23.

19. Relatives of the president, who comes from a poor family, are reported to be among Tunisia's richest citizens.

20. J. D. Ojo, "The Police Under the Nigerian Constitutions," *African Notes* 17: 1 and 2 (1993), 21.

21. R. P. Boyes, "A Report on the Ghana Police Service, Following a Survey by R. P. Boyes QPM, Deputy Chief Constable, Mid-Anglia Constabulary," 1971, 233. It is telling that the Ghanaian officer concerned was influenced by an attachment to the English Metropolitan Police Force in 1968. He knew of their plans for dealing with large-scale demonstrations.

22. John Okello, *Revolution in Zanzibar* (Nairobi: East African Publishing House, 1967); *Keesing's Contemporary Archives* (1964), 19951–19953. The new revolutionary government published a number of decrees in March 1964 that included empowering the president to detain any person considered to be a threat to good order. No court of law had powers to question such an order.

23. Christian Potholm, "The Multiple Roles of the Police as Seen in the African Context," *Journal of Developing Areas* 3 (January 1969), 142; Raymond G. Hunt and John M. Magment, *Power and the Police Chief: An Institutional and Organizational Analysis* (London: Sage, 1993), 32.

24. Potholm, "Multiple Roles," 157.

25. Ibid., 147.

26. *Africa Research Bulletin* 29: 11 (1992), 10799; *Guardian*, 8 December 1994.

27. BBC Monitoring Service, *Summary of World Broadcasts* SWB 2675, 27 July 1996, 3. The army role included maintaining public order.

28. Stephen Riley, "Africa's "New Wind of Change," *World Today*, July 1992, 116–119.

29. In 1995, for example, Oliver Furley identified thirty-two conflicts in progress and a further 118 minor armed conflicts. He considers the causes to include the inadequacy of African state structures, the resurgence of ethnicity as a political force, and the lack of logic in the drawing of national borders by colonial powers. Oliver Furley, *Conflict in Africa* (London: Tauris, 1995).

30. Police were not mentioned. See *Africa Confidential* 38: 2 (1997), 8. The shoot-on-sight policy was never announced, but it was publicly acknowledged by

the president. According to *Africa Confidential,* the International Federation of Human Rights Leagues (FIDH) believed the situation raised significant questions about the security and military training assistance France had provided to Chad.

31. Crime is different from deviance. It requires specificity and punishability. See Hernando Gomez Buendia, ed., *Urban Crime, Global Trends and Policies* (Tokyo: UN University, 1989), 7.

32. J. M. Lee, *African Armies and Civil Order* (London: Chatto & Windus for the IISS, 1969), 2.

33. Henry Bienen, ed., *The Military Intervenes: Case Studies in Political Development* (New York: Russell Sage Foundation 1968), 37. This is separate from examples of the breakdown of civil society. The latter is more accurately described by Richard Sandbrook in his article "Patrons, Clients and Factions: New Dimensions of Conflict Analysis in Africa," *Canadian Journal of African Studies* 5: 1 (March 1972), 109: "Where a society's impersonal legal guarantees of physical security, status, and wealth are relatively weak or non-existent, individuals seek personal substitutes by attaching themselves to "big men" capable of providing protection and even advancement."

34. Lee, *African Armies,* 3.

35. Yezid Sayigh, *Confronting the 1990s: Security in the Developing Countries,* Adelphi Paper 251 (London: Brassey's for the IISS, 1990), 3. As Jackson showed, these concerns can be said to have characterized cold war security concerns, too; see Robert H. Jackson, Quasi-states: *Sovereignty, International Relations and the Third World* (Cambridge: Cambridge University Press, 1990). For a discussion of the conceptual issue involved, see David A. Baldwin, "The Concept of Security," *Review of International Studies* 23: 1 (1997), 5–26.

36. *Sudan Update* 9: 1 (13 January 1998), 1.

37. *Financial Times,* 5 March 1998. Nigeria's civilian elite also proved incapable of operating a stable system during its two periods of office (1960–1966 and 1979–1983).

38. Quoted in Robert Fatton*, Predatory Rule: State and Civil Society in Africa* (Boulder, CO: Lynne Rienner, 1992), 142. Since the World Bank report *Sub-Saharan Africa: From Crisis to Sustainable Growth* (Washington, DC: World Bank, 1989) was published, the crisis in the state is often discussed in terms of the wider debate on governance.

39. *Africa Report* (1991), 59. For definitions of good governance, see Gordon Crawford, *Promoting Democracy, Human Rights and Good Governance Through Development Aid: A Comparative Study of the Policies of Four Northern Donors,* Working Papers on Democratization (Leeds: University of Leeds, 1996).

40. See J. F. Maitland Jones, *Politics in Ex-British Africa* (London: Weidenfeld & Nicolson, 1973), 15.

41. Asked if he had put money into Switzerland, President Godfry Binaisa of Uganda said, "Yes, that's true, but much less than the press has written. As a President working diligently for his country, I had a right to a bigger compensation. That's democratic." *Africa Diary* 20: 6 (1980), 9878.

42. See Jan Kooiman, *Modern Governance: New Government-Society Interactions* (London: Sage, 1993), 43. It is informative to compare the complexity of Western understandings of governance with the Ghanaian multiple understanding of government in the 1970s. See John Dunn and A. F. Robertson, *Dependence and Opportunity: Political Change in Ahafo* (Cambridge: Cambridge University Press, 1973).

43. Robert H. Jackson and Carl G. Rosberg, *Personal Rule in Black Africa:*

Prince, Autocrat, Prophet, Tyrant (Berkeley: University of California Press, 1982), 21.

44. Goran Hyden and Michael Bratton, eds., *Governance and Politics in Africa* (Boulder, CO: Lynne Rienner, 1992), x.

45. Ibid., 29.

46. World Bank, *Demobilization and Reintegration of Military Personnel in Africa: The Evidence from Seven Country Case Studies,* Report IDP-130 (New York: World Bank, 1993), 22.

47. The Koevoet was a police (rather than an army) counterinsurgency unit, and its 300 white officers were almost all South African policemen. See Dennis Herbstein and John Evenson, *The Devils Are Among Us: The War for Namibia* (London: Zed Books, 1989), 68. For political reasons, the Koevoet was absorbed into the police as a counterinsurgency force before the end of the conflict. It continued to patrol repressively in armored and heavily armed convoys in the northern region until a special United Nations Security Council resolution (640) called for its disbandment.

48. See Bienen, *The Military Intervenes,* 35. An indigenous human rights movement may be emerging in a state such as Uganda, but human rights are mainly the concern of an urban middle class whereas most Ugandans are the rural poor. See the *Economist,* 4 April 1998.

49. *West Africa,* 17 December 1966. Section 1(2) of the Police Service Act 1970 expressly provided that police officers should take orders only from senior members of the Ghana Police Service.

50. The rule of law is held by some commentators to establish "principles that constrain the power of government, oblige it to conduct itself to a series of prescribed and publicly known rules." See Neil J. Kritz, "The Rule of Law in the Postconflict Phrase: Building a Stable Peace," in Chester A. Crocker and Fen Osler Hampson, with Pamela Aall, *Managing Global Chaos: Sources of and Responses to International Conflict* (Washington, DC: U.S. Institute of Peace Press, 1996), 587–606. Others recognize the central place of law. Ugandan president Yoweri Museveni in 1986, for example, said, "We are fighting for the democratic rights and human dignity of our people. . . . Our women shall no longer be raped by bandit soldiers . . . Nobody, not even a tramp on the road shall be killed, unless so condemned by the Courts." Quoted in R. Cohen and H. Goulbourne, *Democracy and Socialism in Africa* (Oxford: Oxford University Press, 1991), 125.

51. Indeed, Nigeria did not have the preventive detention acts common elsewhere, but all the constitutions dating from independence in 1960 (that is, those of the first republic of 1963, second republic of 1979, and Third Republic of 1989) had elaborate sections on fundamental human rights.

52. Enloe's work is an exception to this general rule.

53. Rob Midgley and Geoffrey Wood, "Community Policing in Transition: Attitudes and Perceptions from South Africa's Eastern Cape Province," *Low Intensity Conflict and Law Enforcement* 5: 2 (1997), 165–181.

54. Gilber M. Khadiagala, "Uganda's Domestic and Regional Security Since the 1970s," *Journal of Modern African Studies* 31: 2 (1993), 231–255. For the political instrumentalization of disorder, see Patrick Chabal and Jean-Pascal Daloz, *Africa Works: Disorder as Political Instrument* (Oxford: James Currey, 1999).

55. John Wiseman, "Leadership and Personal Danger, *Journal of Modern African Studies* 31: 4 (1993), 657–660. Compare Henry S. Bienen and Nicolas van de Walle, *Of Time and Power: Leadership Duration in the Modern World* (Stanford, CA: Stanford University Press, 1991); Henry S. Bienen and Nicolas van de

Walle, "A Proportional Hazard Model of Leadership Duration," *Journal of Politics* 5: 4 (1992), 693; Baker, "The Class of 1990: How Have the Autocratic Leaders of Sub-Saharan Africa Fared Under Democratisation?" *Third World Quartley* 19: 1 (1998), 115–127. Baker finds that half of the autocratic rulers in power in 1990 successfully transformed themselves into "democratic" rulers.

4

Models of African Policing: Evolution and Conversion

The characteristics and workings of the processes underpinning the model set out in Chapter 3 are best illustrated by reference to policing in specific states. I have chosen Uganda, Ethiopia, Eritrea, Namibia, Somalia, Somaliland, and Congo (Zaire) because each exemplifies a major trait of police systems, and each illustrates the types of relationships that existed between internal policing and regime types from approximately 1990 to 1996. Each provides evidence with which to judge the effects of liberalization on police systems. In this chapter I look at the themes of evolution and conversion in terms of the experiences of Uganda and Ethiopia. Chapter 5 focuses on the construction and integration of police systems in Eritrea and Namibia. Because of the unique importance of fragile transitional environments to policing, reconstruction operations, and international organizations in Africa in the 1990s, I cover the examples provided by Somalia, Somaliland, and Congo (Zaire) separately in Chapter 6, where I consider conflict, fragmentation, and transition.

Model 1—Evolution: Uganda

The evolutionary nature of police systems is recognized in the first phase of the model. At the most general level, all existing police systems can be said to have evolved since independence, but the theme warrants closer analysis because it directs attention to three important aspects of police systems. The first is that the evolutionary model is dominant, especially in the mature and comparatively sophisticated police systems of states such as Kenya, Nigeria, and Uganda. The second is the legitimization (understood in terms of both sanction by law and general acceptance) of the brutality seemingly inherent in many African states, in which harsh methods are institutionalized and thus become more predictable. The third is the progression of policing through cycles of repression and reform, in which brutality acts in tandem with state institutional reconstruction. This process is particularly noticeable in the case of Uganda, where policing displayed continuity in resources and status at the same time it reflected regime developments. Contemporary policing needs to be seen within these dominant themes.

The Legitimization of Brutality: Policing Before 1990

The new central government of Uganda assumed full responsibility for public safety and order once independence was gained in 1962. The Uganda Police Force (which had been established as a civil force with some paramilitary duties) was large and well organized, though the semi-autonomous federal states of Uganda initially kept their own small police forces.[1] Training for the Uganda Police was provided by Britain and other democracies during the 1960s and early 1970s, but it seems likely that the independence and integrity of the state police was compromised as early as 1966.[2] In a speech to the bar of Uganda in 1991, Herbert Karugaba (director of CID at police headquarters) detailed misuses of police powers under the Emergency Powers (Detention) Regulations of 1966 and concluded that the legitimized abuse of police powers was considered permissible at the official level because police actions could not be officially questioned; they were seen as actions of the executive, under the constitution, in the interest of peace and order.[3] The 1967 constitution further institutionalized brutality by protecting the police from judicial scrutiny; the harsh methods of policing were effectively sanctified by repressive laws.

It is not surprising that civilian institutions proved unable to address the problem. Several hundred thousand Ugandans died during the resulting military regime of Idi Amin (1971–1979), many of them at the hands of the security forces and paramilitary organizations.[4] In Kampala, for example, all the military barracks, the maximum security prison, and "nearly all the police stations in and around the capital were also torture and murder centres."[5] The military were most heavily implicated but it is clear that many police were also involved. The majority of the police and prison forces tended to be drawn from the same northern Nilotic tribes as the army, with the Acholi, Itseso and Lango strongly represented in all forces. Amin despised the police, who tended to be Obote supporters. Many of the best officers were killed, but the system remained relatively unchanged because it was easily—and legitimately—exploited and absorbed into the military. As I noted in Chapter 2, assimilation tends to happen in such conditions.

Repression and Reform

The fall of Amin was marked by the first of many attempts institutionally to separate the police from the (para)military by means of reconstructing police recruitment (though the legal system remained fundamentally unaltered). Such "reform" was also prompted by the determination of the Obote II regime (Obote's second term, 1979–1985) to purge Amin's people and ensure its dominance. The resultant policing problems straddled the three categories of issues confronting Uganda since the 1970s: those which predated Amin (primarily tribal rivalry), those he created (such as a brutalized police), and those caused by war and an inexperienced government with no firm domestic power base. The last of these encouraged Obote to rely on coercive forces at the same time he needed to prevent the creation of other powerful organizations. Policing was bound to reflect Obote's unpopularity as a ruler.

The situation also presented problems to the police in that the economy was damaged in order to keep the army content and political instability resulted in the murder or exile of most of the professional classes, thus adding to general insecurity and rising crime. Certainly the police (and the army) appeared unable to control the crime wave. Indeed, the security of the government at that point could be guaranteed only by the support of Tanzania, and 1,000 Tanzanian policemen arrived in Uganda at the end of September 1979 to bolster the ill-equipped and badly disciplined Ugandan force. The Tanzanians provided an initial safety measure for the Obote government, which (with the inefficient and corrupt police working in a shattered economy and derelict infrastructure) remained in power until 1985. Repression was generally politically motivated under Amin, whereas under Obote II it was more criminal or personalized.

Uganda Since 1990

After a succession of short-lived regimes that failed to restore stability, Yoweri Museveni's National Resistance Army (NRA) seized power in 1986, pledging to end political upheaval and introduce national reconciliation. It was the first guerrilla movement to force out an African rather than a colonial regime.

Museveni had not had regular military training, but he was the head of an armed insurgency who fought his way to power. In 1991 he made it clear that he has no faith in political pluralism and that he relies substantially on the army as the ultimate guarantor of national unity and stability. His attitude is predictable, given the critical importance of conflict in the region and the repeated overthrow of Ugandan governments by insurrection.

Whether "no-party" democracy is essentially autocratic rule enforced by the military is debatable, but the prominence of the military in the regime is hardly surprising, as it was clear by 1990 that attempts to implement economic and social reconstruction would be slowed by ethnic rivalries and a rebel opposition. Indeed, Museveni has faced prolonged insurgent action by three major groups since the mid-1990s. The result is that accommodation to pressure, such as demands for increased political participation, have encouraged him to try to manage transition by limiting political participation and competition and restricting the independence of the judiciary and certain rights so as to ensure his regime's survival. The police have been an obvious instrument for achieving this.

National unity. The first political theme to emerge was that of reconciliation and national unity. Once the National Resistance Movement (NRM) had established itself in Uganda, it tried to strengthen this presence—and its own hold on government—by including representatives of other organized political forces in its decisionmaking bodies. This strategy was balanced to some extent by the development of resistance councils, established originally as small-scale support groups during the NRM's guerrilla struggle. The NRM defended the resulting intricate structure (stretching from the village to district level) as being essentially more democratic than the earlier political parties, operating at the territorial level, which had made independence tense by deliberately encouraging ethnic, regional, and politico-religious differences.

When Museveni became president in 1986, he pledged to end the army's tyranny and reform the criminal justice system. He granted greater autonomy to the courts, but this was offset during counterinsurgency operations in northern and eastern Uganda, when several thousand suspected opponents were arrested. Further, the National Resistance Council (NRC) passed a constitutional amendment in late 1988 giving the president the power to declare any region of the country to be in a "state of insurgency." Subsequent legislation allowed the government to establish separate courts in these areas, authorized the military to arrest insurgents, and permitted magistrates to suspend the rules to allow uncorroborated evidence.[6]

Order and pluralism. The second political theme of these years is tension between order and pluralism, reinforced by considerations of regime and state insecurity in the face of pressure for liberalization. Uganda was again confronted with the classic dilemma of choosing between reconstructing the state, using all available resources, and accommodating demands for political participation and multiparty politics. The government's solution was to insist on no-party democracy and a ban on party politics yet invite rivals to adopt a nonadversarial role within the NRM structure.

The form of democracy Museveni pioneered was a pyramidal and hierarchical system of resistance councils (RCs) and resistance committees, which were directly elected at the village level, with each council electing the membership of the next-tier parish, country, and district levels, up to the National Resistance Council, which had originally acted as a temporary parliament and legislature. The RC system has succeeded in creating a broadly based government (with members of all the important political parties being given cabinet posts). It also appears to be acceptable to the West, for Uganda was on U.S. president Bill Clinton's itinerary during his trip to Africa in April 1998, and Uganda is the first beneficiary of the World Bank's debt reduction program for heavily indebted poor countries.

At the same time, Uganda enjoyed a relatively free press and independent judiciary, though power became increasingly concentrated in the hands of Museveni and a group of officials and army officers from his home region. The army, administration, and ruling secretariat are dominated by his Ankole tribe, and the head of counterinsurgency is Salim Saleh, his half brother. But despite the NRM's efforts to show itself as a viable alternative to a multiparty system, Uganda saw resurgence of past political struggles during the 1990s, and a strong police presence was evident at all important opposition rallies.

Museveni's view was that a competitive political system of the type associated with liberalization would destabilize the fragile national consensus achieved by his no-party political system. In May 1993 he therefore banned the activities of all other political parties, accusing them of refusing to abide by government orders, though he insisted (before the 1993 elections) that there was no danger of Uganda's "sliding back into dictatorship."[7] Only nonparty presidential and parliamentary elections (using a secret ballot) were proposed for 1994, after which Uganda would hold a national referendum to decide on a more permanent system of government.

That Museveni's control was tight, if less brutal than previous regimes, was evident in the presidential elections of May 1996. Museveni set the rules and manipulated the electoral process, making it impossible for him to lose to the two candidates running against him.[8] He controlled the government's publicity machinery and how the elections were conducted, for elections were organized through local council administrations rather than an independent electoral commission. More significant, Museveni's candidates were backed by the police who continued to act with the army and security forces in harassing opponents. Indeed, the minister for state security, Colonel Kahinda Otafire, said that if anyone except Museveni won the presidential elections, the newcomer would be overthrown within twenty-four hours.

The tenuous nature of Ugandan stability was shown by the strong tribal undertones of much of the rhetoric employed by all sides during the

1994 elections—such as the NRM's claim to legitimacy based on the fact that its inclusive policies removed tribalism. It is noticeable that there is a divide between the north and south, with most of the insurgency taking place in the north of the country. Traditional alliances and divisions remain strong, as does the memory of Amin's regime, though the majority of Ugandans may well vote in favor of prolonging the status quo when the NRM system is put to a national referendum in 2000. This has implications for the police, because even weak policing enforces both the regime's response and the order considered necessary for regime credibility (and survival) and is at the same time reactive to old and new pressures. Reaction is further accentuated by the spillover of many (linked) social problems from the 1980s into the 1990s: Demobilization, conflict, refugees, environmental degradation, AIDS, and policy reforms such as market liberalization remained significant.

Policing in the 1990s

The continuing importance of regime security in the face of persistent warfare as well as themes of reconstruction and continuity are reflected in the organization and practices of the Uganda Police.

In 1986 the NRA assumed responsibility for internal security. The value of the police was unquestioned by the NRM; indeed, a number of senior NRA members had been police officers. The force, controlled by the Ministry of Internal Affairs, was reorganized and expanded from 5,000 officers (for a population of 15 million) to about 8,000 officers and 5,000 new recruits in 1989, by which time law and order was enforced in most districts. Ambitions for the size of the NRA were as unrealistic as they had been in the 1970s; a force of 30,000 was thought appropriate, though the total strength in 1994 was still only 17,000 (or 1:1,000 of population).

The result was that by 1990 the Uganda Police were a multitribal, nonpolitical armed constabulary of 12,000–15,000 men of all ranks. The British training teams dealing with police management at this time considered the Ugandans to be the most efficient force in East Africa. The ratio of police to population remained one of the lowest in Africa, though this varied according to the district concerned; it was 1:10 in Kampala but 1:10,000 in Kigezi.[9] Such figures could be the result of the degree of government control of territory or, more likely, reflect the southern bias of the regime. The force was commanded by an inspector general appointed by the president on the advice of the Public Service Commission. The inspector general was assisted by four regional commanders and a police council that oversaw all aspects of recruitment and service. The inspector general's acts were exempt from judicial inquiry or review, and he reported directly to the minister of internal affairs and the president. Officers performed both regular and paramilitary police duties and were divided into branches or units covering conventional duties, such as the uniformed branch (dealing with mainly urban matters), special branch, CID, dog section, and a public safety unit. They also conducted most public prosecutions in criminal courts.

Reconstruction was initially a major theme, accelerated by the removal of unsuitable officers at all ranks and the "exceptionally high turnover of officers of Assistant Inspector and above."[10] Increasing recruitment became a priority, though the training of recruits was never given the resources necessary to change the culture of the force. The director of training was also responsible for recruitment, on which he concentrated at the expense of training. Training styles varied, as training was provided by France, North Korea, and Britain, the British government having pumped "huge resources into Uganda Police" before 1990.[11] The style of policing remained paramilitary, so although a British team was asked to review public order capability in 1989, there was already a commitment to more vigorous policing; trainers from the French CRS had earlier arrived in Uganda.

The problems of consolidation. By 1990 reconstruction was, however, inappropriate because it was superseded by the need for consolidation. In early July 1989, for example, there was a massive redeployment of senior police management, including the changing (overnight) of almost all regional commanders. This resulted in a lack of continuity that made it difficult to assess previous work, and the pursuit of economy resulted in a chronic lack of facilities, accommodation, and pay for recruits. Many police stations lacked paper and pens, let alone typewriters and desks, and everywhere the lack of transport and communications made crime prevention and detection difficult.

There were conscious attempts to avoid past failures and to adopt NRM philosophy by involving local communities and RCs in areas such as crime prevention, though this was not a structured part of policing. Much depended on the interests and skills of individuals. In 1989 the Old Kampala Police District, for instance, had a female district commander who was both positive and innovative. In fact, NRM philosophy had some influence on formal policing. In 1992–1993, for example, the force issued a "strategic statement of aim" for its intention "to provide an enlightened and motivated police force that is efficient and accountable to the people. It is intended to make the conditions and standard of service better for us personnel and laudable by the local community for whose purpose the police force was formed."[12] The force accordingly formulated two sets of objectives to "ensure force discipline and duty performance through improvement of performance at all levels." In the first set, for 1992–1993, the force hoped to reduce the incidence of certain types of crime (such as vehicle and street crime) by stepping up patrols, improving policing skills, and campaigns to increase public awareness. The second set of objectives, for 1994–1995, referred to achieving a 10 percent decrease in targeted crime, encouraging public participation in crime prevention, reducing traffic accidents by 10 percent, carrying out a training needs analysis, initiating appraisal systems, and improving staff welfare. In other words, the three main problems confronting the force in the early 1990s remained poor training, scant resources, and low public support.

Training has always been undervalued, and the lack of resources has been a constant theme in Uganda as elsewhere. Some officers displayed great ingenuity and improvisation; others showed less commitment. Many training instructors were appointed on completion of their recruit training (when they had no operational experience), and classes of more than 100 were common. Uganda Police standing orders place a responsibility at district level for holding lectures, and these (varying enormously in frequency and content) were effectively the only further training an (unpromoted) constable received during his service.

Museveni's government controls the budget, providing about 65 percent of the police budget. But in 1993, of the total budget of 45.3 billion shillings, only 14.3 billion were actually approved, whereas 1.2 billion shillings were approved on a budgeted 29.1 billion for capital expenditure. In 1994 less than half (14.2 billion shillings) was approved out of 30.2 billion claimed, and 1.1 billion shillings were received for capital against the 8.6 billion budgeted for. What was approved was not necessarily released; the police saw only 11.3 million of the 62.3 million shillings released for training. A new phase of support to the police began in 1993, focusing on training policy, community policing, and improving communications, but the police never received much of the promised funding.

Inadequate resources had implications for operational policing, for officers were badly paid. An inspector earned about $120 a month in the early 1990s, a sergeant $110, and a senior constable about $33 (for an annual income of $391). The government provided housing, medical attention, police insurance, and interest-free loans, but the cost of living was high and bureaucratic delays reduced such benefits. "When interviewed, how they make the difference, many said they have to rely on the village for food and their wives who do mini business for to keep the fire burning."[13]

Accommodation continued to be a problem. Nsambya police barracks on the eastern side of Kampala (the biggest in east and central Africa), was, for instance, home to officers and men from different units around the city, but lodging meant for 1,214 families actually housed 1,600 families.[14] The presence of more than 3,000 residents resulted in poor sanitation and crime. And in 1994 many officers considered their situation to be worse than that of the police in Botswana. Botswana's population of 1.4 million had 5,000 police divided among thirteen districts. Inspectors earned $1,100 a year, sergeants $1,000 and constables $900, and their remuneration included a risks allowance and free housing. These were, in fact, comparatively low rates, for Botswana's per capita gross national product (GNP) was about $3,600 in the mid-1990s, whereas Namibian salaries (which Ugandans, too, considered attractive) were much higher.

Lack of resources influenced operational techniques as well. Basic methods of policing, such as fixed point guards, were relied on. Transport had always presented problems, so the few vehicles available tended to be confined to Kampala, Tinja, and Entesse. Response times were bad—formally at least one to two hours in the city and three to twenty-four hours in rural areas—as transport police workshops in Kampala in 1994 showed fewer than 120 vehicles available to operational commanders for the 238,000 square kilometers of districts and divisions of Uganda. Most districts had at best two vehicles for all duties, even though some areas were huge (Kanga was 11,113 square kilometers, Kirgum 16,136 square kilometers). Fuel was hard to come by, so many senior officers did not tour their districts annually. Bicycle patrols were considered best for villages, but the few bicycles available were poorly maintained. Such conditions probably had a negative impact on discipline.

The failure of ideals. The Uganda Police inevitably failed to live up to its proclaimed ideals. They were formally "an effective and efficient law enforcement agency to serve the people," but in practice the police had little contact with the general public, even though this was an essential part of the government's philosophy. Some officers (echoing their Western colleagues) thought the public did not appreciate them. A chief assistant superintendent, for instance, said that traffic police, generally the first to be corrupted, are "usually smart, punctual, brave the sun for 8 hours a day and rarely withdraw from their points of duty." He complained that the public regarded them as "the most corrupted and lucrative section of the force."[15]

A significant test of Ugandan policing is to ask how it measures against the respect for human rights that Museveni made a cornerstone of government policy when he took power. The government acknowledged that not only must governmental excesses be checked but human rights abuse by state functionaries cannot occur without sanction. Unfortunately, the inspector general of government appointed to investigate the government's record on this score concluded that "Despite a far more transparent environment and the formal declaration of human rights observances as one of our objectives, there has been little fundamental progress since 1986."[16] This shortfall may result from both resource limitations and political direction.

That the lack of progress in human rights reflects adversely on policing is further emphasized by Amnesty International's inclusion of Uganda among states (such as Kenya, Tanzania, Zambia, and Zimbabwe) that have developed a pattern of human rights violations "in which governments publicly committed to political pluralism adopt methods of curbing domestic opposition and criticism which are designed to minimise the likelihood of international disapproval and keep their democratic credentials intact."[17] The police play a part in this repression because they cancel rallies and enforce charges of sedition, subversion, possession of classified documents, and holding meetings or demonstrations without an official permit—all the techniques used to restrict or intimidate critics of the regime. Amnesty International describes the political use of torture as still common in Uganda and believes the police use excessive force as a routine operational method of investigation and as a means of collecting evidence; abuse remains a serious problem throughout the country. Although both Amnesty International and the U.S. State Department point to repeated examples of such brutality, both concede that it is no longer systematically and officially sanctioned in Uganda.

The Ugandan government has in turn admitted past failures but affirmed its genuine commitment to improving its record. It has also defended itself by pointing out that it cannot be realistically judged against the same standards as, say, the United States. It refers to extenuating circumstances such as the economic situation of the country, particularly after twenty years of civil war, by attributing abuses to ignorance rather than intention: "The army simply did not understand what *habeas corpus* is all about. They did not know how to draw a return on writ of *habeas corpus* to present to court."[18] It avoided the temptation to refer all such abuses as criminal acts and highlighted its cooperation with Amnesty International and the International Committee of the Red Cross (ICRC).

In a live radio broadcast in 1998, Museveni defended his no-party system and referred to the danger that tribalism might hijack the multiparty system. Speaking on the twelfth anniversary of his coming to power, he said: "We are doing what we can to rebuild the institutions such as the police, the judiciary, the prisons, and create others such as [a] human rights commission to oversee the observance of human rights and to enforce the rule of law."[19] The Uganda Police thus continue to evolve, for that rebuilding process is unlimited. Policing in Uganda mirrors this surface ambiguity as it goes through cycles of reorganization, inertia, and repression. Because it reflects politics, it represents regime reactions to events or trends and lacks strategic direction. Reform remains unconsolidated.

Model 2—Conversion: Ethiopia

The experience of countries such as Uganda add significantly to our knowledge of the workings of African police systems and their relationships to regimes, particularly after periods of conflict. But I now turn my attention to a state that exemplifies a very different approach to development after seemingly entrenched brutality and conflict: Ethiopia. The new regime, like that in Uganda and neighboring Eritrea, came to power as a result of an insurgency. Ethiopia (like Eritrea) considered itself to be starting afresh. Dawit Yhannes, a legal adviser to Ethiopian president Meles Zenawi, said, "There is no country called Ethiopia, no state that defends the interests of this multi-ethnic community grouped under the name Ethiopia. That's why we've been immersed in wars for the last 30 years. So we must start again, from scratch."[20]

But Ethiopian policing, unlike that of Eritrea, did not truly start from scratch: It was shaped by the heavy inheritance of a failed centralized autocracy and a brutal dictatorship. In this sense the policing system has been ideologically, politically, and operationally converted rather than created afresh. Both Ethiopia and Eritrea are peculiar in that the Haile Marriam Mengistu regime (1974–1991) was replaced through insurgency, not urban protest. But policing in Ethiopia has evolved differently from that in Eritrea, mainly because of "the structure of the Ethiopian state itself and the difficulty of reconciling democratic accountability with state survival."[21]

The first official trial (in 1996) of the alleged perpetrators of harsh purges against opponents in 1977–1978 underscored the difficulty of reconciling the determination to change a brutal police system with the realization that conversion of any police system is severely limited by political and cultural factors. Meles said in 1994 that "it's very important to prove to Ethiopians that those who mess around with the law, human rights law, those who consider themselves above the law, are not really above the law—that there will be some day of reckoning."[22] A Special Prosecutor's Office had been established in 1992 to create a historical record of the abuses during Mengistu's government and to bring to justice those criminally responsible, but courts did not begin to hear the accounts of witnesses until 1996. According to the special prosecutor, "We are using our national law, national courts, prosecution and defence lawyers for all the cases. This process . . . is the basis for an established sequence of state accountability."[23] Many of the defendants had, however, been held without charge for over five years.

The key to resolving the tension was adaptation on the part of the ruling party and, only then, by policing. The Ethiopian People's Revolutionary Democratic Front (EPRDF) established a transitional government in Addis Ababa in July 1991 after Mengistu fled to Zimbabwe. The EPRDF coalition, formed in 1989, was dominated by the Tigray People's Liberation Front (TPLF) under its general-secretary, Meles. The EPRDF leadership was flexible. It had grown out of a popular revolt and at first demanded autonomy or independence for its region, adopting an Albanian Marxist model as its chosen form of centralized organization until 1990.

But this did not result in support from the former eastern bloc, so the TPLF widened its appeal by means of a series of revisions to include a broad commitment to democratic rights and a pluralist political system. Of necessity the new government had also to address the means of transition from war to peace, including the demobilization of one of the largest armies in Africa, the reconstruction of infrastructure destroyed during civil war, and perhaps most important, the enforcement and maintenance of the order and law without which little could be achieved.

Ethiopia is the first country in postcolonial Africa where part of the state has been allowed to break away and where the political structure of the state is being reorganized from above on ethnoregional lines.[24] Organizations such as Amnesty International continue to condemn Ethiopia's human rights record, though the police that evolved in response to Ethiopia's needs were by 1996 part of a recognizably changed system. The fundamental relationship between state and police is, however, unchanged, and policing is (as elsewhere) as much an instrument of regime control as ever.

Political Developments, 1991–1996

That operational policing techniques have changed while the relationship of the police to the state has not is a reflection of the EPRDF's political requirements.[25] When it, together with other groups active in the anti-Mengistu struggle, took power in 1991, it adopted a national charter establishing a Transitional Government of Ethiopia (TGE). Since then the TGE, headed by Meles, has presided over the introduction of a federal constitution in which power is devolved to nine regional states, based largely on ethnic groupings. In practice authority rests with the president and perpetuates the strong Ethiopian bias toward authoritarianism expressed through policing. Indeed, Clapham argues that when the values and structures of the northern highlands are associated with those of the state, they invariably result in hierarchical and inegalitarian structures:

> These relations culminate in a political hierarchy which has enabled highland Ethiopia to maintain a recognisable state over a vastly longer period than anywhere else in sub-Saharan Africa: but they create attitudes to authority which are difficult to reconcile with the exercise of open criticism and legitimate opposition that characterize multi-party democracy. In particular, it has been difficult to criticize any individual in a position of authority without appearing to challenge that authority.[26]

Such authoritarianism was so firmly entrenched that the TGE felt secure enough to implement its planned devolution of authority to regional governments and, moreover, held elections in June 1995 for the 548-seat constituent assembly. This body was responsible for approving the new constitution (which was ratified in December and replaced the interim national charter). Although the TGE handed over the mantle of power to a popularly elected government, the policy of promoting ethnic identity and regionalism has increased the ascendance of Tigrayans and discontent among the Amharas, who traditionally controlled centralized power. The new constitution of August 1995 promoted a multiparty system and limited the role of the future central government to the preservation of the constitution, defense, and foreign policy, but all the major opposition parties boycotted the June constituent assembly elections and accused the TGE of manipulating the political process. For the framework of the new federal democratic republic was erected under the transitional government, and EPRDF power remains significant, given its monopoly in both the federal government and the nine regional states. The states have legislative, executive, and judicial powers that include all powers not given separately to the federal government. With a majority of ministers from EPRDF, political considerations continue to influence decisions concerning policing.

But the TPLF position, based on the party and regionalism, is difficult. Tigray itself is desperately poor, and Tigrayan speakers form only one-tenth of the state, so (as Clapham points out) "any elected central government would thus . . . be unlikely to accord any great weight to the Tigrinya-speaking population, while a devolved regional government would result in each ethnic administration controlling a high proportion of its own economy and leave Tigray dependent on the charity of other regions."[27] In addition, society was militarized, weapons were easily available, and the EPRDF had always been opposed to the articulate elite concentrated in central institutions such as the bureaucracy and Addis Ababa University. In other words, the regime could not allow its opponents to win the first multiparty elections that took place in May 1995. The elections were to be the final step in the EPRDF's plan to turn the country into a federal republic with a wide range of powers devolved to the regions, but the main opposition parties boycotted them, claiming that arbitrary arrests and the closure of their offices made campaigning impossible.

The results reflected Ethiopia's political reality. The EPRDF dominates Ethiopia, controlling the regions through the party; decentralization has merely meant dispersing the opposition. Party control is ultimately guaranteed by the Tigrayan core of the army and, at a lower level, by the police.

Policing in Ethiopia, 1991–1996

Although contemporary policing has consciously rejected much of the past, the system shares many of its predecessors' cultural characteristics. Everything to do with contemporary policing is in practice measured against the Ethiopian police force during the Dergue's rule (the army has nevertheless continued to be heavily involved in policing). The result is conflict due to hatred for the Dergue's practices, party control, and a bitter police force determined to possess personal independence even though individual members appear to dislike making decisions.

Ethiopia has always been a difficult society to police. The arbitrary exercise of authority and the role of provincial armies in internal security meant that a civil police never formed part of traditional society. The relationship of the state to the peasant, for instance, was repressive, exploitive, and corrupt, so popular notions of good government revolved around a benevolent patron rather than fair enforcement.[28] Formal police forces existed in the 1930s, and police posts were found in the cities and larger towns and at strategic points along the main roads in the countryside. But although recruits were usually local men familiar with the social values of the areas in which they served, and despite imperial proclamations that granted police authority to provincial governors, operations were usually punitive and local control was minimal. A centralized national force was established by the British army in 1941 and was combined with a number of separate city forces to form a single department answerable to the Ministry of the Interior in the 1950s. The force received assistance from Britain, Germany, and Sweden until the early 1970s, but it remained a paramilitary organization controlled by the Central Bureau in Addis Ababa, which acted like an army general headquarters. The situation was similar in 1996.

As in 1991, the overthrow of Haile Selassie in 1974 saw the new (Marxist) government severely limit police authority because it was identified with the old regime and regional interests.[29] It is significant that in the 1970s as in the 1990s public order was enforced by the army rather than by the police, whose status and resources were low. Distinctions between political opposition to the government (which was defined as a criminal activity) and crimes against persons and property were blurred, and army security services assumed police functions. Local law enforcement was delegated to the civilian paramilitary People's Protection Brigades.

Policing before 1991 was bureaucratic, punitive, paramilitary, and political; in the mid-1990s it remained essentially punitive and reactive.[30]

The Police System, 1991–1996

The army was disbanded after the EPRDF came to power in 1991, but a new EPRDF force was initially entrusted with policing urban areas because of attacks by roaming armed gangs, most of whom claimed to be acting for the EPRDF. The Interior Ministry referred to the "anarchy" caused by 42,000 thieves, 35,000 unemployed, 27,000 former soldiers, and many escaped prisoners.[31] The police were powerless in such circumstances, so order was enforced by the military expedient of shooting looters and leaving their bodies on display.[32] This measure succeeded, and the curfew imposed by Mengistu was finally lifted in 1992.

The need for a police force does not appear to have been questioned, and the TGE published a "proclamation to provide for the development of the state defence army of the central transitional Government and for the establishment of the Police Force" in the *Negarit Gazeta* (no. 8) in 1992. This stated that "there shall be established a new police force in each National/regional Self-Government which shall be under the direction of the latter, be responsible for the preservation of peace and security, and the maintenance of law and order of the Self-Government." This implied the creation of fourteen new regional forces, though numbers changed later. The proposed organization provided for a federal police and eleven regional forces; though two of these (Addis Ababa and the town of Dire Dawa) are directly controlled by the central government (see Figures 4.1 and 4.2). The duties and responsibilities of the federal police were contained in a document, titled *Police Force Organizing Policy and Central Bureau Structure and Job Description,* which was published by the Police Central Bureau (Commissioner's Office) in 1996. Further police regulations planned for 1997 were still awaited in 1999. In addition, the Ethiopian Police Proclamation was nearing completion, after a lengthy consultative process, and its publication was expected by the end of 1999. This enabling legislation is expected to generate the promulgation of twenty to thirty sets of procedural requirements over the next few years.

In fact, the police were not reestablished or deployed until mid-1994, with the EPRDF military wing continuing to act as both the national military and an internal security force. The military dealt with the policing of low-level operations to counter the actions of the Oromo Liberation Front (OLF) and Islamic fundamentalist movements, especially in the Oromo and Somali regions, where periodic clashes with insurgent and bandit groups occurred. The TGE continued to demobilize TPLF soldiers during 1994, integrating some into the new local and regional police forces that were increasingly responsible for law and order. There were also moves toward ensuring that the army should be representative and nonpolitical, as when the fourth TPLF congress in December decided to ban TPLF military commanders from party membership. But it is difficult to judge the effects this had on the police, given the tensions between regional independence and continuing party control. Internal politics and political considerations certainly affected internal promotions and postings, and political priorities still informed practice. The national charter, the new constitution, and the

Figure 4.1 Ethiopia: Federal Police Structure

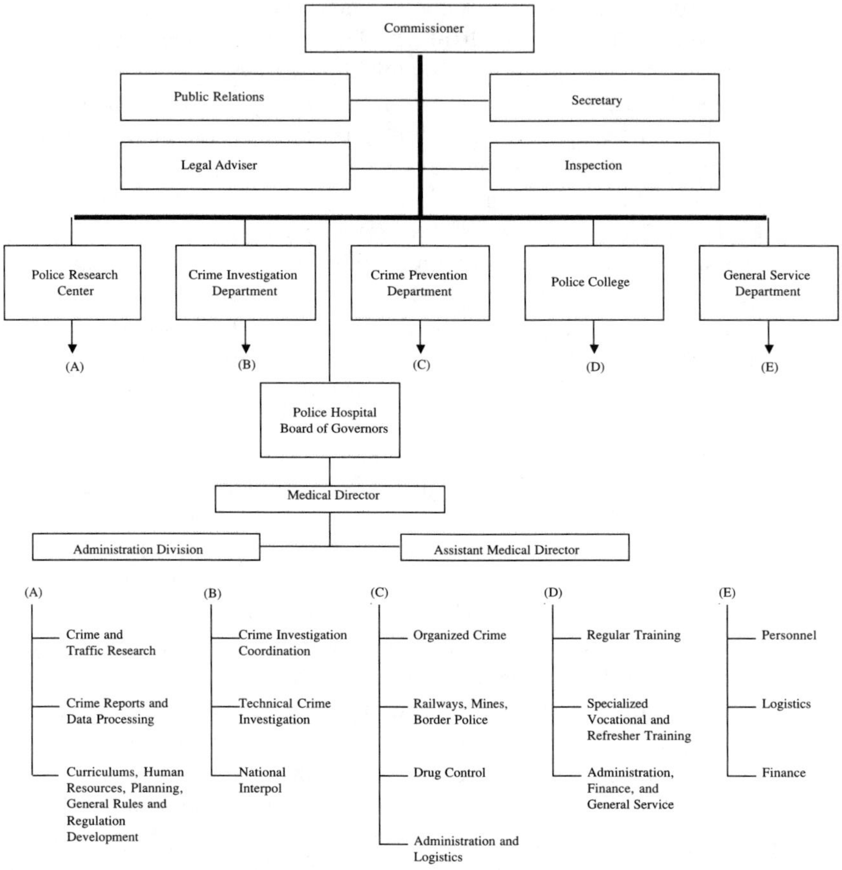

```
                                    Commissioner
                    ┌───────────────────┼───────────────────┐
            Public Relations                            Secretary
            Legal Adviser                               Inspection
    ┌───────────────┬───────────────┬───────────────┬───────────────┐
Police Research  Crime Investigation  Crime Prevention   Police College   General Service
    Center          Department          Department                          Department
     (A)               (B)                 (C)               (D)               (E)
                                    Police Hospital
                                  Board of Governors
                                    Medical Director
              ┌─────────────────────────┴─────────────────────────┐
      Administration Division                              Assistant Medical Director
```

(A)
- Crime and Traffic Research
- Crime Reports and Data Processing
- Curriculums, Human Resources, Planning, General Rules and Regulation Development

(B)
- Crime Investigation Coordination
- Technical Crime Investigation
- National Interpol

(C)
- Organized Crime
- Railways, Mines, Border Police
- Drug Control
- Administration and Logistics

(D)
- Regular Training
- Specialized Vocational and Refresher Training
- Administration, Finance, and General Service

(E)
- Personnel
- Logistics
- Finance

criminal and civil codes prohibited arbitrary arrest and detention, for instance, but the government arrested and detained individuals without charge throughout 1994.[33]

The most significant changes in 1994 were the December adoption of the new constitution and the national and regional elections that followed, because these resulted in the handing over of power to the elected government of the Federal Democratic Republic of Ethiopia (FDRE) in August 1995. The EPRDF remained dominant; the government continued to devolve authority to the regional governments, but it was constrained by the underdeveloped nature of the local police, judicial and administrative systems, and the imperatives of party control.

Figure 4.2 Ethiopia: Regional Police Structure

REGIONAL POLICE STRUCTURE (A)

REGIONAL POLICE STRUCTURE (B)

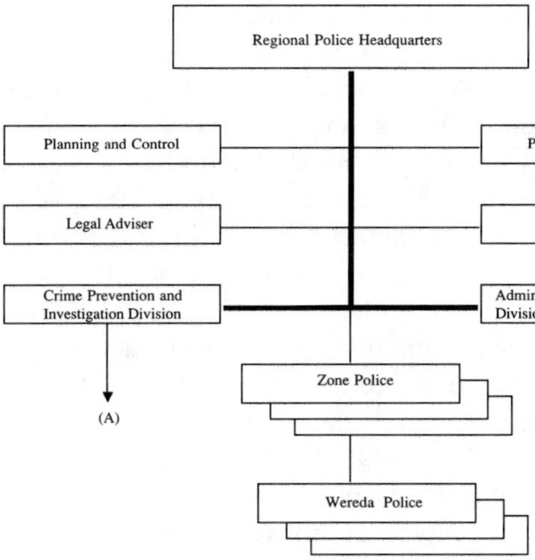

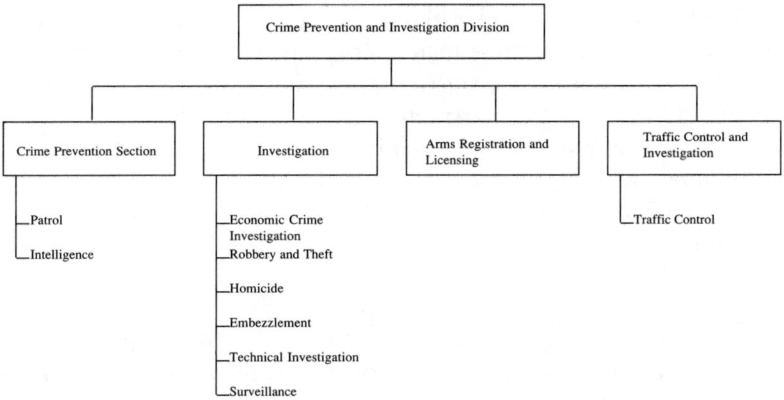

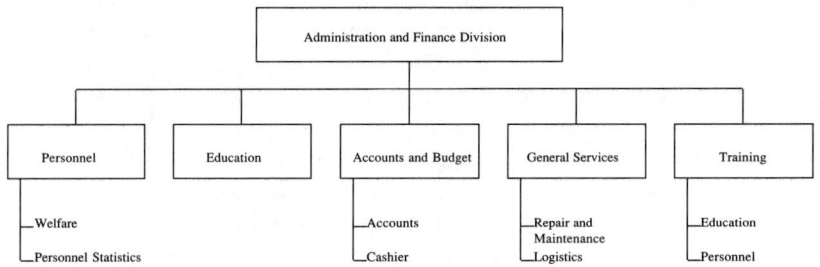

The maintenance of order shifted even more from the EPRDF's military wing to the police. The Ministry of Internal Affairs was abolished in August 1995, and the national police organization was subordinated to the Ministry of Justice as a response to the government's goal of enhancing quality and performance. The changes did not amount to much. Though a security, immigration, and refugees authority was created under a general manager, the manager (who had previously been vice minister of the interior and head of TPLF security) reported directly to Meles—who retained his own security team under a member of the TPLF central committee. These moves may also represent a battle for political influence, for several former military officials, such as the head of security and immigration, were understood to be uneasy about the growing influence of civilians on the prime minister. Former officials did not appreciate the rise of those who had spent the war years in exile.[34] The shift toward civilianized policing was evident throughout 1996, but ongoing violence on the continent (such as the attempted assassination of Egyptian president Hosni Mubarak by members of an Egyptian terrorist group in Ethiopia) ensured that the EPRDF military wing was kept as an internal security force.

As in Eritrea, many aspects of policing derived specifically from the war. Rank is a case in point. Titles remained militaristic, and individuals' war service counted for more than their formal rank, so that a lieutenant or colonel with an impressive war record could outrank a brigadier general.[35] The adoption of such a rank structure may also owe something to the military, for U.S. pressure had resulted in the army's redesign along more orthodox lines. After a visit from the U.S. deputy assistant secretary for defense, who recommended a formal structure of army ranks, Ethiopia reintroduced conventional military ranks and announced eight formal promotions to brigadier general.

Other wartime habits persisted. The *gime gema* system of confessional accountability, for example, involved criticism of police performance by all ranks in a station or department, sometimes for days on end at monthly intervals; policing in a particular area or location (such as the central garage) would stop for the duration. One session, in which eighty officers sat on benches facing three managers, lasted for a week. Two notetakers recorded everything that was said, and the notes were then forwarded to the next level of the hierarchy.[36] The system aggravated shortcomings in policing, for such ritual systems stifled decisionmaking and initiative and allowed major practical problems to revolve around the arbitrary exercise of authority and personal preference.

It is difficult to tell how local commanders carried out recruitment (generally involving recruits between eighteen and twenty-five years old). Politics, party concerns, and provincial arrangements were undoubtedly influential. There were no formal conventional selection procedures, though commanders undoubtedly canvassed community leaders from a candidate's region. When asked why they had joined the police in 1996, new recruits said they wanted to "help our country."[37] Some may have been deliberately chosen by their community, for applicants were often discussed by local groups, who decided if individuals were suitable. But it is unclear how the process worked because there is no means of checking—there is no central record system. The federal government has been careful to preserve an ethnic balance in the army, and the same is probably true of the police, but it is hard to determine how antagonism between the Tigrayans and Amharans, for example, was reflected in the police or what the reaction was to the several thousand TPLF demobilized fighters who become policemen (with a 50 percent pay raise for the ranks).[38] Indeed, it is difficult accurately to judge the relationship between the police and the military, though the relationship is likely to be close.

By 1998 a training pattern had emerged.[39] Once selected, recruits spent five months at a regional training center. After practical experience in the region in which they were to serve, they returned to the training center for two more months before becoming constables. There was also a fast-track system, by which certain recruits could go straight from school to the police staff college at Sendafa, training there (and in the regions) for nineteen months. Training standards for recruits in general were uneven, as the government made no provision for regional training. Some northern schools had very low expectations, even by regional standards, though training was often good in the south in the mid-1990s, in part because of the regional training school for 700 students that Germany had built near Addis Ababa. The school had enthusiastic students, aged about twenty-two to forty, from all over the region. The quality of its female students was considered less satisfactory by Western visitors, however. This was important because women had been of more significance in the Dergue police than in the army, and many had been rehired by the TGE police force. Overseas aid alone could not improve the situation with regard to this or other policing weaknesses, such as financial management.[40]

The conditions of service in the various federal and regional forces vary, though the police, along with other civil servants and officials, represent a significant proportion of Ethiopia's wageworkers. Officers get paid for an eight-hour shift even when personnel shortages mean that they must work twelve-hour shifts. They cannot join unions or strike. The policing standards adopted are adequate by regional criteria, with police station detention cells, for instance, usually providing enough food and water. But policing remains an essentially urban activity, even though 85 percent of the population still lives in rural areas where the economy is based on smallholder agriculture. Rural police posts are self-sufficient, as they were under Mengistu.

Problems Confronting Ethiopian Policing

The police budget in Ethiopia, as elsewhere, is underfunded, and regional budgets are strongly tilted toward Tigray so as to ensure an effective Tigrayan control over the security and political apparatus. The loyalist TPLF fighters who led the war against Mengistu remain at the apex of the military, and their influence can no doubt be paralleled in the police structure.

Ethiopian policing is confronted by chronic insecurity. Guns are everywhere; as Meles said in 1992, "any person has an easy access to arms. Guns and poverty have bred banditry."[41] The wide availability of automatic rifles meant that violence often seemed a quick way for things to be done or taken. This inevitably resulted in a degree of breakdown in order and law, given that the nearest police or army posts in many border areas, for example, are many hours' walk away. Banditry and religious tensions increased in volatile areas such as Zeila, and low-level military operations continued throughout 1994 in an effort to counter OLF and Islamic fundamentalist groups, especially in Oromo and Somali regions. Such violence remained a serious problem throughout 1995, with police often being killed during robberies. Some police raids against bandits may have resulted in suspicious deaths, but bandits were often armed with automatic weapons and hand grenades. Ethiopia is also a transit hub for heroin and cocaine.[42]

Fatal incidents occur regularly in the frontier regions. Armed attacks on government units at Kombo in eastern Harrarghe province (blamed on an Oromo liberation movement) involved the kidnap of the police commissioner and the town's civilian administrator; military members of the EPRDF were wounded. In another typical incident, a military depot in the Borona region was looted and attackers stole about 100 rifles that government forces had previously confiscated from Gedo and Guji tribesmen involved in armed confrontations. According to the German-based Solidarity Committee for Ethiopian Political Prisoners (SCEPP), the government is obsessed with the prospect of an armed opposition and used police coercion against publishers and journalists belonging to opposition groups.[43] The SCEPP said that the accusations were intended to criminalize certain opposition groups and their supporters by implicating them in so-called preparations for terrorist operations in Addis Ababa without bringing any proof to support the charges.

Other problems Ethiopia shared with its neighbors include those exacerbated by its borders with Somalia and the Karamoja region of northeast Uganda and Kenya, with their plentiful supplies of arms; the existence of large numbers of refugees, such as the 32,000 repatriated from Djibouti since November 1994; and, at a lower level, street children.[44]

The new constitution provided for an independent judiciary. The central courts have, in fact, shown some judicial independence, but the judiciary was weak, understaffed, and subject to political pressure. There was a severe shortage of judges, lawyers, and the clerks and buildings needed to support the police. There were also serious financial constraints and no clear demarcation between central and regional jurisdictions—all of which kept the judiciary weak. In 1994, for example, officials in Jinka claimed that regionalization gave them complete autonomy over local affairs, and they ignored orders from the chairman of the southern region's supreme court. There was also a perceptible climate of grudge settling following a number of mysterious assassination attempts in early 1996. A former chief of the police and prison service was reportedly arrested in connection with the manner in which their investigation was carried out, and a police major was relieved of his duties and sent back to Tigray.

Extrajudicial killings have not abated. There was no governmental investigation after a certain Alebatchew Goji died in suspicious circumstances in police custody in the town of Orhessa near Dessie in 1994; he had been detained and interrogated for six days about a fugitive uncle's whereabouts. After his death, the police left his body on public display. There was, however, no evidence to support occasional rumors of killing squads even in the eastern Somali region's conflict, though numerous disappearances were reported in the press in 1994. There were reports of the dismissal or imprisonment of officers jailed for infringing human rights and other offenses (such as forty in Arsi zone), but it was difficult to tell if they were scapegoats. In September 1994, ten were dismissed in the central zone of Tigray for bribery and brutality, but this was unusual, for there are seldom convictions of guilty police. The government claimed that police officers suspected of excessive brutality were detained in custody while investigations were made, and that it was unhelpful to confuse occasional human errors with deliberate human rights violations.

Police officials usually dismissed reports of torture and disappearances made by organizations such as the Ethiopian Human Rights Council (EHRC). The police authorities stressed instead that all regional police chiefs and senior prison officials attended a seminar on prisoners' rights in September 1995, and the national police underlined the responsibility of local authorities to guarantee the basic human rights of prisoners. They therefore claimed that some deaths in July 1993, to take one example, were those of ordinary criminals, whereas those described by nongovernmental organizations (NGOs) as the result of torture, the authorities blame on a malaria epidemic.

It is difficult to judge the accuracy of such allegations. Ethiopian policing was always brutal, and the linkage between internal security and regime concerns was always tight. Politically motivated arrests were common and probably remain so, for senior judicial officers privately acknowledge government pressure on judges to deal leniently with EPRDF defendants. The TGF's opponents have been harassed and their relatives tortured as a result of politicians' abusing their positions. But against this can be set known examples of individual police refusing instructions from EPRDF officials to imprison opponents and even offering to take victims to the hospital. Again, the crowd-control techniques used at a violent riot at the Grand Anwar Mosque in Addis Ababa in 1995 were measured nonlethal response rather than gunfire. Whatever the case, human rights concerns are likely to focus increasingly on the regions because their combination of autonomy and weak administration, policing, and judiciary means less accountability. This appears to be the case even though autonomy is often illusory and Tigrayan groups dominate many of the relevant organizations.

The evidence for this judgment is anecdotal rather than statistical, but it suggests that police conversion has limits. The government may be forceful in its verbal commitment to human rights, but serious problems remain, and human rights organizations, political opponents, and the general public have made numerous allegations against the Meles regime that the government flatly denies. When at a 1997 press conference Meles was challenged regarding several deaths, he said blandly, "Show me where those people are detained and I will take measures."[45] Extrajudicial killings appear to be prevalent in rural areas where the OLF is increasing its resistance, and a number of Oromo intellectuals, businesspeople, students, and peasants have allegedly been harassed, tortured, or illegally detained because they refuse to join the EPRDF or its surrogate Tigrayan-dominated parties.[46]

Policing continues to reflect political developments, with the Central Bureau dictating policy to the regions, just as the party and the Meles government dominate politics. Centralizing tendencies remain vigorous. There has been no assessment of policing needs as such, and regional ministers (all of whom are political appointees) retain autonomy over local issues. There is no strategic planning, even though the short-term developments introduced into policing cannot provide lasting solutions unless integrated into a long-term framework. Policing is as underresourced as elsewhere on the continent, and problems are likely to result from the stagnant economy and persistent high levels of unemployment and internal migration.

So the situation in Ethiopia is complex. The many imponderables make it unclear whether policing has changed fundamentally since 1990, but change seems unlikely. There has been a visible attempt to convert and civilianize the inherited system, and by 1994 the police appeared to be less of a political tool than their predecessors, yet that conversion appears limited. Indeed, it is more likely that the force has reestablished rather than converted or civilianized itself.

Notes

1. Many areas of Uganda experienced widespread riots immediately after independence that had to be controlled by large deployments of police and units from the King's African Rifles.

2. The United States provided for general duties, India for traffic control and accident investigation, Australia police administration, and Kenya CID.

3. Herbert Karugaba, "The Role of the Uganda Police Force in the Criminal Justice System of Uganda," unpublished paper. This can be compared to the state of emergency declared in western Sudan, ostensibly to curb armed robbery and lawlessness in the late 1990s. The decree effectively empowers Sudan's police, army, and other security agents to deal with suspects and directs the formulation of instant courts to dispense swift justice. See *Sudan Update* 9: 1 (13 January 1998), 1.

4. *Africa Research Bulletin* and *Africa Diary* provide excellent material on security developments. The former is especially useful for identifying cycles of repression and reform in the police.

5. Tibamanya mwene Mushanga, "Twenty Years of State Violence in Uganda," in Tibamanya mwene Mushanga, ed., *Criminology in Africa* (Rome: UNICRI, 1992), 60. In 1972 the Ministry of Internal Affairs was brought under the umbrella of the Ministry of Defence so that the police and prison services would not be able to act as independent forces.

6. An administrative police, under the district administrators and intended to strengthen security in rural areas, was also announced. *Africa Research Bulletin* 26: 2 (1989), 9154.

7. Ibid., 30: 5 (1993), 11009. See also ibid. 30: 1 (1993), 10851.

8. *New African,* quoted in ibid. 33: 3 (1996), 12206.

9. George Thomas Kurian, *World's Encyclopaedia of Police Forces and Penal Systems* (Oxford: Facts on File, 1989), 389. The ratio is important because crimes are not reported in areas without police stations; the crime rate is usually directly proportional to the ratio of police to the population.

10. D. W. Love, "Final Report of the British Police Training Team Seconded to Uganda from 16 October 1988 to 5 May 1989," West Midlands Police, 1989, 14. See also Metropolitan Police, "Report of British Police Training Team in Uganda, April–November 1989," Metropolitan Police Force, 1989.

11. "The British view is that help in rebuilding the Ugandan police force is far more valuable than the usual areas into which aid is poured in third world countries." *Daily Telegraph,* 10 Sept. 1979. This no longer appears to be the case.

12. Richard Edyegu, "To Review the Operational Policing Problems Within the Uganda Police with Respect to the Strategic Statement of Aims; to Make Comparisons with Selected Other Countries; and to Make Recommendations," unpublished paper, Overseas Command Course, the Police Staff College, Bramshill, England (1994), 11.

13. Ibid., 20.

14. Given the total staffing levels of the national force, this represents a considerable concentration.

15. Edyegu, "To Review," 15.

16. Quoted in J. Oloka-Onyango, "The Dynamics of Corruption Control and Human Rights Enforcement in Uganda: The Case of the Inspector General of Government," *East African Journal of Peace and Human Rights* 1: 1 (1993), 23–51. Oloka-Onyango argues that some human rights abuses are lawfully committed,

insofar as existing law permits acts that violate fundamental precepts of democratic government. Successive governments since Amin have made reference to the legal provisions passed then but have done nothing to repeal them. See also U.S. Department of State, Bureau of Democracy, Human Rights, and Labor, *Uganda Country Report on Human Rights Practices for 1996* (Washington, DC: U.S. Department of State, 1997); *Journal of African Law* 40: 1 (1996); Mubiru Musoke, "Human Rights, Politics, War and the New Constitution in Africa," *Uganda Quarterly Review* 2 (1993), 49–127; Human Rights Watch, *Human Rights Watch World Report 1995: Events of 1994* (New York: Human Rights Watch, 1995); UN Department of Humanitarian Affairs, *Humanitarian Situation Report on Uganda*, Integrated Regional Information Network, 4 December 1996.

17. Amnesty International, *Kenya, Tanzania, Uganda, Zambia and Zimbabwe: Attacks on Human Rights Through the Misuse of Criminal Charges* (London: Amnesty International, 1995), 1.

18. Republic of Uganda, *Observations by the Government of Uganda on Communication No. 92/4/6, 719 in Respect of Human Rights Violations to the United Nations by Amnesty International* (Kampala, 1995).

19. BBC Monitoring Service, *Summary of World Broadcasts* AL/3136, January 1998, A/2–3.

20. *Financial Times*, 5 May 1995.

21. Quoted in Christopher Clapham, *Transformation and Continuity in Revolutionary Ethiopia* (Cambridge: Cambridge University Press, 1988), 134. For pre-1990 policing, see John Andrade, *World Police and Paramilitary Forces* (Basingstoke, UK: Macmillan, 1985); James Cramer, *The World's Police* (London: Cassell, 1964); Kurian, *World's Encyclopaedia of Police Forces;* Ernest W. Lefever, *Spear and Scepter: Army, Police, and Politics in Tropical Africa* (Washington, DC: Brookings Institution, 1970). For decentralization, see John M. Cohen, "Decentralization and 'Ethnic Federalism' in Post–Civil War Ethiopia," in Krishna Kumar, *Rebuilding Societies After Civil War: Critical Roles for International Assistance* (Boulder, CO: Lynne Rienner, 1997), 135–153; John Young, "Ethnicity and Power in Ethiopia," *Review of African Political Economy* 70: 23 (1996), 531–542. For human rights organizations in Ethiopia (and Namibia), see Claude E. Welch, *Protecting Human Rights in Africa: Strategies and Roles of Non-Governmental Organizations* (Philadelphia: University of Pennsylvania Press, 1996).

For an overview of events in 1991–1993, see Alex de Waal, "Rethinking Ethiopia," in Charles Gurden, ed., *The Horn of Africa* (London: UCL Press, 1994), 25–46; Economist Intelligence Unit, *EIU Country Report: Ethiopia, Eritrea, Somalia, Djibouti* (London: EIU, 1995); U.S. Department of State, Bureau of Democracy, Human Rights, and Labor, *Ethiopia: Human Rights Practices* (Washington, DC: U.S. Department of State, published annually).

22. *Africa Research Bulletin* 32: 5 (1994), 11449. There was no shortage of evidence; the special prosecutor's office set up to oversee the trials had received 250,000 pages of government documents by then. The Mengistu regime was highly bureaucratic, and when the EPRDF moved into Addis Ababa on 28 May 1991, it found the government's files virtually intact (only prison service files had been destroyed). The security service, trained by former members of the East German Stasi, kept meticulous records. *Africa Confidential* 32: 22 (1991), 8.

23. *Africa Research Bulletin* 34: 3 (1997), 12619.

24. Compare the situation in the self-proclaimed republic of Somaliland in northern Somalia, which is ignored by the international community.

25. The continuity is emphasized by publications by organizations such as Amnesty International and Human Rights Watch, which cite alleged abuse. For

criticism against the government's record in early 1997, for example, see *Africa Research Bulletin* 34: 3(1997), 12579.

26. Clapham, *Transformation,* 118.

27. Ibid., 131.

28. Eva Poluha, "Democracy in Africa—an Interpretation of Priorities," *African Anthropology* 27: 1 (1995), 17–44. Universalist claims for the concept of democracy often conflict with prevailing indigenous values. Compare Leonardo A. Villalón, "The Moral and the Political in African Democratization: The *Code de la Famille* in Niger's troubled Transition," *Democratization* 3: 2 (Summer 1996), 41–68.

The 1961 criminal procedures code (drafted by a British jurist) confirmed that punishment was the pillar of Ethiopian criminal law, but the Red Terror campaign of the Dergue had the greatest impact on the collective mind. The difficulties of policing Ethiopia are indicated by articles discussing regional conflict. See Jon Abbink, "Transformations of Violence in Twentieth-Century Ethiopia: Cultural Roots, Political Conjunctures," *Focaal* 25 (1995), 55–77; David Turton, "Warfare, Vulnerability and Survival: A Case from Southwestern Ethiopia," *Disasters* 15:3 (1991), 254–264.

29. The federal system may itself generate a policing system seen as an alien imposition in many regions.

30. In June 1996, for example, the *Indian Ocean Newsletter* (724, 22 June 1996, 3) reported the disappearance of a number of people suspected of having links with opponents of the EPRDF. Relations between the EPRDF and the main Oromo opposition party, the Oromo Liberation Front, also provide instances of punitive policing. In early October 1997, there was a fight between OLF "remnants" and security forces. Two days later the editor and assistant editor of the Oromo weekly newspaper *Urji* were arrested after questioning the EPRDF version of events. *Africa Confidential* 38: 21 (24 October 1997), 8.

31. See Paul Collier, "Demobilisation and Insecurity in Ethiopia and Uganda: A Study in the Economics of the Transition from War to Peace," in Jackie Cilliers, ed., *Dismissed* (Midrand, South Africa: Institute for Security Studies, 1995), 104–111. The lack of gun control in the context of recent warfare is a strong theme in Ethiopia, Eritrea, and Uganda. The senior Ethiopian officers Collier interviewed thought that demobilization had initially caused an increase in crime, especially rural banditry.

The crisis escalated with the war between the EPRDF and the OLF in summer 1992. Although low morale, overcrowding, and minimal policing resulted in low security in the holding camps (inmates in Bahir Dar resorted to a vigilante justice system), the situation improved in 1993. Major factors contributing to the improvement were the quick response of the TGE, some donors, and NGOs in civilianizing ex-combatants and the establishment of law and order by the TGE at state and regional levels.

For demobilization, see Mats R. Berdal, *Disarmament and Demobilisation After Civil Wars: Arms, Soldiers and the Termination of Armed Conflicts,* Adelphi Paper 303 (London: Oxford University Press for the IISS, 1996); Nat J. Colleta, Markus Kastner, and Ingo Wiederhofer, *Case Studies in War-to-Peace Transition: The Demobilisation and Reintegration of Ex-Combatants in Ethiopia, Namibia, and Uganda* (World Bank, Washington, DC: 1996).

32. The situation in early 1992 is described in *Africa Research Bulletin* 32: 2 (1992), 10468.

33. The extent of this is debatable, but "serious problems remain" according to the U.S. Department of State, Bureau of Democracy, Human Rights, and Labor,

Ethiopia Human Rights Practices, 1994 (Washington, DC: U.S. Department of State, 1995).

34. *Indian Ocean Newsletter* 733 (27 September 1996).

35. There are constables, corporals, sergeants, and shift leaders. Ranks then progress through warrant officer, sublieutenant, lieutenant, captain, major, lieutenant colonel, brigadier general, major general, and general.

36. *Police Review,* September 1995, 16–18.

37. Private conversation, London, 1997.

38. The integration appears to have had more to do with the inclusion of the police in the demobilization program—which was dictated by the TGE's security, political, economic, and fiscal policy—than with donor plans.

39. See *Police Review,* 15 January 1999, 22–24.

40. A number of states provided support to the TGE for the development of a civil police force. Britain (unlike, say, Germany) provided expertise rather than equipment. It included technical training assistance in forensic science, police and civilian records, and fleet management (which was probably the most successful part of the program). A financial management adviser, based at the Central Bureau, was also recruited in Britain to improve budgetary procedures (and operational efficiency) in the face of chronic underfunding. The adviser was to look at issues such as developing expenditure norms through balancing capital (including vehicles, equipment, and buildings) and recurring expenditure, as well as salary and nonsalary operating costs. See ODA, *Ethiopia: Country Aid Programme Statement* (London: ODA, 1993). The politically sensitive $8.3 million training project was halted after four years when police killed an unarmed human rights activist in Addis Ababa. It was later reinstated.

41. *Africa Research Bulletin* 29: 5 (1992), 10575. There were about 9,000 paramilitary mobile emergency police plus border guards available to the government in 1996. Police were present, often with a Kalashnikov and a sidearm, in every street and public building in Addis Ababa in 1998. Petty theft was common but opportunistic, and major crime tended to concern extortion and fraud. There were thirty identified murders in Addis Ababa in May 1998. *Police Review,* 15 January 1999, 22–24.

42. Fears of corruption result in officers' being moved around.

43. *Indian Ocean Newsletter* 724 (22 June 1996).

44. Christopher Williams, "Street Shildren and Abuse of Power," *Africa Insight* 26: 3 (1996), 221–228. It is interesting to note that although most police (including those of Namibia) victimize them, "in Ethiopia, street children have reported more kindness than brutality, . . . while those in Sudan have said that police have made a determined effort to be helpful," 224. Williams suggests that the difference in police response toward street children in East Africa (and Latin America) could be based on strong traditional family structures. In Amaharic the children are referred to as *doorry* (literally, "one who belongs to the wilderness and is untamed"), which implies that they are out of control, as in the Ugandan *muya aye* ("out of control"). Max A. Anyuru, "Uganda's Street Children," *Africa Insight* 26: 3 (1996), 268.

45. *Africa Research Bulletin* 34: 3 (1997), 12579.

46. Oromo is the largest regional state, with a population of about 20 million. The government began by saying it would grant autonomy to the region, but since the Oromos boycotted the elections, it has victimized the region instead.

5

Models of African Policing: Construction and Integration

In both Ethiopia and Eritrea, the new regimes were formed from reformist insurgencies that incorporated the insurgents' own organizations into the new governments and their policing systems. Whereas the rejection of the previous system's excesses resulted in the conversion (and to a degree continuity) of the police in Ethiopia, in Eritrea it produced a new force.

Model 3—Construction: Eritrea

The construction of an original police system is atypical; international intervention, for instance, is more likely to result in the improvement or reconstruction (as in Angola and Namibia) of a force than its outright creation. But the example of Eritrea shows that construction can occur if a new state is internationally acknowledged, particularly after an unambiguous military victory.

The Eritrean force directly reflects the political environment in Eritrea rather than external influences. Yet at the same time it is important because it provides additional evidence for linking case-specific police systems to the conventionalities of both policing and order. It shows that the practicalities of policing limit the options available to even new forces.

Postconflict Beginnings: The Political Environment

The capture of Asmara, the provincial capital, and the Red Sea port of Massawa (Ethiopia's only direct access to the sea) in 1991 left the guerrilla insurgent group known as the Eritrean People's Liberation Front (EPLF) victorious after a thirty-year armed struggle for the right to self-determination.[1] Political agreement was quickly reached, partly so as to ensure that Addis Ababa did not experience the disorder seen in Liberia in 1990 or Mogadishu after Barre fled in 1991. The key themes of the new state were to be reconciliation, social cohesion, self-reliance, and the development of institutions necessary for this.

The experiences of insurgency shaped this program, for it molded the state, the regime, the political system, and its police system from the beginning, in terms of legitimacy, experience, and personnel.[2] Indeed, the EPLF's position was legitimized by its continued identification with victory in the war, and its position was centralized by its insistence during 1992 that the army that it had formed would be the agency for national construction—and would be expected to work without pay, as it had done during the war. The EPLF was thus central to national development, and its institutions were not formally separated from those of the government until February 1994, when it changed its name to the People's Front for Democracy and Justice (PFDJ). A minister stated in 1994: "In every state the power of governing and controlling the government must be given to some definite set of people. . . . These rules are the constitution of a state."[3]

The EPLF leadership, left as the de facto government of Eritrea, made it clear that reconciliation and cohesion required political stability to come before multiparty democracy (though democracy was itself linked to stability and the rule of law). As a widely circulated Asmara newspaper, *Hadas Ertra,* commented in 1995: "We hope to make . . . Eritrea a place where peace and prosperity prevail; where democratic culture and tradition flourish; where the rule of law reigns and a democratic system is established."[4] This approach, which was influenced by the recent history of disorder in the region, was a concern shared by donors—which no doubt caused them to be less aggressive in emphasizing the governance agenda in Eritrea.

The pursuit of stability and the institutions required to manage it characterized the transitional period up to the formulation of the government's macropolicy framework in 1994. This can be seen as a preparatory period for the identification of areas of priority in the development strategy, for war had affected or destroyed most aspects of social life, the economy, the administrative machinery, and services in the country. Even successful EPLF policies for education, health, and local government could not adequately respond, and the rehabilitation of existing roads and telecommunications services was the main task in terms of infrastructure. Eritrea was heavily dependent on its human potential, and the government saw the need to train and retrain existing resources as key, for the limited institutional and personnel capacity was a major constraint on development.

The EPLF found the transition from liberation movement to government difficult, and the political difficulties inherent in reconstruction were increased by the EPLF's ambiguous international status during the two years before the referendum on independence in May 1993 and by continued dependence on Ethiopia for links with international institutions. The EPLF announced that it would disband once independence had been achieved and that multiple political parties (but not those based on ethnic or religious differences) would be allowed at that time.[5] Unlike the victorious Ethiopian People's Revolutionary Democratic Front, which encouraged pluralism based on ethnic identity, the EPLF represented a one-party rule that effectively repressed ethnic or religious representation.

Harvests in 1992 were poor, and the flow of international aid was slow, but the EPLF's political supremacy was not seriously contested during the early years of transition. Despite regional differences, there was no real political opposition in the period leading up to the referendum in 1993, which resulted in an overwhelming vote in favor of independence. Issaias Aferwerki (secretary general of the EPLF) became president in 1993, and the EPLF central committee was converted into a national assembly. The new government (with a four-year mandate) had a cabinet of fourteen ministers backed by ten regional governments, but (with one exception) all members of the EPLF politburo remained in the high posts they had occupied in the previous government, though there were fewer direct military representatives in government posts. There was a deliberate emphasis on the division of rule between the government and the PFDJ executive (formerly the EPLF), and the government again spoke of eventually instituting a multiparty political system. In fact, a further transitional government was created, and the introduction of multiparty politics (though not ones based on ethnicity or religion) was postponed.

Some political participation was allowed in the interests of reconciliation, but it was limited. Although the Eritrean Liberation Front–Revolutionary Council (ELF–RC) complained that the government had excluded it from the process of constitutional review, individual members of the ELF–RC and other opposition groups actively participated in the work of the Constitutional Commission. But attempts to reorganize mass organizations (such as youth, workers', and women's associations closed down after 1991) were resisted, as were demands for new independent bodies. Other protests were less political, resulting from the government's inability to pay its former fighters. Pruning the security department also contributed to unemployment, and more than 3,000 of 10,000 or so civil servants sacked during this process were ex-fighters who had been moved there on demobilization. There were few opportunities for dissenting voices to be heard. The government's perception of the requirements of stability inevitably constrained its toleration of independent views, though it is doubtful if the PFDJ feared other rivals.[6]

So by 1994 Eritrea was effectively a single-party state with a powerful military whom it could not necessarily afford to feed or pay. It faced internal divisions and a shattered economy and infrastructure. Public-sector industries operated at only one-third capacity, and drought had devastated agriculture; 80 percent of the population needed food aid, thousands were disabled, and a further 500,000 Eritreans awaited repatriation from refugee camps in neighboring Sudan.

Society remained militarized even though soldiers were hardly visible. The requirements of stability underpinned the pursuit of security and although the government retained a high degree of popular support, the security forces were recognized as (in the words of article 12-2 of the draft constitution of July 1996) "an integral part of society." A close if ambiguous relationship existed among the various parts of the security architecture and the party.

Development of the Police Force

The police system that was shaped by these circumstances was in many respects conventional. Even the innovative arrangements of the first three or four years of the force appear to have resulted from practical concerns rather than ideological conviction as such. Indeed, the need for a police force does not appear to have been questioned. The EPLF had been an extraordinarily well organized and effective insurgent movement, with a developed investigation and prison section.[7] It had the organizational ability, discipline, and legitimacy required to create a police system able to enforce and maintain its understanding of civil order and the social cohesion linked to it. In addition the EPLF argued that its right to independence should follow the principles that had guided postcolonial Africa. The creation of a state police was implicit in this understanding. The creation of the police thus paralleled that of other state institutions and was effectively hived off from EPLF institutional structures.

Initially there was no separate police force. EPLF members performed police duties throughout Eritrea, and the ELPF armed forces (which in 1992 comprised over 100,000 regulars) continued to serve as the main internal security force and agent of national construction. Demobilization of this force began in late 1993 and by the end of 1994 over 40,000 had been released, some of whom formed the cadre for the new police force. Policing was not separated from security until 1996, and even then it appears as though the actual separation of the police from the military function may have been only partial. Continuing tension in the region (and war with Ethiopia in 1998) would also account for the reluctance of EPLF officials to shift policing away from a purely military stance. Details of the force's development are difficult to trace, for it was extremely fluid.

The police function was defined as the maintenance of peace and the protection of property, but all else was implicit rather than explicit in the proclaimed vision of "peace and order" and democratic policing; the police were to "be productive and respectful of the people." Moreover, it is difficult to identify the resources or state expenditure devoted to policing because even as late as 1996 the police budget was notional. Fluidity was also reflected in the system's structure. The system was restructured in 1992, 1994, and 1996, as new priorities were identified; the changes ranged from the appointment of a public relations official to the separation of CID and crime prevention duties.

The many administrative changes pragmatically reflected shifts in requirements and experience. Basic police duties dominated; central or specialized services (such as pathology and a drugs crime investigation subunit) were considered desirable but inappropriate luxuries. This pragmatic approach was exemplified by the general attitude to rank and uniform. Rank remained something that even senior officers were unwilling to discuss in 1996; there had been none in the revolution, though individuals' war record undoubtedly influenced their informal ranking and status. Uniform was similarly ambiguous to external observers, though some senior officers wore blue shirts and epaulettes by 1996. The gradual change during the mid-1990s may reflect that by 1996 the army had been given new security job descriptions, titles, and uniforms, which would emphasize the subordinate role of the police in the security hierarchy.

The new force was a practical organization built on the experience of the ex-fighters. Few Eritreans had policing experience before they became fighters; those who had were given early responsibility.[8] The head of training in 1996, for instance, had been a policeman. He left the front for Yemen before reaching Lebanon, where he worked on finance for the EPLF. The deputy commandant was also an ex-fighter (and graduate) who had run a security and intelligence center. Such a record was not unusual though the problems associated with using ex-fighters were also recognized; the requirements of peacetime policing were different, and good fighters did not necessarily make good provincial commanders. It was partly for this reason that training (provided by Germany, Israel, and the United States) was considered essential, as was the need for senior commanders to cultivate political skills.

The new force was initially small, with about 200 police active in 1991. All (including provincial commanders) received a two- to three-month basic course; there was also a separate five-month course for civilians. Both police and prisons were answerable to the Ministry of Internal Affairs (which was also responsible for the political department, security, rehabilitation, and immigration), but police training was separate, with specialized courses including traffic, driving, public order, photography, investigation, and management. More than 240 ex-fighters completed a five-month training course in November 1994, the sixth such group to graduate.[9] At the ceremony in Balincki, Adi Nfas, at which graduates received certificates and prizes from the commissioner, the deputy commissioner highlighted the value resulting from training conducted since mid-1992. But another advantage was that the police had fewer problems in accommodating social changes than, say, some civil servants who had spent fifteen years out of touch with a money economy in the so-called liberated zones. More than 500 officers had qualified for anticrime and traffic duties, 390 for general duties, and 160 for finance-related crime by 1996.

Police numbers expanded from about 200 in 1991 to more than 1,300 in 1992, after 1,124 fighters joined, but many were dropped when several thousand were later demobilized. It is difficult to make sense of the official numbers of police over the next three years, when figures of 819 are given for 1993 (plus 111 civilians), 314 in 1994, and 162 for 1995, though these are probably for career officers. The population at that time was about 2.5–3 million, in an area of 125,000 square kilometers. After 1994 the police (who had been unpaid) received a nominal salary of about US$10 to pay for electricity, housing, and food. (In 1993, gross domestic product [GDP] per capita was $130–150.) The intention in 1996 was eventually to increase annual pay to $240.

The self-reliance and pragmatism (moderated by party rule) that characterized Eritrea was thus reflected in policing. It was furthered by an emphasis on self-help policing as expressed in the fighting slogans "People serving themselves" and "Never kneel down," which suggested the greater legitimacy of a successful war-fighting party after a liberation struggle. The effects of one-party rule (and, to a declining extent, war records) on this and recruitment are difficult to judge but are probably significant. Official accounts are, however, colored by the weight the EPLF placed on the Ethiopian regime's violations of human rights as it transformed itself from a guerrilla army to a significant political as well as military actor in the region. Governmental perceptions of security and stability stressed the need for control but undoubtedly benefited from a postwar consensus and legitimacy that few African regimes could match in the 1990s.

Immediately after creating the provisional government, the EPLF encouraged regional identifications by establishing ten (decentralized) provincial administrations. Each was to have a certain level of autonomy, with regional assemblies linked in a federal system to the federal government, which maintained total control over defense, foreign policy, and coordination among the different regional structures. The administration was later reformed, but the government was clearly determined to control provinces at all times, especially those with a Muslim majority along the Sudanese border. Policing was part of this, with the politics of internal security taking priority over anticrime policing, though the situation in Asmara was always distinct from that of the provinces. The police, with their old army radio systems, also found it difficult to get information and intelligence from the provinces.

In comparison with Ethiopia, the problems associated with the maintenance of order and (only then) law by the police were slight. As a result of the social cohesion inherited from the struggle for independence, crime levels were remarkably low and did not present reconstruction policies with serious challenges. Disparities in income had yet to develop in 1996, with ministers living in much the same style as taxi drivers, so ordinary crimes tended to range from the theft of water containers to trade in contraband and illegal emigrants.[10] In addition, the experience of insurgency continued to be of positive use to policing; the disciplined fighter mentality was a source of strength among the police, and strong cohesive traditions and goodwill meant that public cooperation was usual. There was an evident lack of vagrancy and disorder, though the state's attitude to problems common elsewhere, such as street beggars and children, was robust—street children were sent to prison if they continued begging after receiving initial state aid. Ministry newspapers featured traffic offenses, robbery, petty theft, fighting, and crimes involving guns.

Most reported crime involved traffic violations, according to an informative annual report issued by the police corps in an Asmara meeting of February 1995, when the police commissioner and his deputy chaired a discussion of the nature of crime in Eritrea.[11] Participants, including the vice minister of the interior and the president of the high court, were told that unlicensed, underage, or careless cart drivers were the main cause of accidents in 1994. There were no comments about corrupt traffic police, even though they are usually the first to be affected. Indeed, complaints about corruption appeared to be rare. The head of the traffic department pointed out that "It is natural for the public to expect efficient service from traffic police," though the wartime legacy of distrust and corruption when justice was sold remained strong.[12] Damage to property over the same period was estimated at more than 7 million birr (about $500,000).

Public disorder was on a small scale. The very quietness of the security situation resulted in bored fighters' (based in areas such as the Sahel) drinking and fighting, simply because there was not enough for them to do. The in-service education programs begun during the war had finished, so the demobilized had little to do except play football and volleyball and drink when they could. Eritrea was, however, awash with illegal weapons even though batons were usual for the police in Asmara, with guns the norm elsewhere. There were few legal weapons, for after 28 August 1991 the Department of Security and Intelligence directed that only EPLF members in possession of a police license and security staff on duty were allowed to keep their arms. It also stated that all EPLF members on a mission in Asmara must carry their provisional identity cards at all times and show it to police on request.[13] But the potential for bureaucracy inherent in this (as in traffic duties) was limited by the shortage of skilled personnel and operational equipment and by inadequate offices.

The rule of law worked reasonably well in the honeymoon period of independence, but several events in 1995 and early 1997 indicated potential future problems such as terrorism, corruption, and illegal drugs. The scale of the problems has remained limited, but the murder of five Belgian tourists at a popular tourist attraction (probably by terrorists rather than bandits) was an indication of the increasing insecurity close to principal towns.

Corruption was also on a small scale. Although Eritreans had been encouraged to fight against the Ethiopians by every conceivable means, including bribery, independence meant that such techniques were considered not only illegal but also offensive to national sensibilities—"it is not our culture."[14] Corruption was, however, also often tied to significant levels of political and economic secrecy amongst the ruling party. The PFDJ (the country's main economic force), for instance, provided funds for private business development in return for a stake of about 51 percent, though, as a signal for an anticorruption campaign in early 1997, President Issaias Afewerki warned that misappropriation of public funds would be punished. This was a reference to the appearance before military courts (and subsequent imprisonment) of officials (from the head down to clerical workers) of the state-owned Red Sea Trading Corporation on charges of corruption and abuse of power and resources.

The Red Sea Trading Corporation had begun with $14,000 in 1983, but by 1995 it was worth $25 million and sold everything from cement to cordless telephones. This capital gave the PFDJ a great political advantage over its rivals, and the head of the PFDJ's economic division was reported as saying that when the rebels took over in 1991, "This country had little but what we owned. . . . We used our money to set up the government. This country started from scratch with our assets."[15] Counterfeiting and drug trafficking also remained on a small scale.

The police appeared generally to observe human rights, and the situation bore no resemblance to the more brutal environment of Ethiopia. Although there were reliable reports that local police regularly picked up private citizens (sometimes holding them for long periods without charge) throughout 1994, there were no reports of politically motivated killings or disappearances, nor were there reports of torture.[16] But the judicial system is overloaded, so although the criminal code provides that detainees may be held for a maximum period of thirty days without being charged with a crime, in practice the police frequently hold suspects for much longer.

Some of those detained by urban police at the disabled center in Asmara (a holding place for beggars and a shelter for the homeless and mentally ill) have spent up to fourteen months without formal charges or a trial.

The precise relationship between the party and the police is unclear, but the reputation of the police is generally good—a reflection of the EPLF's initial popularity. The latter, however, depends on the nationalist fervor generated by independence and cannot be relied on indefinitely. The issues of resource scarcity (as discussed in Chapters 2 and 3) may yet arise in this poor country, too. Much was achieved in the first five years of independence, but just as much remains to be done. The police budget, for example, will take twenty years to develop fully, and it must first become real.

The example provided by Eritrea is unusual but demonstrates that the concerns and organization of police systems reflect the societies of which they are part. The common Eritrean concern for stability, reconciliation, and self-reliance received a pragmatic expression in policing. A number of other significant themes can also be identified in the development of the force. In the short term, there has been a restructuring of the organization, management, and training of officers of all ranks. The organizational fluidity has been the by-product of a genuine attempt to monitor and assess developments and may also indicate the government's intention to develop a technocracy. There has been a conscious enthusiasm for the evaluation of standards, identification of objectives, and provision of basic specialized training within the constraints imposed by limited resources. The aims of the basic training school and national police training college program have inevitably been focused on Asmara, but self-reliance has also been a strong theme, as is evidenced by neighborhood watch and special patrolling schemes.

In the long term, there is a need to civilianize away from a reliance on war experience. Eritreans are less willing to make great sacrifices in peacetime, and the police will need to be regularly paid if corruption and inefficiency are to be avoided.[17] The memories of those policed are also changing, so shared experience can no longer be relied upon—a twenty-three-year-old fighter who joined the EPLF in 1987 would have been six when the USSR replaced the United States in Ethiopia. The police, like the government, need to adapt and evolve. Thus, the main variables here are two. First, the unusual circumstance of armed struggle for independence in a post–cold war context where (unlike Angola and Mozambique) the victors in the war did not face externally funded insurgency meant that the regime could seriously demobilize while benefiting from the residual legitimacy of its success. Second is the much more common problem of a lack of adequate resources to sustain policing institutions. The question now is whether the second of these variables will overwhelm the first and lead to the unhappy outcomes referred to in Chapters 2 and 3.

Model 4—Integration: Namibia

Each regime considered so far fought its way to power under a strong leader whose personality has influenced the postwar conduct of policing. This is also true of Namibia. But Namibia's new regime did not win a war militarily and was forced by a negotiated settlement to integrate the members of an existing paramilitary police into its new security forces. The result was a program marked by reconciliation and crime prevention as aspects of internal security. As the minister of home affairs said in 1991, internal security was "a priority" for the police because of the circumstances of the time: "The country has just emerged from war and there are people who are not happy with independence. They want to do everything possible to bring about disorder and instability. A crucial role of the police is to protect Namibia from such people."[18]

Insecurity was exacerbated by factors such as conflict (which provided easy access to arms and broke down the social fabric), the end of existing means of social and political control, the high rate of unemployment, and the unrealistically high expectations raised by independence. Lawlessness was accentuated by increased theft, assault, rape, and murder thoughout the country; the prevalence of illegal arms; an exodus to southern towns (30,000 people reportedly moved from Owambo to Katura between the elections and independence in March 1990); and a lack of trained police officers. An ex-fighter from the People's Liberation Army of Namibia (PLAN), resettled in the former Ovamboland, expressed this succinctly: "Crime rates were low before independence, because there were road blocks. There was also night curfew, and controls were tough. After independence, crime has increased here because there is less control."[19]

NAMPOL

When Sam Nujoma, leader of the South West African People's Organization (SWAPO), won Namibia's first free election of 1989, Namibia had one of the potentially most productive economies in sub-Saharan Africa, though distribution of income and wealth among the estimated 1.5 million inhabitants, scattered across a vast territory of 825,000 square kilometers (less than half of which was suitable for agriculture), was extremely uneven.[20]

Much of the black population had no regular source of income, schooling and health care were rudimentary, and few owned their own land or housing. But expectations were high for the new unitary, multiparty democracy and its institutions. The new Namibian constitution (which was accepted by the constituent assembly in February 1990) stated that Namibia was to be a republic with a proportional-representation voting system, an independent judiciary, a bill of human rights, and a police system consistent with such standards. Chapter 15 of the constitution ("The Police Establishment of the Police Force") stated that "there shall be established by Act of Parliament a Namibian police force with prescribed powers, duties and procedures in order to secure the internal security of Namibia and to maintain law and order." An inspector general of police (appointed by the president) was to "make provision for a balanced structuring of the police force to ensure the efficient administration of the police force."

That the need for a recognizable public police force was taken for granted is unsurprising. The creation (or rather, conversion) of a police force is always seen as a priority during reconstruction after war, partly because it is thought to have the potential to neutralize violence or military activity comparatively cheaply. The presence of many ex-fighters represents a security problem, and it is better to have some of them policing a community than to leave them disaffected by the fact that independence means they have no job. In this way the police in Namibia were meant to absorb (and thus reintegrate) some ex-fighters as a security measure.[21] Such measures show the uniqueness of the Eritrean example, for they underscore conversion and reintegration as strong themes in forces after conflict. In addition to the above considerations, trained officers are always in short supply (as Namibia exemplifies), and suitable ex-fighters cannot be wasted. There is, however, no assurance that new recruits will behave or think differently than their predecessors, as both are probably recruited from the same social strata and culture.

All these factors were evident in Namibia. The Namibian police force of 1990, NAMPOL, was new in name, uniform, weapons policy, and vehicles but not completely so in personnel: The old South West African Police (SWAPOL) was not disbanded at independence, and its leadership and structure formed the basis of NAMPOL.[22] In this way Namibia's problems were similar to those of South Africa; both states were confronted with the difficult task of integrating two sides from a conflict into a single force.

When SWAPO came to power, Namibia's new force numbered fewer than 800 officers. The most immediate problem was recruitment and training for the new force, which the new government pragmatically tied to the theme of reconciliation. One result was that many senior officers were political appointees. SWAPO had no police experience of its own, but SWAPOL represented an invaluable source of potential officers. Rather than expelling them—or encouraging them to take up arms against the new regime—the minister designate of home affairs insisted they were all "sons and daughters of Namibia." This resulted in a white top echelon, which included the inspector general and the heads of all function branches; regional and district commissioners were mainly black. The sole exception was the deputy inspector general. Indeed, in October 1990 discontented black officers claimed that 82 percent of officers above the rank of inspector were white. The number of retained senior SWAPOL officers was controversial—there were calls for the dismissal of "white thugs"—but could be justified by sound policy reasons, such as the need for their expertise, reduction of the security threat, and as part of the negotiations leading to independence. (The internationally mediated independence agreement compelled SWAPO to employ a certain number of the old regime's police.) Less attention was given to the problems the process caused the police. It was not clear, for example, how the presence of large numbers of personnel from the counterinsurgency force of the old regime affected perceptions of legitimacy in the African community. The official emphasis on reconciliation is unsurprising in the circumstances.

Promotion policies were controversial for different reasons. Those recruited in the north were mainly ex-PLAN and those in the central and south regions ex-SWAPO, whereas the ethnic background of recruits tended to correspond to that of the dominant group in their area of responsibility.[23] As in the 1960s, many whites argued that promotion should be based on merit and that the (political) promotion of ex-PLAN members in particular undermined policing standards. Only a small number of the new recruits were demobilized fighters, some of whom had previously been in SWAPO's armed wing. This was a political grievance, for most SWAPO fighters assumed that the end of apartheid would mean jobs. An estimated 32,000 combatants from PLAN and approximately 25,000 combatants from the South West Africa Territorial Force (SWATF) and its paramilitary units were demobilized in 1989, but only around 1,000 of these were absorbed into NAMPOL, which (temporarily) numbered about 6,000 in 1990.[24]

Most of the ex-fighters had joined the army when they were in their twenties and had stayed in for more than ten years; they tended to have little education, and most were married men with children, with few other job prospects (aside from security guarding) if demobilized. SWAPOL nonparamilitary staff were also incorporated into NAMPOL. The priority given to training acknowledged these concerns and was reinforced by the choice of British police advisers (who were seen as suitable models of professionalism) effectively to legitimize the process: "The value of the British team's involvement lies in its neutrality and experience in conventional policing."[25] The team advised the Ministry of Home Affairs on planning, policy formation, and the design and supervision of a new training program during 1990–1991. NAMPOL officers were reported as generally satisfied with the British approach (though NAMPOL officers criticized the British failure to insist on rigid discipline).

The program was directly related to NAMPOL's mission as a conventional democratic force, reoriented from counterinsurgency to crime prevention. SWAPOL's aim had been to protect the state against the people, but NAMPOL's was to protect the public. The associated problems of training (and image) were addressed by such means as the British training officers at the Luiperdsvallei Police College, where training included courses on human rights. South African–controlled security forces had used unlimited powers of arrest and detention in the northern war zone before independence, so attention to human rights (in both the constitution and practice) was considered crucial.

On the whole this approach seems to have worked in the first years of independence, though two units (the Presidential Guard and the Border Guard) went against it. A shortage of recruits meant that both units were made up of former soldiers, with the Presidential Guard effectively a contingent of 500 former PLAN fighters turned into a police as special constables.[26] The minister responsible for policing claimed not to be too concerned about the tensions surrounding this situation saying, "It is inevitable that some people are suspicious of each other" and that such criticism was a sign of freedom of speech.[27] In the meantime, a substantial number of recruits were enrolled, and special constables were also hired as a temporary measure. By October 1990 NAMPOL was 6,000 strong, but numbers did not grow significantly during the next five years. The central force numbered about 4,200 officers in 1995, with the permanent established force (excluding temporary or special constables) numbering about 2,730 at the end of 1995, distributed in nine districts. There were plans to expand the established force to 4,295 by 2000 (that is, achieve a ratio of 1:300 of population).

The resources allocated to NAMPOL appeared adequate. The budget for the police and prisons during the 1990–1991 financial year was given by South African commentators as 132 million rand (about $10 million), or 5 percent of the total state expenditure. Of this sum, 13 million rand (about $1 million) was for police administration, 108 million rand for combating crime, and 1 million rand for training, whereas 10 million rand was allocated to prisons.[28] The World Bank's figures for public order and safety in Namibia during the early 1990s ranged from 6.40 to 7.20 percent of total government expenditure and from 4.20 to 4.49 percent of GDP.

By 1994 the government met about 70 percent of NAMPOL's proposed budget, which theoretically allowed it to maintain sufficient vehicles, bicycles, and boats for traffic duties and emergency responses and motor and foot patrols, and to claim a response time of ten minutes in urban centers and thirty minutes in rural areas. The government also provided officers with housing, free medical attention, a risk allowance of about $30 a month, and a welfare savings scheme. By 1994 an inspector earned about $260–280 a month, a sergeant $239–260, and a constable about $135–156. Such high rates of pay suggest that the government took a keen interest in ensuring the loyalty of NAMPOL, or, to interpret their motives more cynically, in buying the loyalty of old regime officers and rewarding allies from the freedom struggle.

Such measures have ensured a politically unthreatening force. The regime does not appear to have been concerned that by the mid-1990s it was clear that NAMPOL shared some of the weaknesses of forces elsewhere. Its institutional incapacity, for example, was evident from the few illegal weapons it confiscated in the face of the volume known to be leaving Namibia for South Africa.[29] Although the evidence provided above suggests that NAMPOL did not suffer from an especially severe shortage of resources, it is noticeable that many recent newspaper and conference reports on crime in Namibia refer to NAMPOL's lack of human and financial resources.[30] Inadequate personnel also remains a major problem in areas such as Windhoek, for instance, because most officers have under three years' experience; two-thirds of their time is spent on administration, and bureaucracy causes long delays because everything has to be referred through the hierarchical structure of NAMPOL. Also, some staff are illiterate. The resulting inefficiencies are compounded by delays in court hearings, inadequate facilities in prison cells (where some remand prisoners can spend up to a year), and a lack of cooperation between the police and other agencies in the criminal justice system. Furthermore, increasing levels of (white-collar) crime will present great temptation to such a force, especially where morale is low.

Low morale was suggested by about 1996 by the high absenteeism, few promotions and the failure of training (as elsewhere on the continent) to achieve its objectives. No training strategy existed, and there was no provision for the type of training SARPCCO had identified as necessary to deal with drug trafficking, commercial fraud, and vehicle theft. Training was inadequate at all levels. Junior ranks lacked field training, middle managers received none, and there was no specific training for senior managers (except for overseas command courses such as that provided by the British Police Staff College).[31]

Nevertheless, NAMPOL was officially credited with having a reasonable public image (despite the presence of old regime agents), though a number of officers continued to use excessive force.[32] A police task force unit was responsible, for example, for beating and shooting some ex-combatants of PLAN, SWAPO's defunct military wing, who had been demonstrating against unemployment in October 1995. Part of the government response was to enlist several hundred of them into NAMPOL, thus highlighting the overall role of NAMPOL in the peace process.[33] The home affairs minister responsible for the police said he was satisfied with their work, despite personnel and equipment shortages. The regime evidently considered NAMPOL to be a satisfactory force.

Politics, 1990–1996

The developments in NAMPOL (especially where they concern institutional weakness) reflect President Sam Nujoma's internal security interests and personal position. Nujoma, personally secure in his role as father of the nation, was a survivor of thirty years in exile. Above all, he has mastered the strategy of staying in power by dividing and ruling and that of judging security interests. SWAPO, for example, did not have any emotive issues of its own during independence. Indeed, even promises of a better future were convincing only to the electorate in Ovamboland, which suffered most in the war and obtained the fewest benefits from the interim government. Namibia never had an attachment to clan politics or socialism comparable to that in Somalia or Tanzania, though Nujoma had advocated it before his late conversion in the 1980s. But in general ideological fervor was missing, and the government was able to argue successfully that policy must focus on political stability, reconciliation, and national unity, even at the expense of punishing those guilty of past injustices.[34] Uncovering the past would impede this. It would also draw attention to the ruthlessness of the SWAPO elite. For SWAPO's own security service was notorious for the brutalities it inflicted on its own members in exile in the 1970s and 1980s. Its head, Solomon Hawala, who had been responsible only to Nujoma, became head of Namibia's security service in 1990.

As a result, the key mobilizing factors in the 1990 campaign were money and patronage rather than ideology or emotion.[35] This presaged the later development of what became known as casino capitalism.

Casino capitalism. Controlling corruption and restricting the growth of a society based on extensive state patronage have been identified as the key problems for stable African governments, such as Namibia, where there are also massive bureaucracies. This is particularly noticeable in Namibia, where a 30 percent growth in the size of the bureaucracy has taken place in an economy in serious difficulties. But the situation is more complex and emotive than this would suggest. For those who lived under apartheid assumed that majority rule would bring economic opportunity. Nujoma is expected to deliver it. It is for this reason that bureaucracy has expanded, even though it drags down economic growth. Economic growth of 2.7 percent and 5.5 percent occurred in the first two years of independence, in spite of high unemployment, poverty, and other developmental problems, mainly because of close links to the South African economy, and growth soon faltered from 6 percent in 1994 to 2 percent in 1995. Social problems remained acute, with continuing shortages in areas such as housing.

Though the government made some progress in extending water supplies, health care, and education, there are indications that corruption has begun to seep into some layers of government. Certainly by 1994 corruption was no longer just the civil service problem it had been in 1989.[36] Both the justice minister and the deputy home affairs minister were, for instance, investigated by a public service commission (and a separate police inquiry) over the alleged misuse of government aid. Such corruption (though mild by regional standards) became generally known as casino capitalism because of rumors surrounding a casino being built by Stocks and Stocks, a South African leisure and construction group. The chairman of the Namibian subsidiary of Stocks and Stocks is Nujoma's brother-in-law, Aaron Mushimba, and SWAPO is reported to have substantial holdings. By early 1996 *Africa Confidential* was referring to SWAPO Inc. as "developing a new way to run the economy" and as more comfortable with private investment (often its own) than national reconciliation.[37]

Nevertheless, pragmatism and conciliation characterized SWAPO policies during its first five years in office. It sought to conciliate the 70,000 whites and to maximize economic growth by reducing taxes and introducing incentives for investment in export capacity. But the centrality of state patronage to personal advancement has become typical and, with it, a deterioration in democratic practices, as reflected in the competition of trade union leaders to become MPs and in Nujoma's uncontested assertion in 1994 that he had the right to make thirty-two nominations for the seventy-two places on the party electoral list.[38] The potential for political interference in policing is naturally increased by such developments.

Presidential style. The Namibian constitution was internationally regarded as liberal and democratic, but some commentators argue that "it suffers from one crucial weakness—it places too much power in the hands of the central government."[39] The regions have a right to review laws passed by the national assembly, but their powers are limited. The newly elected regional councils after the end of 1992, for example, had no legislative or executive powers and only limited administrative powers. Such a concentration of power has potential implications for the control—and use—of policing, particularly if crime rates are seen to rise or a president wishes to consolidate more power, as Nujoma did on the eve of Namibia's fifth birthday. Already commander in chief of the defense forces and head of security, he also acquired the new home affairs portfolio in charge of policing and immigration, prisons, and corrective services. Nujoma said he would keep the police portfolio only "for the next year or so" to combat increased crime.[40] In the event, he appointed a new home affairs minister within a matter of months, telling journalists that his campaign to cut rising crime was successful, even in the face of an evident shortage of transport and radio equipment.[41]

Not surprisingly, there was tension between the government and an increasing number of critics who identified arrogance, corruption, and nepotism as major characteristics of the new elite. Nujoma was careful to keep a core of leaders from minority indigenous and white communities in the cabinet to offset such criticisms, but he clearly found the existing constitution (negotiated with opposition parties) restrictive in 1994 when he wanted to seek a third term as president. "We must go for more than two-thirds majority," Nujoma was reported as saying before the elections. "There are some clauses which favour opposition parties and we might want to get rid of those clauses."[42]

In the meantime, Nujoma remains a symbol of national unity (though he was seventy at the time of the 1999 elections); his presidential style is criticized but he appears able to keep corruption and "tribalism" by his northern Ovambo Kwanyama kinspeople (who dominate politics, the military, and state security) within acceptable limits. SWAPO decided to back him for a third term in 1999, with the prime minister, Hage Geingob, stating that as father of the nation he deserved another five years. Geingob equated Nujoma's position with the preservation of national unity. The honor was, he said, "an African way of doing things." Many SWAPO members were lukewarm but thought it would avoid disputes over his successor, perhaps aggravating ethnic tensions.[43] Such tensions may, however, be in the process of becoming more visible, as a secessionist movement in Caprivi, the northeastern region, threatens to raise the prospect of similar pressures elsewhere.[44] The supporters of secession are alleged to include police officers.

After six years of independence, SWAPO and its popular leader remained the personification of national unity. Internal party dynamics may have become more important at the same time the political elite have become less accountable and more clientalist in their relations to other social formations, though they do not appear to have exploited the coercive resources of the police so far. Nujoma retains control of the state coercive apparatus, however, while NAMPOL, supervised by the civilian Ministry of Home Affairs, shares responsibility for internal security with the Namibian Defense Force. Although he did not keep the home affairs portfolio he claimed in 1995, Nujoma has made tentative moves to bring the police under his political control; he heads the police himself and appears to recruit senior officers without a power base of their own. There is a danger that such trends will result in the destruction of state institutions, including policing, seen elsewhere.

Significant problems for policing and the police remain. Independence created a black elite to join whites but it has not narrowed the gap between rich and poor. In 1995 the majority of Namibians earned less than $21 a month—about one-twentieth of the earnings of a constable—and unemployment stood at 40 percent.[45] The pressure to overstaff, as mentioned, is strong. Crime, especially economic crimes, stock theft, burglary, rape, and muggings, are seen as increasing. On 2 August 1995, the pro-SWAPO *Namibian* recorded protest marches by residents over rising crime rates and urged the government to suspend without pay all officers and officials involved in car-theft syndicates. If it is true, it suggests that officers are becoming involved in criminal syndicates. Such a development is worrying because the situation would then be comparable to that in South Africa. For when counterinsurgency units were integrated into the police, they included existing clandestine commercial operations—and the South African "total strategy" counterinsurgency policy in Namibia included the "self-financing" of units through criminal means.[46] And Namibia offers opportunities to exploit this situation: Although South Africa is the center of the region's illegal drug trade, Brazilian cocaine, for instance, arrives there via Namibia.

In the early 1990s, the focus of policing changed from counterinsurgency to civilian concerns such as crime prevention and local initiatives to deal with specific issues in the early 1990s. The *Namibian* has since then reported shocking prison conditions, but the constitutional right to a fair trial (and the presumption of innocence until proven guilty) is generally provided, though delays and inefficiencies in the various judicial systems are a hindrance. The U.S. Department of State's annual reports on human rights for the mid-1990s found no reports of political or extrajudicial killings or disappearances. The abuse of human rights by the police has undoubtedly decreased significantly but probably remains acute in northern areas, such as those where the opposition forces are active.[47] Thus NAMPOL remains reasonably faithful to the regime's initial stated objective of pragmatically driven reconciliation and democratization, even if its institutional capacity to deliver such services in the future is debatable.

Reality and Ideals

By the 1980s, the Namibian conflict had become increasingly brutal, as South Africa imposed martial law on almost half the population. After independence the new government made a notable effort to transform and civilianize policing in the cause of national unity, reconciliation, and more political imperatives, such as elite security. There was an unsentimental acknowledgment of political and policing realities in 1990, which smoothed the conversion of the inherited system to that considered appropriate for the new state. The proclaimed ideals of NAMPOL were perhaps unrealistic, and the caveats referred to above are important, yet the police not only dressed differently but most also behaved differently, and there was a conscious attempt, at least in the early years, to become an accessible service rather than an occupying force.

NAMPOL's ideals were laid down in the mission statement of its first inspector general:

The Police is an important pillar of democracy in our country. Our duty is to ensure a stable and peaceful society. We protect and respect the fundamental human rights enshrined in our constitution. . . . The Police serves without fear or favour and, above all, avoids abuse of authority and intolerance. . . . Every member of the Police is accountable for his or her acts before the law.

This remains an ideal rather than a strategy. NAMPOL inevitably reflects developments in a political system becoming ever more dominated by an elite unfavorably disposed toward participatory democracy. NAMPOL still includes agents with experience in enforcing the authoritarian rule of apartheid. Indeed, its low institutional capacity means that South Africa continues to control areas such as firearms licensing and statistical data. The issues now arising for NAMPOL are more tightly linked to regime interests and a decreasing level of political accountability—to what Good calls the new authoritarianism—than to community protection or public service.[48] NAMPOL's future as a "professional" democratic police service is increasingly threatened by its internal problems and institutional weaknesses, both of which are directly affected by the personalization of power, political control, and corruption evident in Nujoma's Namibia.

Notes

1. For background information, see Christopher Clapham, "The Horn of Africa: A Conflict Zone," in Oliver Furley, ed., *Conflict in Africa* (London: Tauris, 1995), 72–91; United Nations, *The United Nations and the Independence of Eritrea* (New York: United Nations, 1996); Ruth Iyob, *The Eritrean Struggle for Independence: Domination, Resistance, Nationalism, 1941–1993* (Cambridge: Cambridge University Press, 1995); Eritrea, Ministry of Foreign Affairs, *Eritrea: Rising from the Ashes* (Asmara: Eritrea Ministry of Foreign Affairs, 1995); UN Research Institute for Social Development, "War-Torn Societies Project: Eritrea," Asmara, 1996.

2. Christopher Clapham, "Ethiopia and Eritrea": The Politics of Post-insurgency," in John Wiseman, ed., *Democracy and Political Change in Sub-Saharan Africa* (London: Routledge, 1995), 116–136.

3. "What Is a Constitution?" *Eritrea Profile* 1: 31 (1994), 3.

4. Quoted in Ruth Iyob, "The Eritrean Experiment: A Cautious Pragmatism," *Journal of Modern African Studies* 53: 4 (1997), 651.

5. BBC Monitoring Service, *Summary of World Broadcasts* ME/0859, 3 September 1990, B6/7.

6. Two categories of people have been consistently detained: those suspected of human rights violations under the Mengistu regime and those allegedly associated with certain political or terrorist organizations. See Amnesty International *Annual Report 1996* (London: Amnesty International, 1996).

7. See James Cheek, "Ethiopia: A Successful Insurgency," in Edwin G. Corr and Steven Sloan, eds., *Low-Intensity Conflict: Old Threats in a New World*

(Boulder, CO: Westview, 1992). Little is known of EPLF intelligence operations, though they appear to have been effective. Compare the National Patriotic Front of Liberia in 1990, which had a security organization, G-2, that gathered intelligence, authorized travel and medical treatment, and, in the absence of a civil administration, acted as a form of local government.

8. Eritrean nationalists in the Eritrean police and Sudanese police and army formed the second batch of fighters in the ELF. David Pool, "The Eritrean People's Liberation Front," in Christopher Clapham, *African Guerrillas* (Oxford: James Currey, Fountain, Indiana University Press, 1998), 23.

9. *Eritrea Profile* 1: 37 (1994), 8. Sixteen thousand of the 54,000 ex-fighters were women, but it is unclear how many joined the police or the administration (a quota was reserved for them).

10. A newspaper column called "Hizb'n Police'n" in *Hadas Ertra* (People and police) lists legal violations.

11. *Eritrea Profile* 1: 49 (1995), 8. This is, however, an official newspaper.

12. He had twenty traffic officers in 1995, whereas there had been more than 100 in 1970.

13. *Indian Ocean Newsletter* 492: 7 (September 1991), 5. This information was supported in conversation with several officers.

14. Iyob, "Eritrean Experiment," 654, n. 29.

15. *Economist,* 6 May 1995.

16. See U.S. Department of State, Bureau of Democracy, Human Rights, and Labor, *Eritrea: Human Rights Practices 1994* (Washington, DC: 1995); Amnesty International, *Report 1994* (London: Amnesty International, 1994). Amnesty International had little information about political arrests or political prisoners. Although policing before independence was undeniably brutal, some local police units in Asmara (suspected of secessionist sympathies) allegedly stayed at their posts for some time after their dismissal by the army in January 1975 in order to protect civilians from attack by soldiers.

17. National service was reintroduced, with the first contingent of 10,000 youths conscripted in May 1994. *Africa Research Bulletin* 31: 4 (1994), 11448.

18. Laurie Nathan, *Marching to a Different Drum: A Description and Assessment of the Formation of the Namibian Police and Defence Force* (Bellville, South Africa: University of the Western Cape, 1990), 23. In some respects, the Eritrean force had more in common with Namibia than with Ethiopia. In an interview in 1994, Bereket Habte Selassie, chairman of the Constitutional Commission of Eritrea, said, "We can learn a lot from our neighbour Ethiopia, and from Namibia which has a similar history to that of Eritrea, in terms of colonisation, struggle and so on." See Eritrean Development and Information Network, 15 August 1994, Dehai Web site.

19. Nat J. Colleta, Markus Kostner, and Ingo Wiederhofer, *Case Studies in War-to-Peace Transition: The Demobilisation and Reintegration of Ex-Combatants in Ethiopia, Namibia, and Uganda* (Washington, DC: World Bank, 1996). See also *Namibian,* 26 January 1990. For background information see Lionel Cliffe with Ray Bush, Jenny Lindsay, Brian Mokopakgosi, Donna Pankhurst, and Balefi Tsie, *The Transition to Independence in Namibia* (Boulder, CO: Lynne Rienner, 1994). Prime responsibility for law and order and the administration of Namibia during the transition period lay with the existing South West African Police under the supervision of UN officials. A civilian component of police, administrative, legal, and electoral officials monitored the elections. But Namibia stands out in terms of resources. In contrast, Eritrea did not face the problem of integrating opposing forces into one organization.

20. The Economist Intelligence Unit (EIU), *Namibia Country Profile: Annual Survey of Political and Economic Background, 1991–92* (London: EIU, 1991). See also the volume for 1993–1994.

21. The policy has continued. In 1997 the Special Field Force was established in order to absorb some of the 10,000 ex-PLAN combatants still unemployed. They are used to perform security sweeps in secessionist areas in the northeastern Caprivi region.

22. Some South African legislation has remained in force. In April 1998, for example, police arrested a number of protesters under proclamations AG 23 and AG 26 of 1989 (AG 23 was approved by President P. W. Botha). "Critics thus have a reason to compare SWAPO to the colonial government run by South Africa." *Pointer: Jane's Intelligence Review,* July 1998, 10.

23. *Namibian,* 19 October 1990. See also *Namibia Brief* 12: (1990), 56f. Henning Melber argued that the "Namibian way" of reconciliation was used as a means of silencing controversy. This is true but it is not unusual. After the Touareg rebellion, the Niger government demobilized 5,900 Touareg fighters; 200 were integrated into the army, fifty into the national gendarmerie, and 100 into the police force. Others went to forest services, customs, and the republican guard. And in Congo (Brazzaville), where reorganization of the security forces was politically sensitive after the politicoethnic troubles of 1993–1994, approximately 4,000 members of party militias from both opposition and the Presidential Tendency Party had been integrated into the police and gendarmerie by 1997. This no doubt stopped when civil war began again later that year.

24. Colleta, *Case Studies,* 2. The members of PLAN were of predominantly Ovambo ethnic origin, SWATF was more diverse, including Ovambo, Herero, San, and Caucasians. SWATF members seemed to have found employment easier, with significant numbers being hired as security guards by private companies. This employment opportunity was not present in other cases considered here (except, to a limited degree, in Uganda). In contrast, security is the fastest-growing industry in South Africa.

25. See Laurie Nathan, "From a Police Force to a Police Service: The New Namibian Police," in M. L. Mathews, Philip B. Heyman, and A. S. Mathews, *Policing the Conflict in South Africa* (Gainesville: University Press of Florida, 1993), 121–132. Other European approaches to aid were different. The German government, for instance, later provided computers and radio equipment but not the training required for their use.

26. The protective unit composed of ex-combatants who acted as border guards and provided general protection has been renamed the Special Field Force and now covers public disorder as well. It is essentially a distinctively uniformed and specially trained paramilitary unit, with its own command structure inside the force; it is not integrated into main policing. In early August 1999, a brief secessionist uprising in the northern Caprivi strip resulted in members of the Special Field Force beating detainees in a police station. Members of the force were described as drunk and undisciplined. See the *Financial Times,* 30 August 1999.

27. Nathan, *Marching to a Different Drum,* 32.

28. Figures are taken from Nathan, *Marching to a Different Drum,* 24; Colleta, *Case Studies,* 128. The public sector, which has 67,000 Namibians on its payroll, is by far the largest single employer. Its numbers have increased by at least 50 percent since independence.

29. The unit dealing with firearms and smuggling activities in 1996 consisted of about half a dozen people. Glenn Oosthuysen, "Shooting the Golden Goose," in Robert I. Rotberg and Greg Mills, eds. *War and Peace in Southern Africa: Crime,*

Drugs, Armies, Trade (Washington, DC: Brookings Institution and World Peace Foundation, 1998), 64–88.

30. A useful source for such material is to be found on the University of Pennsylvania's major Web site, http://www.sas.upenn.edu.

31. Forty-three overseas officers attended the 1992 overseas command course at the college. They included a deputy inspector general of the Gambia Police Force (whose task was to merge the Gambian gendarmerie and police force), a colonel of the Ethiopian force, and a deputy commissioner from Eritrea charged with establishing a police force in that country. In 1992 two former members of courses held in 1990 and 1991 took command of the national forces of Namibia and Uganda.

32. Africa Information Afrique (AIA/Protasius Ndauendapo), "NAM Police Have Good Image," Windhoek, 16 February 1996.

33. It also emphasizes the (regionwide) failure of demobilization plans to provide for the social integration of ex-fighters. See Rotberg and Mills, *War and Peace in Southern Africa*.

34. See Africa Watch, *Accountability in Namibia: Human Rights and the Transition to Democracy* (New York: Africa Watch, 1992). SWAPO did not acknowledge that during the struggle it had said it would impose justice on South African abusers. Neither has it confronted the killing and maltreatment of several thousand SWAPO members labeled as South African "spies" by the party elite during its exile in Angola in the 1980s. Independence celebrations in 1996 were notably soured by the publication of *Wall of Silence* by Siegfried Roth, a German Lutheran clergyman. The book detailed the torture and murder that took place during this period.

35. *Africa Confidential* 31: 2 (1990), 1–2. "Nevertheless local Swapo leaders may remain faithful to the organization not least because of the patronage it has dispensed over the years." *Africa Confidential* 30: 18 (1989), 2.

36. See, for example, *Africa Confidential* 35: 23 (1994), 5. Compare a recent case in Zimbabwe. Seventeen years after independence, cabinet ministers, MPs, and others closely associated with the ruling Zimbabwe African National Union-Patriotic Front (Zanu-PF Party) were alleged to have claimed more than half of the $36 million war veterans' compensation fund, treating it as a slush fund to reward those close to the ruling party. *Africa Research Bulletin* 34: 4 (1997), 12650.

37. See *Africa Confidential* 37: 8 (1996), 4. *Africa Confidential* estimated that SWAPO companies, employing about 6,000 (mainly in the fishing, construction, property, hotels, entertainment, and transport industries) controlled about N$100 million in capital assets. Though a fairly small percentage of the country's total of N$9,000 million, local firms complained that the government gave preferential treatment to those with the right connections. SWAPO businesses operate on commercial lines but are clearly regarded as the source of questionable profits for politicians and their relatives.

38. *Guardian,* 8 and 9 December 1994. The main opposition party, Democratic Turnhalle Alliance (DTA), which described unemployment as a "simmering volcano," believed job creation was possible if the government stopped spending money on luxuries and expensive trips abroad. *Namibian,* 3 November 1995. The DTA supported the employment of former PLAN fighters in the police force.

39. *AI Bulletin* 33: 1 (1993), 2. In a discussion of the "steep decline in state capacity, and a marked deterioration in democratic practice" in South Africa, Kenneth Good suggests that the rise of a "predominant party system, and elitism . . . is present too in Namibia, with similar consequences." Kenneth Good, "Accountable

to Themselves: Predominance in Southern Africa," *Journal of Modern African Studies* 35: 4 (1997), 547.

40. *Africa Review,* May/June 1995, 11. According to 1996 estimates, the combined personnel availability for the national defense force and police was 377,687, with 224,682 males fit for military service. The defense expenditure for 1995/1996 was about $64 million.

41. *Africa Research Bulletin* 31: 9 (1995), 11976–11977.

42. *Financial Times,* 6 December 1994.

43. *Africa Research Bulletin* 34: 9 (1997), 12819. Ethnic tensions have increased since then. The government had originally sponsored legislation recognizing Namibia's traditional tribal authorities, but by 1998 the DTA and the leadership of the Herero (the second largest ethnic group) claimed that SWAPO had politicized the legislation in its favor. See *Pointer: Jane's Intelligence Review,* July 1998, 10.

The future may be more complex without Nujoma as external factors (such as multinational corporations, drugs, and AIDS) affect Namibia.

44. According to some commentators, SWAPO has deliberately inflamed ethnic tension by selectively supporting progovernment tribal groupings. *Africa Confidential* 40: 1 (8 January 1999), 6–7.

45. *Facts and Reports: International Press Cuttings on Southern Africa* 1: 25, c (10 February 1995), 9.

46. For South African forces in Namibia, see Ros Reeve and Stephen Ellis, "An Insider's Account of the South African Security Forces' Role in the Ivory Trade," *Journal of Contemporary African Studies* 13: 2 (1995), 227–243. I am grateful to the anonymous reviewer who pointed out that the illegal trade in ivory and rhinoceros horn was investigated, with specific reference to Namibia, in the South African government's judicial Kumleben Commission of Inquiry report.

47. U.S. Department of State, Bureau of Democracy, Human Rights, and Labor, *Namibia, Country Report on Human Rights Practices for 1996* (Washington, DC: U.S. Department of State, 1997). See also publications issued by the Namibian National Society for Human Rights, http://www.iwwn.com.na/nshr/publications.html.

48. He judges this to have potentially greater permanence than *apartheid,*" and quotes Swilling: "If the old racial authoritarianism is replaced by a new populist authoritarianism, then all that will be initiated is a new era of stagnant, unimaginative, fear-driven uniformity." Good, "Accountability to Themselves," 573.

6

Models of African Policing: Transition

Many years of conflict in sub-Saharan Africa have been accompanied by economic, political, and social dislocation that, taken in conjunction with the uncertainty resulting from the end of the cold war, reduced many commentators to judgments expressed in pathological terms.[1] The apparent irrational breakdown of recognizable order has meant that attention to policing has been slight even though contemporary conflict is characterized by developments (such as the mobilization of children) that will have implications for policing.[2] Of greater importance for this study is that it is in such extreme circumstances that the attributes of police systems are most clearly seen.

No matter how depressing, such circumstances are rarely beyond hope, so I call the fifth phase of the model "transition," rather than borrowing a term from pathology. It is based on situations that combine a fragmented state, endemic tension or conflict, and a disintegrated police system. It may involve both crisis and recovery. It is an artificial classification—Uganda in 1986 could qualify for inclusion—but it is taken to apply to situations where there has been a continuing absence of central state authority and institutional capacity. Policing in this context is consequently seen as a local effort or as part of factional politics, in the absence of a single dominant unifying organization (such as Museveni's NRA).

I use three very different examples to illustrate the main arguments associated with the model: Somalia, the self-proclaimed republic of Somaliland, and Congo (Zaire). I turn first to policing in Somalia because it provides the most extreme example of what happens to a national police force once conflict has broken a state apart, leaving it existing in name only. I contrast the situation with that in Somaliland, where societal groups took over policing directly, just as they do on a smaller scale in other societies. For the way in which the police force disintegrated as political power in

Somalia fragmented provides a key to the evolutionary and tenacious nature of police systems. It raises the following questions:

- What happens to the organization and activity of policing when the institutions and processes on which it is predicated for existence and opportunity fragment?
- How self-sustaining is the acquisition and maintenance of coercive power in the absence of state institutions?
- What are the means of transition?

In common with all categories of the model, the transition phase seeks to identify how the function and role of the police mirror state developments.

The focus of the chapter is on policing in Somalia and Somaliland, but I present the example of Zaire (before President Mobutu's death in 1997 brought an end to thirty-one years of authoritarian rule) for comparison. Congo (Zaire) shows how a fragmented police system, in a situation of general economic and personal insecurity, may be the result of deliberate regime choice. Somalia and Congo (Zaire) exemplify the ways in which structure and order may unravel in contemporary African states.

Fragmenting African States in the 1990s

Before reviewing the fragmentation of policing in Somalia and Congo (Zaire) in the 1990s, we must look at events in those countries in the context of recent state failures that result from the actions of the second- or third-generation regimes now dominating the states established at independence.

State fragmentation is not a recent phenomenon. Indeed, "It might be said that contemporary African history began in state collapse, in the . . . events associated with the collapse of the colonial state in the Congo (now Zaire)."[3] In the 1990s the fragmentation of a state referred to a failure of central rule that leaves a regime unable (or unwilling) to perform the functions required of it; competing groups vie for power and the state may (for a time) cease to exist as an empirical, functioning order. Using this notion, a recent examination of eleven cases of the disintegration of legitimate authority in African states identifies two waves of collapse in established states ruled by nationalist regimes.[4] The first took place around 1980, when regimes that had replaced the original nationalist generation were overthrown (as in Uganda in 1979–1981) by military regimes that proved unable to exercise power effectively, or when state authority (in Chad, for example) collapsed and what remained of the administration lost contact with its agents. The second round of collapse ten years later is typified by

Somalia and Liberia. "Collapse" implies a more extreme prostration than "fragmentation," but it is the term used (synonymously) by many authors.

The collapse of a state is never straightforward. Although colloquial definitions of collapse usually employ medical analogies, Zartman (who finds it difficult to establish an absolute threshold for state collapse) identifies consistent patterns comparable to a long-term degenerative disease. He identifies signposts such as the devolution of central power and a breakdown in a regime's ability to perform expected statist functions such as the provision of security—which would include the capacity to field a police force. Even though there is an absence of clear turning points or warning signals, Zartman characterizes the collapsing state as one in which "The normal politics of demands and responses atrophies; the political processes for popular legitimization are discarded or prostituted; politics and economics are localized; and the center becomes peripheral to the workings of society."[5]

A flaw in this view is that many areas of life (including policing) in which centralization is taken for granted in the West were outside the scope or reach of African regimes in the 1990s, as they were in the 1960s. As Bienen wrote in 1968:

> In the power realm, nation-wide political structures are either non-existent or too weak to enforce the will of ruling national elites, no matter whether they are of traditional lineage groups, civilian bureaucracy, or the military. . . . Highly localized determination of political life need not be synonymous with disorder, anarchy, and chaos. In fact, it may be the only way to avoid these conditions in certain circumstances.[6]

The imposition of a state police system on such an environment means that police systems invariably disintegrate along with the state infrastructure that maintains them. In fact, the level of stateness has been low at some point in all the cases discussed so far in this study (except, perhaps, Namibia). Nonetheless, it is possible to make distinctions of degree. If conflict levels are high, neither the status nor the resources of the police allow state policing.[7] For instance, the police cannot operate as a public force in the type of situation common in parts of Sierra Leone in the mid-1990s. Several shadowy armed groups were active in the countryside around Freetown in 1996, mostly operating for profit. The groups included Sobels, operating in groups of thirty to fifty, who were soldiers by day and rebels by night; irregulars, or bands of fifty to seventy young fighters under the patronage of senior army officers; 80–100 escaped prisoners from a jail in Eastern Province; bands of fifty or more Revolutionary United Front (RUF) dissidents who manned freelance roadblocks for money; and, from Liberia, 50–100 old fighters from the United Liberation Movement for Democracy. On the government side, there were various foreign forces filling gaps left by the army. These included about 1,000 Nigerian troops, men from the security company Executive Outcomes, and traditional hunters from the south and east.[8] In addition, the national army was badly trained, badly fed, and demoralized.

Such a situation does not, however, necessarily mean that the regime has lost control of its coercive agents. Such a situation may result from regime choice. A category of regimes has discovered that they can best control rivals through the promotion of violence on the part of nonstate actors rather than try to control it or apply it directly through state institutions such as the police. Furthermore, a regime (such as Amin's) may through recruitment tactics still retain sufficient control to impose its policies and stave off collapse in such circumstances through the pursuit of a noninstitutional strategy.

The African state is at best a fragile construct, and degrees of fragmentation are characteristic. Fragmentation may represent a separate shadow state, or it may result in a parallel universe associated with activities outside state control, which performs two related (but analytically distinct) tasks, both of importance in understanding the environment of policing. At the primary level such a universe is concerned with survival strategies, and at the official level it encourages patronage and corruption. A further function, operating at a secondary level, may be identified as a recovery of space from the state by means such as a black market, which deprives the state of revenue and weakens its controls. Though these trends are usually seen in terms of economic or political participation rather than those of coercion, they have relevance to policing. They also offer subversive potential for the police as individuals. The practical result is that personal, family, and group security are at a premium and self-defense measures are employed to fill localized security vacuums. The police may become a part of this process by hiring themselves out as guards, but the desideratum is small-scale security in which the activity of policing plays a more important role than the police. This is the key to policing in conflict-ridden societies, for policing develops in response to circumstances and is rarely formally defined in an institutional or a (Weberian) legal-rational sense.[9]

Model 5—Transition: Crisis and Recovery in Somalia and the Self-Proclaimed Republic of Somaliland

Somalia provides a classic example of the fate of a police system in such a failed state for five reasons:

First, the Somali force had a reputation for excellence because it appeared to stand above internal conflict. Commenting in 1969, Lee, for instance, referred to Somalia's "remarkable success" in integrating the separate administrations of British Somaliland and Italian Somalia into a new police.[10] Indeed, such was British confidence in the workability of the multiclan system that it was thought the principle of clan balance would work against any attempt to set the army against the police or vice versa. Accordingly, the British authorities in British Somaliland made no serious attempt to destroy the predominance of clan loyalties. When the Illalos (the district police force recruited from local clans) were called upon to stop an interclan fight, Lee describes how the police restored order by dividing into their own clan groups, each of which fired on the opponents of its own kin. Police coherence was retained because individuals were never called upon to oppose their own families.

Second, by the spring of 1991 the fragmentation of Somalia's infrastructure emphasized that security problems in African states result from internal sources.[11]

Third, Somalia demonstrates that political instability is more concerned with the absence of an agreed set of rules than simply with changes of government or high levels of violence—blood feuds being an accepted way of settling clan disputes.

Fourth, Somalia shows that the existence of a central authority may be negated by political and social structural factors. In other words, centrifugal forces are more characteristic of Somali political power than are centralizing ones.

Fifth, events in Somaliland show how policing, as a consequence of this and (more important) as a measure of the relationship between citizens to a public authority, may take different paths.

The Somali Police Force

Policing, the military, and politics were tightly related in Somalia before 1990. The Somali Police Force (SPF) grew out of the forces established by the colonial powers in British Somaliland and Italian Somalia and was (like the state) funded by cold-war-driven foreign aid. The colonial forces also produced the senior officers and commanders who led the SPF after independence in 1960.[12] Indeed, Siad Barre had been a policeman for the Italian force prior to World War II, before becoming a chief inspector for the British, and then again an officer under the Italian mandate. After independence he became chief of police, then was appointed vice commander of the army and commander in chief in 1965. At the time of a constitutional crisis in 1969, following the assassination of the president, he had seemed a natural figurehead for the army officers responsible for the coup. The coup was an army affair, but six high-ranking police officials were invited to join the twenty-five-member Supreme Revolutionary Council

(SRC). There was a further abortive attempt at overthrowing the council in 1970, probably led by General Jama Ali Korshel, vice president of the SRC and a former police commander.

Under Barre's regime, several police and intelligence organizations were responsible for maintaining public order, controlling crime, and protecting the government against domestic threats. These included the SPF, the People's Militia, the National Security Service, and a number of intelligence-gathering operations, most of which were headed by members of the president's family. The SPF was distinct from the military, but both performed the same general control functions; in 1965, for example, a serious dispute over water and grazing rights caused the police to declare an emergency and adopt infantry tactics to restore order. Although the government used the SPF to counterbalance the Soviet-supported army, no police commander opposed the 1969 coup, and by the early 1980s Somalia was effectively a garrison state where power lay exclusively with the military, with former (military and police) officers firmly entrenched in the civilian institutions of state even though Barre's authority no longer extended beyond the main towns.[13] Policing was predictably repressive. During riots in July 1989, for example, troops with heavy machine guns cleared the streets by shooting at anything that moved, and units from the loyal presidential guard and military police were deployed when demonstrators, chanting antigovernment slogans, tried to march toward the parliament buildings. Control was not handed back to the police for four days.

In the late 1980s, the SPF numbered about 15,000 officers, 6,000 of whom were in the mobile and heavily armed force called Darawishta, which was designed to stop clan warfare. The force remained theoretically divided into eighteen regional districts, with about ninety police stations in the districts and more than 100 police posts in smaller towns, but it had already begun to disintegrate. It may be wrong to assume that normal police procedures were abandoned, though, for the police seem to have been less corrupted and politicized by the Barre regime than the judiciary.[14]

The Disintegration of National Policing

The severe government response to fighting in late 1990 prompted a popular rising in which several thousand people died. Artillery fire had already destroyed or damaged most of the capital, Mogadishu, and armed gangs roamed the streets. There was widespread looting, electricity was cut off, and food and water were in short supply. The police had ceased to exist as a coherent organization by the time Barre fled Mogadishu on 27 January 1991.

Many police apparently returned to their clan areas, but it seems unrealistic to suggest that officers carrying out routine duties (particularly in the northeast) unintentionally created de facto regional police forces.[15] Precisely what happened to the police during this period is unclear, but when police officers reemerged, they did so along local lines—and were thus better able to adapt to the decentralizing conditions than the judiciary was. The pattern was repeated in Hargesia in the northwest, though a new authority was instituted there that proved able to police the community. (There was no comparable government in the old Italian section of Somaliland.) The police undoubtedly lacked transport and communications, and there are no reports that senior police officers acted like the group of generals who established an action committee January 1991. The resulting interim government in Mogadishu, however, soon tried to reestablish the police force for internal security duties, using guerrillas. Its first task was to try to disarm the many groups of armed civilians still on the streets and restore civil order in Mogadishu, but no one could ensure public safety.[16] Protection rackets flourished, and intense fighting broke out between factions throughout the year, resulting in further destruction.

Fighting, famine, intimidation, and extortion characterized the situation. Crime was entrenched; NGO drivers stole food, drug trafficking and prostitution increased, and UN food stores, peacekeepers, and aid workers were attacked. It is hardly surprising that most plans for the future included the formation of a state police. At the beginning of March 1994, for example, a conference of twelve factions of the Somali Salvation Alliance in Cairo proposed that an interim government and a transitional national council be formed to govern Somalia; in the meantime it proposed that the Salvation Council would be responsible for a police force, disarmament, legislation, a judiciary, and courts. Tight links between politics and former police officers continued, with some prominent politicians having served in the SPF. General Mohamed Abshir, chairman of the Somali Salvation Democratic Front, whom the United States considered a potential president of Somalia, was one such. He had been police chief to the new president, Mohamed Ibrahim Egal, of the self-proclaimed republic of Somaliland. Both men were regarded as pro-American.

Although the SPF collapsed when Barre fled, individual officers retained a policing memory—though it is difficult to tell whether the force would have been resurrected without external prompting. For example, at the request of the UN—strongly prompted by the United States—three police consultants (from France, Germany, and Italy) arrived in Mogadishu in January 1993 to examine restructuring the SPF. The mission was delayed because the French and Germans disagreed, but the United States continued to press for a new force, arguing that 2,400 of the old force of 3,500 could be rehabilitated and used in a new force. The argument for this "indigenous solution" was based on a judgment that the old force was never totally under Barre's control and was made up of older men "wise and careful in their behaviour" who were "still widely respected in the country."[17] This seems debatable in the circumstances. But whatever the case, a Somali police officially began operations in Mogadishu in February 1993, for the first time in two years, with more than 2,000 of all ranks taking part in general relief activities such as the distribution of assistance, food convoys, and collecting arms.

Ganzglass says the police were well trained, disciplined, and generally nontribal. If this was the case, then he is right to suggest that the nucleus for a Somali police, acceptable to Somalis in the regions where they were stationed, already existed. Certainly General Ahmed Jama, the last commandant of the SPF, had suggested to Mohamed Sahnoun (the UN secretary-general's special representative for Somali) in 1992 that the police should be used to maintain law and order in the sectors of Mogadishu where they were accepted by the population. And General Jama Mohammed Ghalib (also a former police commandant from Barre's early days) had, when asked by the Council of Elders of Somaliland how the police should be rebuilt, advocated a decentralized police to replace UN troops then deployed in the northwest.[18] Nonetheless, such proposals were premature because, as a UN consultant noted, without "government revenue there is no security. Where there is no security it is difficult to generate revenue."[19] Some form of limited decentralized policing could have been valuable, but the fundamental problem remained that policing was essentially about clan and regional and international politics. Indeed, the contention surrounding it was not about ethnic power so much as state power itself, which the clans saw as a source of revenue.

Although Sahnoun resigned before any of these ideas were put into practice, it is unlikely that such policing could have represented more than isolated examples. The police in Mogadishu could not, for example, function throughout the city, which was in any case divided into war zones. In late 1992 General Ahmed Jama suggested an incremental approach, with the police being reestablished in areas under the control of the American-led Unified Task Force (UNITAF), which had been authorized by UN Security Council Resolution 794 of 3 December 1992. His ideas appealed to the U.S. special envoy, Robert Oakley, who wanted to start organizing the police by district and regions, without addressing the more controversial and difficult problem of combining such commands into a national force. The means through which Ahmed Jama proposed to achieve this was a police committee in Mogadishu to which each faction would nominate police officers. An arrangement was then brokered between the faction leaders General Mohammed Farah Aideed and Ali Mahdi Mohammed, with the result that by March 1993 Mogadishu had a force of 3,000 (plus 2,000 in the remainder of the UNITAF zone), and police began arresting criminals again after a two-year gap.[20]

This force represented a positive step forward, with the subcommittee agreeing on selection criteria, such as two years' service with the Somali National Police, some literacy, and the assurance that candidates had not committed any tangible offense.[21] Furthermore, it was intended that the force should be paid from the operational funds of the second UN operation in Somalia (UNOSOM) after May 1993, Security Council Resolution 814 of March 1993 having requested UNOSOM II to "assume responsibility for the consolidation, expansion and maintenance of a secure environment throughout Somalia." But because there was no budget, the force was unpaid, except in terms of food. (The consequences of this on discipline are unclear.) There was no planning, and no thought was given to expanding the concept of the police committee to the rest of the country. So in the absence of a national government, it remained merely one force among many offering policing. It was an essentially factional arrangement to which UNITAF became a part, as Ahmed Jama recognized when he refused command of the Mogadishu force in January 1993.

International concern remained focused on a future national force, but as events showed, the political will was lacking. Some moves were unambiguous. For example, Security Council Resolution 814, crafted largely by the United States, laid out the tasks required to establish long-term peace and stability. It mandated the UN to undertake the reestablishment of national and regional institutions and civil administrations throughout the country and assist in the reestablishment of Somali police. And the UN sent a small technical team to look at an auxiliary security force, which, it was claimed, had 4,000 members from the SNF capable of dealing with short-term requirements for order and public safety. The UN team met three former Somali National Police commandants and the Mogadishu police committee during its three-week visit. The team concluded that a national force should be established at its pre-civil-war level of 18,000–20,000, monitored by and assisted by a 500-strong UN civilian police (UNCIVPOL); that the new force should be built around former police and extended to the northwest; and that a special unit should be established within the force to cope with cross-border security problems.[22]

But these recommendations existed in a vacuum: the UN secretary-general took no further action, and no UNCIVPOL team was sent. The funding for the 5,000-strong Mogadishu force (with a notional budget of $12.6 million for an initial six months) proposed by the U.S. team was unclear. The source of pay for officers was obscure—UNITAF had used food from relief agencies in lieu of salaries. UNOSOM I eventually made some funds available for equipment, uniforms, and salaries, but the force was effectively without uniforms, transport, and stations. There was admittedly nothing unusual about this, but in the context of Somalia the result was the "preposterous situation of an open air arms market in Mogadishu existing under UNITAF, and armed guards of NGOs serving as security personnel during the day and moonlighting as bandits at night, while UNITAF struggled to find funds for batons, berets and whistles for the police."[23]

There were pockets of policing excellence, such as that promoted by Australian troops in the southwestern Bay region.[24] They arrived with a comprehensive civil affairs program and quickly set up an auxiliary police force in Baidoa to deal with the "entrepreneurial banditry" of the area, using former members of the Somali National Police whose names were vetted by the police committee in Mogadishu. The local elders then proposed a police commander for Baidoa who was acceptable to both the community and the Australians. Later the Australians set up a CID unit of former CID officers that was considered exceptionally effective. Police equipment (which came from UNITAF) included typewriters, stationery, VHF radios, uniforms, batons, whistles, and transport; the 25 percent of the force who were armed also received training. Other units were set up throughout the Bay region once those in Baidoa were established, and the police station was rebuilt in the same compound as a court and small prison. By the end of the Australians' tour of duty, the region was considered secure by the Australians. How long the effects of this work lasted is not known, but it is clear that the 260 police concerned could not stop militias from moving back into the region once the Australians left, for police forces remained at the mercy of factional leaders, militia, and UNOSOM—the last of which had allowed the special problems of Mogadishu to dictate its agenda for the entire region.

Factors Influencing the Shape of Policing

Somali policing was shaped by factors resulting directly from the collapse of the central state and its institutions, compounded by the fact that although new social groups emerged, traditional cultural patterns (based on kin and Islam) were eroded, and there was no authority or leader capable of sustaining the order a national police force needs.[25] It was also shaped by the great size of the country (more than 620,000 square kilometers), its small population of 5 million, the vast distances between urban areas, the scarcity of resources, clan rivalries, and the differing histories of the north and south of the country. Policing in Somaliland is on too limited a scale to meet such serious challenges.

The collapse of the central state cannot be blamed solely on Barre's inadequate political leadership. The various faction leaders deliberately exploited clan animosity and resources for their own purposes. Although Somalis seemed willing to pay taxes at the local level (where immediate results are visible and authorities appear accountable), the resources needed to fund a state police force, for example, could never be collected at a national level. Accordingly, clashes between the Egal administration in the northwest and the Issa were prompted by Egal's attempt to take over Issa taxation of local commercial traffic. Years of war and looting (and the absence of foreign aid) have reduced the resources available, but more importantly, the essentially centrifugal nature of clan politics has overwhelmed efforts at reunification and national policing. Somaliland, where a clan coalition, tax system, and police force exist, is the sole exception. In the past, a combination of foreign patronage and military coercion overcame the centrifugal forces, but none of the present leaders have the security resources of a Barre. The result is that although they can intimidate local communities, their resources and activities are on a comparatively small scale.

In addition, many leaders have a vested interest in fragmentation. Factions and individuals profit from the existing economy of plunder, with its extortion rackets. The power base of numerous militia leaders depends on conflict and mobilization. The status and wealth of many individuals would drop dramatically in peace; some businesspeople would lose out if trade was opened up to newcomers, and entire clans would stand to lose considerable property as a result of national reconciliation. Fewer would gain. They include businesspeople, who would benefit if major roadways and ports were kept open, and the political class of former civil servants, high-ranking officers, and ministers whose place was within the state apparatus.[26] The state-centric diplomacy of the international community has only a limited role as a centralizing force. Centripetal forces are weaker than centrifugal ones.

The growth of private policing. Local communities have adapted to the prolonged collapse of the state by developing informal systems and mechanisms that provide some of the minimal functions of day-to-day government. Policing is one such function.

By 1995 Somalia had a variety of overlapping and fluid local authorities—ranging from militia to clan elders, Mafia-like rackets, and fundamentalist mosques—that provided forms of private policing. They reflected the "mosaic of fluid, highly localized polities" filling the security vacuum.[27] In 1993 local policing in Kismayu (in the southwest) included gray-uniformed, truncheon-wielding police led by a former officer in Barre's CID who supported General Mohammed Hersi Morgan, Barre's son-in-law and leader of the Somali National Front. Belgian units enforcing a weapons-free zonal policy in the area recognized the police. Again, local councils in Baidoa, in the southwest, in 1994 ran a local police force that allowed some businesspeople to profit from Somalia's tax- and duty-free conditions, setting up private telephone exchanges, passport offices, and franchises for the export of goats and fruit. In contrast, some clans and subclans in the self-proclaimed republic of Somaliland had recourse to their own traditional structures in the absence of de facto state institutions, with heads of lineage groups expanding into the void left by the collapse of Barre's administration. Traditional systems of governance, however, rely primarily on the moral authority of lineage and clan leaders, and the power of such systems to prevent crime and violence is limited.

Other schemes operated in areas such as the Medina neighborhood in Mogadishu, where several security and judicial systems overlapped. One was a neighborhood watch system, a crime prevention scheme in which residents blew whistles if armed outsiders were seen or crime suspected. Many Medina neighborhoods also provided payments to local armed youths to serve as private security forces.

Another scheme was provided by fundamentalist mosques that imposed *shari'a* law (of approved Muslim behavior) through the use of armed young men in different clan areas, such as north Mogadishu, Luuq (where they existed even before UNOSOM II), and Kismayu. In general the *shari'a* authorities have been established, with the consent of local faction leaders (often when they have been unable to bring security to an area), to perform basic governance tasks. *Shari'a* authorities thus gained popularity because they were able to deliver security. Such authorities in Mogadishu performed policing functions, for example, with several armed trucks, known as technicals, being converted to police vehicles.

The authority of the factions was not directly challenged by the development of *shari'a* authority, but several Islamic leaders indicated that *shari'a* had a political base because of its Pan-Somali nature (which went beyond clan divisions).[28] This may result in future tension, as the *shari'a* pursuit of integration represents a (latent) centripetal tendency. In the meantime, Islamic jurisdiction affects other secular systems of policing and adjudication. *Shari'a* courts traditionally ruled in cases of civil and family law, but their jurisdiction was extended to criminal proceedings in some regions in early 1994. In Bosasso, for example, the authorities turned criminals over to the families of their victims. In the northwest, Somaliland continued to use the pre-1991 Somali penal code, so courts in Bardera applied a combination of this and *shari'a* law. In contrast, court decisions in areas such as north Mogadishu and part of south Mogadishu were based solely on *shari'a* law.[29] Amnesty International described the punishments imposed by Islamic militia as inhuman and degrading, but execution as a form of punishment was retained by all existing court systems in Somalia, whether secular, Islamic, or traditional and clan based.[30]

According to Menkhaus and Prendergast, "collectively this web of radically privatized, quasi-vigilante security arrangements provides reasonable deterrents to crime—for those who can afford them, and who hail from sub-clans with adequate power to reinforce the deterrent factor. . . .

However imperfect this security system may be, it is and will remain far superior to any police force in coming years."[31] It is inaccurate to describe such policing as routine extortion, but its development suggests a gray area linking extortion and taxation that falls into the general theories about state building proposed by commentators such as Tilly and Olson.[32]

Militia. The links among policing, enforcement, and crime is made explicit by militia groups in such conflict scenarios. Militia are not police as such, though they may well enforce order in their territory. They may or may not include individual police acting as entrepreneurs, but they undoubtedly represent a common policing problem.

We may distinguish three categories of militia. The first comprises those operating on behalf of a recognized clan, ethnic, or ideological leader such as Aideed; these may be called personal militia.[33] The second covers what are best described as clan militia. These are armed groups, loosely recognized as private clan armies, that look after the general interests of their specific groups (rather than a particular leader). Such militia usually run the areas controlled by their clans or lineage and may work with the armed kinsmen who often operate in areas controlled by their lineage. In their 1993 analysis of Somaliland, for example, Farah and Lewis identified forty militia-manned checkpoints (divided among more than ten lineage groups) along two trade routes commonly used by *qat* trucks.[34] They refer to militia "squadrons" extorting cash from passing private trade and *qat* from *qat* trucks in what the militia see as legitimate taxation and compensation for their unpaid services. The trade associated with *qat* has also led to agreements between militia and dealers for the former's armed trucks to act as protective escorts for the latter's consignments. Such activity has implications for future organized crime.

The third category of militia is that of freelance militias plundering and destroying in an opportunistic fashion. They are not police, but they are undoubtedly a policing problem. They are often left behind after the dispersal of recognized forces, and in Somaliland are usually composed of teenage boys and unmarried males, without livestock, who hate the elder generation and all that it stands for. Their plunder of property and stock threatens security in both urban and rural areas.

All militia groups represent a significant obstacle to the reconstruction of a legitimate police force, but the fragmentation associated with their existence has resulted in more than one variant of the transitional model.

District Policing in Somaliland

The situation in Somalia exemplifies the low end of the spectrum of state institutional capacity. It emphasizes the way in which policing may be used as a measure of the relationship between citizens and a public authority. It also provides evidence of the ways in which societal groups arise to take over policing directly. This phenomenon is especially clear in Somaliland, where a belief in the importance of institutional capacity is evident on the part of a few prominent men, albeit on a limited scale. For although the UN thought almost exclusively in terms of relief, Somaliland's aim was security. In 1993 President Egal insisted that there was an urgent need for better internal security.[35] He said this required an effective administration, possibly along the lines of the Anglo-Indian administrative model, capable of limited revenue collection. He did not think this would necessarily make the development of Somaliland possible, but he did think it would enable a government to subsist and, with it, a police force able to manage security.

In 1993 Egal could do little more than hope to survive. Soviet-U.S. rivalry had turned the country into a vast arms dump, covered with ammunition dumps and unexploded ordnance. Security deteriorated steadily after Somaliland's supposed liberation of May 1991, but a turning point was reached in October 1992, when clan elders negotiated an end to clashes in the Berbera area. The following year the assembly, the Gurti, negotiated a comprehensive peace agreement for the whole of Somaliland, drawing up a constitution with a two-tier government and choosing Egal (briefly British Somaliland's prime minister and architect of unity in 1960) as president.

Internal stabilization was a clear priority, and policing was seen as an appropriate response to the new situation in which looting remained a significant problem. This was most obvious in the town of Hargeisa, which formed a district police force specifically to deal with looting; its 300 recruits were promised clothing and salaries by the president at a mass rally in November 1992.[36] A British aid worker, Rob Turnbull, described how local people gathered in front of the townhall to hear an address from the president, the minister of defense and others, with "the high spot of the proceedings being when 300 newly recruited Hargeisa District Police marched smartly on parade to the beating of drums and following the flag." Another mass rally was held on 25 November in which 150 prominent elders and thirty militia commanders drawn from every clan took an oath of allegiance to the state and pledged to maintain and protect peace and public order.

Armed units loyal to President Egal continued to engage members of the militia throughout the following months, but by early 1993 Hargeisa was enjoying significant commercial freedom. This provided an opportunity for policing. There were few visible guns—"Whenever the people spot an armed man, they hoot at him in unison . . . They can't abide the sight of weapons"—though the police evidently avoided confronting the group of chain-smoking armed militiamen (extorting money from passengers as an easy option) who represented security at the airport.[37]

By 1994 the police force numbered about 400 (though Egal reckoned 3,700 were needed to cover the country). Funding and a lack of resources remained significant problems, tying the police closely to sections of the town. The force was paid for (in kind rather than cash) by local people, so it was local to the elders of the region rather than the self-proclaimed government. Local businesspeople apparently welcomed it, for they ran a small electricity grid using two bulldozer engines and gave free current to police stations, courts, mosques, ministries, and main streets. Police pay was in rice, oil, and powdered milk, and the force got its first vehicle (a loaned, secondhand Toyota) from one of a group of volunteers supplying food to the Hargeisa jail.[38] UNOSOM's sole contribution was green uniforms, for the UN claimed that to give more would have amounted to recognition of Somaliland.

International recognition may have been lacking, thus affecting offers of aid; mililtias were a major difficulty, and clan power struggles continued to encourage conflict, but by 1995 Egal's position was reasonably strong. The government was widely considered to have received its mandate through the relatively democratic process of the 1993 Booraame conference, and Somaliland saw the beginnings of institutionalization in October 1996, with the third national conference. This organized a supreme court and formalized the roles of the president and cabinet.

Serious administrative problems remain. There is no banking system, public accounting, school system, health care, or reliable tax base. The small civil service is underpaid, and the large army is (like the police) unpaid; neither is there cash to demobilize it. Yet there is a modest government structure and a reasonably secure environment in which district police forces and localized policing have played a part.

Fragmentation: Regime Choice in Congo (Zaire)

The collapse of the Somali police mirrored that of the state, and the fragmented nature of policing since then reflects the localization—or regionalization—of Somali politics. But the policing of fragmented states may also result directly from expediency or regime choice. In Zaire, for example, President Mobutu Sese Seko (whose authority rested on his control of key security forces) used conflict for personal political ends, and the resulting (mis)management of the apparatus of government caused an almost complete collapse of the economy, infrastructure, and policing.[39]

The situation in Zaire presented a further variant on the theme of evolution and adaptation by police systems in fragmented states. For its recent history of policing emphasizes the importance of context and complexity in understanding the coercive state.

The collapse of the Congo in 1960, with the instant Africanization of the Territorial Police (there was no national force), meant policing standards deteriorated dramatically. The UN force that arrived in the Congo in 1960 acted as an emergency police substitute, but no reliable force was developed. Although each province maintained its own force, the departure of the experienced Belgian officer corps meant that some soon became private armies while others disintegrated. The UN imposed limited order; the rehabilitation of the police, however, proved difficult. Despite training provided by Belgium, Nigeria, and the United States, continuing conflict in the mid-1960s limited its impact, as did the political decision to increase the number of provinces from six to twenty-one. The resulting new provincial police forces rapidly expanded until they once again resembled armies.

Mobutu stopped this process when he came to power in 1965. The police played no special role in the 1965 coup, nor indeed in the Mobutu regime. He soon removed the police from provincial control, standardized their organization and equipment, removed unreliable elements, and centralized control under the Ministry of the Interior in December 1966. The reorganization reduced paramilitary threats to the regime and lessened the influence of local politicians, tribalism, and regionalism, but the reputation of the force remained at best one of brutal, urban mediocrity. Mobutu then gave new roles to specialized security forces as a deliberate divide-and-rule policy. In 1972, for example, the National Police was dissolved and merged with the (rural) gendarmerie into a single force, the National Gendarmerie. This significantly increased the size of the national force and made it equivalent to the other security services. But by transferring control of the force from the Ministry of the Interior to the Ministry of Defense, Mobutu effectively brought the police under his direct control. Yet, as Schatzberg noted, the process should not be overestimated, for one of the striking conclusions to emerge from his study of coercive forces in Zaire was the extent to which the state left military and police commanders in the field on their own. Up to 30,000 of the local police remained outside governmental control, acting on their own behalf or at the behest of military authorities. This encouraged brutality and corruption, for the gendarmes were rarely paid, and the state rarely punished those guilty of abuse; only the lowest-ranking officers suffered the exemplary punishments of losing their positions, fines or imprisonment. Even the chief of staff of the gendarmerie admitted (in a speech in 1993 on the anniversary of its founding) that roads were insecure because of banditry, murder, extortion, and armed robbery committed by gendarmes. Thus, rather than being a monolith, the state under Mobutu was a "complicated congeries of only imperfectly controlled organizations and institutions, each motivated by different imperatives."[40]

The disintegration of policing happened easily. Extrajudicial executions and unlawful killings by the police were regularly reported. Amnesty International noted:

Beatings and other forms of torture and ill-treatment are routine for anyone arrested or refusing to surrender money demanded by military or other authorities in Zaïre. It is so commonplace that both victims, civilian and military authorities appear surprised to learn that it is actually prohibited by Zaïrian law and the Constitution.[41]

Many basic security or guarding tasks were performed by locally recruited untrained individuals, and the activities of the existing (often unpaid) police rarely made reference to regional, let alone national, objectives. Police squads were more likely to be hired to settle personal vendettas. The resulting ambiguity of identity is indicated by the following report from the border region between Zaire and Rwanda: "The few soldiers and police stationed in the area have themselves frequently profited from the situation, looting from the various sides and essentially selling their services to the highest bidder."[42] As Schatzberg observed of Zaire in the 1980s, "Coercive power without significant control increases insecurity among both rulers and ruled."[43]

Mobutu's Zaire was replaced by the Democratic Congo of Laurent Kabila in 1997, but the nature of policing remains unchanged. Human rights records continued to deteriorate as Kabila's treatment of the opposition became reminiscent of his predecessor's. At first, though, the police system had a potentially more coherent profile, because issues related to law and order constituted Kabila's main worries. Kinshasa was destabilized by unpaid soldiers and the influx of 30,000 refugees from fighting across the river in Congo-Brazzaville. "The local Berci polling firm found that 70 per cent of citizens approve of the Kabila government's rapid intervention police squads, which ruthlessly pursue robbers."[44] More significant, the nature of political power remains unchanged, the police suffer the same desperate lack of funding as under Mobutu, and Kabila soon created a new gendarmerie, the Special Security Group of the President, to strengthen his own power.[45]

Conclusion

Events in Somalia (and, to a lesser extent, Zaire) during the 1990s present two apparently contradictory features. The first is that police systems disintegrate or dissolve when the political processes on which their organization and activity are predicated fragment; police functions and roles reflect political developments (see Table 6.1). The second is that police systems are able to survive conflict and the fragmentation of a state. These features return us to functional questions related to the point at which a private or state militia is no longer a police force. It may be that *public good* (such as security or crime investigation) must be defined as a precondition or that there is a requirement for the police to have the capacity to deliver such a public good. Egal's forces seem to fit both criteria, whereas those in Baidoa (let alone freelance bandits or Mobutu's "police") do not. In any case, the permitted employment of coercion does not automatically mean groups are police agents.

The two features are in practice linked by the activities of the international community in states such as Somalia. This suggests that a police system will eventually be reestablished because the police are considered an attribute of the contemporary state. Furthermore, the experience of Ethiopia shows that even a formally decentralized Somalia may yet have a single system (by means such as confederation, federation, regional autonomy, or nonterritorial friendly association).

The example of Somalia indicates that a state force cannot, however, exist in a security vacuum but will remain confined to a specific locality (such as Hargeisa). This is reinforced by the localization of Somali politics, which itself represents a significant social adaptation to the collapse of the centralized state. It is a reflection of the new types of fluid power structures, situational in nature, noted by commentators. In this way, some recently developed local authorities are a response to the internal needs of

Table 6.1 State Policing Requirements

Phase	Function (requirements)	Role (agents and their activities)
Strong central government	Enforcement and maintenance of civil order Regime representation Regulatory activities	National public police performing conventional duties
Fragmentation	Functions limited by absence of single civil order Authority and power devolve to regions	Formal police force replaced by informal localized policing provided by other suppliers (e.g., militia, mosques, security companies)
Collapse	Formal police system either collapses (and there is a failure to fill the void with formal or de facto police) or its functions are militarized	Localized policing replaced by various armed groups

clans to organize local affairs, whereas the development of such local authorities along clan lines (to guard the interests of the clan from external threats) accentuates the division of the state into smaller entities.[46] Islamic power structures must also be accommodated. Such a situation may in turn accelerate localized recovery from conflict because recovery is "facilitated by the lack of a functioning civil government, with its potential for crippling levels of taxation and bureaucracy."[47] This represents a central paradox, for the lack of government also prevents the re-creation of a single police force in the absence of international pressure.

It is tempting to emphasize the continuing importance of centrifugal tendencies in Somali policing at the expense of other factors, but their existence did not prevent the emergence of a centralized coercive system in the past—political contingencies and leadership factors were also important. Moreover, the acquisition and maintenance of coercive power appears to be almost self-sustaining at both local and central levels; all leaders value it as a tool and aspire to the legitimizing prestige it attracts. The function and role of policing thus continue to mirror juridical state developments; for policing is localized when politics is, but a residual national system is retained during transitional periods in the form of individual memories and aspirations.

Notes

1. The best known of these is Robert Kaplan, whose influential essay began and ended with Sierra Leone. Robert D. Kaplan, "The Coming Anarchy: How Scarcity, Crime, Overpopulation, and Disease are Rapidly Destroying the Social Fabric of Our Planet," *Atlantic Monthly,* February 1994, 44–76.

2. See Alex de Waal, "Contemporary Warfare in Africa: Changing Context, Changing Strategies," *War and Rural Development in Africa, IDS Bulletin* 27: 3 (1996), 6–16.

3. I. William Zartman, ed., *Collapsed States: The Disintegration and Restoration of Legitimate Authority* (Boulder, CO: Lynne Rienner, 1995), 2.

4. Ibid., 1. See also Mohammed Ayoob, "State Making, State Breaking, and State Failure," in Chester A. Crocker and Fen Osler Hampson with Pamela Aall, *Managing Global Chaos: Sources of and Responses to International Conflict* (Washington, DC: U.S. Institute of Peace Press, 1996), 37–51.

5. Zartman, *Collapsed States,* 6.

6. Henry Bienen, ed., *The Military Intervenes: Case Studies in Political Development* (New York: Russell Sage Foundation, 1968), 36.

7. States that can no longer support bureaucratic structures cannot support centralized national police systems. This has implications for the wider study of policing because the creation of a force is often attributed to an emerging dominant class seeking to control access to scarce resources. See Cyril Robinson and Richard Scaglion, with J. Michael Olivero, *Police in Contradiction: The Evolution of the Police Function in Society* (Westport, CT: Greenwood Press, 1994), 4.

8. *Africa Confidential* 37: 13 (1996), 6.

9. That the absence of institutions may sometimes be an advantage is suggested by the ICRC's judgment that recovery from the civil war has been eased by the absence of a functioning central government and taxation system. International Federation of Red Cross and Red Crescent Societies, *World Disasters Report 1994* (Geneva: IFRCRC, 1994), 87. Hashim suggests that alliances and bargaining between clan groups may actually represent state strength rather than weakness. Alice Bettis Hashim, *The Fallen State: Dissonance, Dictatorship and Death in Somalia* (Lanham, MD: University Press of America, 1997).

10. J. M. Lee, *African Armies and Civil Order* (London: Chatto & Windus for the International Institute of Strategic Studies, 1969), 81.

11. There have been few interstate wars, and the boundaries of states inherited from colonialism have been preserved no matter how unrealistic they may appear. See Jeffrey Herbst, "The Creation and Maintenance of National Boundaries in Africa," *International Organization* 43: 4 (1989), 673–692. Paradoxically, Somalia violated this taboo when it attacked Ethiopia in 1997.

12. For details of the force before 1990, see John Andrade, *World Police and Paramilitary Forces* (London: Macmillan, 1985), James Cramer, *The World's Police* (London: Cassell, 1964); George Thomas Kurian, *World's Encyclopaedia of Police Forces and Penal Systems* (Oxford: Facts on File, 1989).

13. In 1989, U.S. State Department officials described Somalia as disintegrating. *Africa Research Bulletin* 26: 10 (1989), 9424.

14. Ganzglass thinks that the fact that many former police emerged on UNTAF's arrival—and tried to restore law and order unarmed and without clan protection—supports this. Martin R. Ganzglass, "The Restoration of the Somali Justice System," *International Peacekeeping,* 3: 1 (1996), 113–138.

15. See Refugee Policy Group, *Hope Restored? Humanitarian Aid in Somalia, 1990–1994* (Washington, DC: Refugee Policy Group, 1994). Ganzglass provides a particularly useful account of this period. He notes that police policy had been never to send a serving commanding officer to his home area.

16. *Warsidaha Ururka Ingiriiska Iyo Soomaalida: Journal of the Anglo-Somali Society,* May 1991, 3.

17. *Indian Ocean Newsletter* 561 (6 February 1993).

18. Ghalib had learned to read and write in Hargeisa before joining the protectorate police in the 1950s. He has been Egal's critic and opponent since then. Jama Mohamed Ghalib, *The Cost of Dictatorship: The Somali Experience* (New York: Lilian Barber Press, 1995). UN officials who discussed the option of a national police force evidently thought it would create many problems. See Mohamed Osman Omar, *Somalia: A Nation Driven to Despair; A Case of Leadership Failure* (New Delhi: Somali Publications, 1996). The UN was expelled from Hargeisa.

19. John Drysdale quoted in Ganzglass, "Restoration," 115. Drysdale proposed that the way out of this circle was to support and pay a nontribal Somali police force as part of a plan with "revisions to ensure that the continuity of the force is assured." See also n. 9 above.

20. Aideed nominated five former police officers to represent his group, but Ali Mahdi nominated only one. The other four (who were unchallenged) were either from Siad Barre's National Security Service or the army. Aideed became convinced the committee was being marginalized in favor of UNOSOM action according to *Warsidhaha* 13 (1994), 39.

21. An excellent account of policing at this time is given by Lynn Thomas and Steve Spataro, "Peacekeeping and Policing in Somalia," in Robert B. Oakley, Michael J. Dziedzic, and Eliot M. Goldberg, eds., *Policing the New World Disorder:*

Peace Operations and Public Security (Washington, DC: National Defense University Press, 1998), 175–214.

22. Ganzglass, "Restoration," 120, 124. Approximately $42 million was eventually budgeted for rebuilding the police force nationally, with the goal of having a force of 18,000 in operation by March 1995. By early 1994, the United States had earmarked $37 million to equip and train an 8,000-member force. It was to receive 5,000 M-16 rifles, 5,000 pairs of handcuffs, 358 vehicles, and 2.3 million rounds of ammunition even though there was no government to direct it. *Daily Telegraph,* 25 March 1994.

23. Ganzglass, "Restoration," 135, n. 52.

24. See Michael J. Kelly, *Peace Operations: Tackling the Military Legal and Policy Challenges* (Canberra: Australian Government Publishing Service, 1997).

25. See Terence Lyons and Ahmed I. Samatar, *Somalia: State Collapse, Multilateral Intervention, and Strategies for Political Reconstruction* (Washington, DC: Brookings Institution, 1995).

26. Key faction leaders in Mogadishu later formed a coordinating committee to establish a single administration in important areas such as the seaport and international airport. BBC Monitoring Service, *Summary of World Broadcasts* AL/3140, 2 February 1998, A/2, A/3. The Mogadishu peace committee also tried to establish multiclan control over the seaport and airport.

27. Ken Menkhaus and John Prendergast, "The Stateless State," *Africa Report* May-June 1995, 25; *Economist,* 18 February 1995.

28. In 1997 Somalia's main Islamist organization, Al Itahad al Islami, said it intended to become a political party. *Africa Confidential* 38: 2 (1997), 3.

29. U.S. Department of State, Bureau of Democracy, Human Rights, and Labor, *Somalia: Country Report on Human Rights Practices for 1996* (Washington, DC: U.S. Department of State, 1997).

30. Amnesty International, *Annual Report 1996* (London: Amnesty International, 1996), 273–274.

31. Menkhaus and Prendergast, "Stateless State," 25.

32. See Charles Tilly, "War Making and State Making as Organized Crime," in Peter B. Evans, Dietrich Rueschemeyer, and Theda Skocpol, eds., *Bringing the State Back In* (Cambridge: Cambridge University Press, 1985), 169–191.

33. An *Economist* report on Liberia (13 April 1996) typifies this understanding. The article describes how five main factions, recruited from young, semiliterate villagers, emerged from the conflict following the death of Samuel Doe. They were motivated by "ethnicity, greed, drugs, magic and fear of magic. . . . The battlegrounds were trade and aid routes, ports and diamond mines." Their actions were orchestrated by leaders described elsewhere as "warlords" (*Financial Times,* 13 April 1996) and "rival militia chieftains with political agendas of their own" (*Sunday Times,* 18 February 1996). But the new police force Charles Taylor sent to arrest Roosevelt Johnson (leader of a rival faction) in March 1996 was similarly described as composed mainly of "Taylor militia-men" by the *Sunday Times,* which suggests a formalization of some aspects of the relationship among conflict, security, and law enforcement. The implication is that militias act in a fluid but close relationship to clan or faction leaders in conflict-ridden societies.

34. Ahmed Yusuf Farrah, with I. M. Lewis, *Somalia: The Roots of Reconciliation. Peace Making Endeavours of Contemporary Lineage Leaders: A Survey of Grassroots Peace Conferences in "Somaliland"* (London: ACTIONAID, 1993), 61. *Qat* (or *quat*) is a mild narcotic used throughout the Horn. See *Africa Confidential* 33:7 (1992), 2.

35. *Warsidaha* 12 (Spring 1993), 8f.

36. Ibid. Turnbull's visit of November 1992 was described in *Warsidaha* 13 (1993), 9. Compare the situation in Bosaso in the northeast region of Bari, where a police academy provided refresher courses for 125 former police officers in 1998.

37. *Warsidaha* 14 (Autumn/Winter 1994), 18. The airport was controlled by 'Iidagale militia and Force 111, the old guerrilla army of the Somali National Movement, until early 1994, when government forces took it back. Force 111 (headed by general Jama Gahalib, a former police general and former interior minister in Siad Barre's regime) levied a tax on all airport users. See *Indian Ocean Newsletter* 643 (22 October 1994), 2.

38. The individual concerned also supplied food to Zairean jails. *Africa Report* (January/February) 1994, 36–38.

39. See William Reno, *Warlord Politics and African States* (Boulder, CO: Lynne Rienner, 1998), especially 147–182; IPS, "Zaire: Mobutu Seen as Abetting Anti-Tutsi Attacks," Comtex Newswire, 31 July 1996; *Jane's Intelligence Review, Crisis in Central Africa*, Special Report 13 (1996), 14.

40. Michael G. Schatzberg, *The Dialectics of Oppression in Zaire* (Bloomington: Indiana University Press, 1988), 69.

41. See Amnesty International, *Report 1996*, 330; Amnesty International, *Zaire: Human Rights Activists Under Threat* (London: Amnesty International, 1996), 5; *Guardian*, 25 March 1997.

42. Human Rights Watch/Africa in New York and the Fédération Internationale des Ligues des Droits de l'Homme (FIDH), Comtex Newswire, 31 July 1996.

43. Schatzberg, *Dialectics of Oppression*, 70.

44. *Africa Confidential* 38: 19 (1997), 1.

45. International Institute for Strategic Studies, *Strategic Comments* 4: 6 (July 1998), Congo.

46. Ken Menkhaus and John Prendergast, *Political Economy of Post-Intervention Somalia*, Somalia Task Force Issue Paper 3, www.antro.uu.se/bh/nomadnet/menkaus.html, April 1995; Ken Menkhaus, "Somalia: Political Order in a Stateless Society," *Current History*, May 1998, 220–224; *Africa Research Bulletin* 33: 10 (1996), 12446.

47. International Federation of Red Cross, *World Disasters 1994*, 97.

7

Models of African Policing: Adaptation

The World Bank refers to a crisis of statehood in Africa, which has led to a spiral of insecurity and crime.[1] Indeed, the World Bank considers that most African states, with the exception of a few countries such as Botswana and Uganda, now have a lower "state capability" than at independence. A comparable evaluation has led French researcher Perouse de Montclos explicitly to relate the problems to those of the police in Africa. He suggests that African police are mere shadows of their former selves, that the prevalence of repression is symptomatic of their loss of control; and that systematic corruption and brutality are now fundamental to African policing.[2]

Following Montclos, we might point to a more general failure to define the distinct interests of the state, as opposed to the private interests of the individuals or groups that staff its agencies. Herein lies a distinction among bandits, private militias, politician's action groups, and the real public police, which (in a Hobbesean notion of the state) provide nonexclusionary security or (in a Lockean notion) offer a public good in a more explicitly contractarian fashion. The police may be brutal or abusive in all cases, but a definition of their interest, public or private, is crucial.[3]

Perouse de Montclos argues that brutal behavior by the police can no longer be regarded as an aberration. The police are consistently the biggest suppliers of arms to criminals, and poverty is no longer the sole explanation for their susceptibility to bribery. The notorious venality of the Nigerian police, for example, is probably an indirect consequence of the prosperity attending the oil boom, though the situation has since worsened with the collapse of oil prices. But the relationship between corruption and poverty is not straightforward, and it is more likely that poverty is a cause of corruption than the sole cause. Like many commentators, Perouse de Montclos judges that state authorities could not stop police banditry nor mitigate their repression even if they wished to—and some do not wish to—and that the judicial and prison systems of most states merely reflect the wish of regimes to make examples of criminals. The punishment of criminals, especially when it is a public spectacle (as in the "Palm Beach shows" of Lagos, when thieves are executed on the seashore), appears to be related more to the display of power than the operation of justice. In other words, the political interests of a faction are pursued through the guise of crime fighting.[4]

Moreover, Perouse de Montclos thinks that police repression results directly from their powerlessness in the face of increasing crime. Basing his comments on a UN investigation, he says three out of four Africans in South Africa, Tanzania, and Uganda have been the victims of violence (the UN investigation did not even consider notoriously violent states such as Congo [Zaire]). Such a judgment results from the belief that crime prevention and detection, rather than the enforcement of order on behalf of a regime, should be the prime function of African policing. As I show, this is debatable, for policing is most affected by the special kinds of crime that are seen to threaten political order. Policing increasingly responds to internal security threats to a regime's hold on power rather than to the pursuit of a broader state interest in providing security for its citizens. To the extent that a population rejects a regime's legitimacy, these two objectives become mutually exclusive pursuits. The more serious the threats are seen to be, the more oppressive the police response; repression is thus directly related to regime perceptions of security. Furthermore, although the judgment that African police are ineffective at providing security is understandable, its dismissal of the scale and ubiquity of communal violence in many societies (which police cannot conceivably manage) does not advance an understanding of the relationship of policing to political development.

Perouse de Montclos asks the question, Should the police in Africa be abolished? His answer is a qualified yes. He does not question the need for a formal state institution charged with maintaining order, but he thinks there should be a radical reform of security systems. His argument is not linked to pressures for liberalization so much as the need to confront the inadequacy of existing state policing and the value of self-help policing. He acknowledges that the state, which has never had a monopoly on the violence proper to a state of law, is made fragile by the increase in self-help policing, but he is convinced that the populace should be made to participate in the provision of citizen security through means such as neighborhood patrols. The suppression of existing police systems would then, in his view, address the contemporary crisis of statehood. It would signal a positive step toward the creation of a legitimate authority capable of serving a public (as opposed to a regime) interest in security. By this argument, unrecognized Somaliland and even episodes of neighborhood policing by communities in Baidoa represent stateness more accurately (in a classical, contractarian sense) than does an arbitrary regime such as Abacha's Nigeria.

But this argument does not engage with the tenacious and evolutionary nature of police systems; it does not confront the possibility that the police will adapt to such developments and will remain as a recognizable state system for the foreseeable future. Neither does it address the possibility that policing may instead become a more, rather than less, exclusionary activity, especially in states that are themselves becoming privatized. It does not confront the fact that there is little motivation for public—or local—forces to provide security to a community as a non-exclusionary or public good.

Model 6—Adaptation: Changing Relationships

There are important implications for policing if commentators such as Perouse de Montclos are right in suggesting that the relationship between governments and people has significantly changed. But the events of the mid-1990s make this seem increasingly unlikely. Coercion remains a potent instrument of policy. The 1990s have not proved to be Africa's decade of democracy, and liberalization, in the form of multiparty politics and market-driven economic policies, has been weakened by continued corruption, coups, and conflict. Police systems have (like regimes) already accommodated at institutional and individual levels many manifestations of the demands for liberalization. In the long term, a greater challenge may lie in the alternative state systems symbolized by the so-called privatization of security and the contemporary integration of commerce and violence.[5] It is for reasons such as these that the sixth phase of the model underpinning this study specifically concerns the adaptation of the police to developments likely to shape policing during the next decade. The developments involve the rise of so-called alternative states, commercial security, various forms of self-policing (such as vigilantism and community policing), pressures associated with liberalization and "civil society," and external influences such as overseas aid. I use the case of Lesotho to caution against assuming the blanket applicability of such factors.

Before considering such developments in more detail, we need to note that application of the word *privatized,* commonly used in this context, is often problematic. It can be used to make distinctions between degrees of stateness or the degrees to which security forces pursue popular interests as opposed to acting for themselves. *Privatized* can legitimately be used to describe the guards and mercenaries hired from commercial companies by regimes, local political factions, and international companies in weak states. But although foreign private security firms are usually an adjunct to the predatory states that hire them, they may also be used to restore public order and law enforcement. This may see them provide a public "good." In contrast, units of a predatory state's public police may privatize coercion in the sense of subordinating it to themselves or to the personal interests of a politician. Most of Zaire's security agencies during the thirty-two years of Mobutu's regime, for instance, served the personal interests of their members (loot) and those of Mobutu himself (survival and power). Indeed, the state and its resources are often privatized in predatory fragmented states.

Such a situation may be contrasted with the privatized self-policing that arises in response to a community (or public) interest. When this is the case, certain vigilante groups, for instance, may become public rather than private forces. Their use then raises questions about the point at which such a group, formed to provide a community (rather than a group or personal) benefit, becomes a public force. In all cases, it is sensible to use a definition that hinges on the interests of the agents concerned rather than their formal title. Although all policing acts against the interests of someone, privatized policing is exclusionary in a way that—ideally, if not realistically—public policing is not.

Alternative States

As Perouse de Montclos emphasizes, other forms of protection and survival must be found when the central institutions of state fragment and regimes prove unable or unwilling to provide security. The phenomenon of the big man is as strong as ever: "Where a society's impersonal legal guarantees of physical security, status, and wealth are relatively weak or nonexistent, individuals seek personal substitutes by attaching themselves to 'big men' capable of providing protection and even advancement."[6]

Any police force notorious for corruption, greed, weakness, violence, or partiality will be seen as part of the security problem by most of the population. One result is that police systems are usually bypassed by those who want security. Some aspects of this type of enforcement may be taken over by the military, who are able to operate in more extreme circumstances—hence the use of the military to "police" Rwandan refugee camps in Zaire. But other aspects of policing are effectively privatized, either in terms of self-policing, roughly divided into vigilantism and vigilance (the distinctions between the two are likely to be imprecise), or, if they are sufficiently profitable, taken over by specialized international companies, such as Military Professional Resources in Angola and Defence Systems Ltd. (DSL), though these are armies, protecting regimes or international corporations, rather than police forces protecting property or citizens.

Again, the distinctions between private and public are ambiguous, and *exclusionary* may be a better term to describe such policing.

This development is particularly evident in what Reno calls the shadow states.[7] Shadow states present alternative forms of structure, power, and profit in which regimes draw authority from their ability to control markets and resources rather than territory or coercive agents. "Weak state rulers willingly relinquish direct control over coercion. They abandon attempts to impose a comprehensive internal order. . . . Thus weak state rulers try to rule through control over commercial syndicates, abjuring contractarian ties to citizens. . . . The purpose of governance is not to provide a foundation for order and security."[8] There is no attempt to provide a public good, though the pursuit of regime security may be compatible with its provision.

Yet the public police continue to be used by most if not all regimes, even though their role is less clear-cut than that of the military; the substitution of foreign mercenaries and advisers for a national army is unparalleled in policing (much will depend on how a regime uses them). Tanzanian police were used in Uganda, but there has been nothing comparable in policing to the Ghurka Security Guards in Sierra Leone, who "worked within Strasser's formal state structure, co-ordinating their efforts with the army, virtually the only major functioning state agency."[9] Commercial policing is not sufficiently profitable for many companies to want to be involved, and those that are involved provide security (especially guarding) rather than the representational roles identified by Potholm. In other states private policing (in the sense of commercial policing) may supplement public policing, even though private security is more expensive. In Angola, for instance, low-ranking police officers earn $5 a month, whereas security companies are quoted as paying their staff about $100–200 a month.[10] In South Africa the private sector was reported as paying double, sometimes treble, what a constable could expect in the SAPS in late 1998. Individual police officers are naturally well placed to exploit their relationship with security guards and the military, selling their services to the highest bidder and blurring distinctions between public and private activity. Paradoxically, an Angolan may have less to fear from a private security guard than a national police officer *if* the higher income translates into better-disciplined behavior.

Order within the state is a fragile construct, and a cluster of associations and activities not directly under state control has developed to accommodate this fact. Such organizations are nothing new in states such as Nigeria, where there have long been specialized private societies; independence encouraged this, with special nonstate organizations assuming responsibility for the defense of politicians and for public security in several large southern Nigeria cities. Yet as Fatton points out, the developments of the 1990s have opened what is "potentially a highly subversive space . . . where new structures and norms may take hold to challenge the existing state order."[11] The result is small-scale security in which private security, various forms of self-policing, and vigilantism play a role. This growth may in turn be linked to Reno's suggestion (in his study of contemporary Sierra Leone) that the last decade has seen the erosion of the postcolonial state and a return to the enclave economies and private armies of earlier years.

Reno argues that the ties between foreign firms and African rulers in Sierra Leone, where politicians and warlords use private networks to enforce their demands and extend their powers of patronage, have played a dominant part in the conflict in that country. He does not address policing as such but argues that corruption is fundamental in states such as Sierra Leone (and, as I suggest, Congo [Zaire]), and that it is disconnected from individual morality and the failure of state institutions such as the police. (The implication is that police are not present in the conventional sense, regardless of how a regime describes its agents.) A parallel shadow state has then emerged from the institutional decay. Reno claims that it is wrong to see this as disengagement because this presupposes what African states should be rather than what African political authority is. He suggests that it is this new order that reflects post–cold-war configurations of political authority in which weak regimes distribute resources to commercial companies, all of whom use coercion for mutual gain. The use of *privatized* in the colloquial sense may now be inaccurate. For regimes no longer need formal state agencies; instead, they exploit their dependency on the foreign firms, mercenary troops, creditors, and aid organizations contributing the resources sustaining them. If state police are not yet included within this framework, it must be because they are considered too weak, ineffectual, and unprofitable.[12]

Commercial Security

In countries such as Angola, South Africa, and Congo (Zaire), "the poor do without electricity, decent roads, working telephones and are robbed by the local gendarmes. The rich have generators, four-wheel drive vehicles, mobile phones and security guards."[13] Security is therefore one of Africa's growth businesses, with the East African sector expanding by about 28 percent a year by the mid-1990s. There is no shortage of recruits in countries such as Angola. Most of those in the 500-strong Guardasegura in Luanda, for example, who have five to ten years of army service, are paid the equivalent of $250, about ten times a university professor's salary. And an important contributing factor to the growth of the industry has been the demobilization of security forces from the apartheid era in South Africa and Namibia; ex-soldiers sell their skills, especially in counterinsurgency, to new customers.[14]

The boom in commercial security services (such as risk assessment and the guarding of personnel or property by companies such as DSL, Group 4, Saladin, and the Control Risks Group) is not, however, policing as such. This is a critical point. For such Western- or white-owned companies tend to focus on specific work related to foreign investments, which they protect against banditry, kidnapping, and other crimes. None of them provides a public good except insofar as it is incidental to the private protection of property. They are also expensive and temporary. The same is true of the crime prevention services offered by companies such as Kroll Associates, Network Security Management, and Asmara. Their investigations concentrate on crimes against companies (such as extortion and fraud) and operate at a significantly different level from conventional policing. Neither do security or crime prevention companies fulfill policing tasks (such as fingerprint analysis), for which state forces lack expertise and equipment, because it is unprofitable.[15] Such companies do not serve a political or public role related to remedying state collapse.

The expansion of urban settlements and the inability of the state to control crime in cities such as Nairobi has also resulted in burgeoning numbers of local commercial security companies. There were about eighty security firms providing services to individuals, embassies, businesses, and banks in Nairobi by the late 1980s. Their services included radio installation, fire alarms, the guarding of premises and cash in transit, patrols, and investigations—all with the implication of protection of persons and property against crime.[16] A random sample of forty-five such companies showed that the largest firm, Securicor (K), was established in the 1970s, and the remaining originated between 1980 and 1983. The equipment used in the companies ranged from clubs and helmets, whistles, torches, dogs, and bows and arrows to radios, alarm systems, cars, and motorcycles. Their size varied from two to forty-seven administrative staff members and five to 4,000 security staff members. The companies do not, however, offer policing, though their numbers may include officers and their activities are a result of policing inadequacies.

The staff of private security companies may also have been trained by state police. The national training school of the Zambia Police, for instance, provides such training in order to generate income. Significantly, the badly paid Kenyan police, who by 1998 found it difficult to contain riots, increasingly rely on the many private security companies set up by retired policemen and army officers.[17] Once again, the boundaries between public and private policing are blurred, as police forces adapt to or exploit changing circumstances.

Self-Policing

Self-policing is a further variant on the provision of small-scale security. It takes many forms, from being incorporated into a state strategy to vigilantism, but the emphasis in such policing (which is not necessarily self-protection) is on the activity of policing rather than the police as such.

The best-known examples of semiformal self-policing during the early 1990s occurred in South African townships. Once again, such policing raises definitional issues related to private and public activities, for the provision of security within the confines of such a community was not necessarily a nonexclusionary (public) benefit. Commentators describing it during the early 1990s acknowledged its violent potential but believed that it should nevertheless be subsumed within a constitutional framework incorporating some form of power sharing by the state police. Brogden and Shearing accepted the need for a strong state police force in South Africa but argued that it should be located within "an equally strong self-policing civil society."[18] Their work was concerned with making policing accountable (in terms of popular social justice) and was based on a belief that although "the SAP could be transformed towards orthodox Western policing," policing does not necessarily mean state policing, with its specialized functions located in a separate institution (as it is in parts of Somalia). They rejected models derived from liberal consensus policing, advocating instead a dual policing in which self-policing played a part. Police powers and operational planning should, they argued, be decentralized, at the same time as the use of force should be restricted to the state police. Policing could then be understood as a "popular enterprise to which everyone can and should contribute." It would be a development of the traditional, informal, and noninstitutionalized social control systems common in many societies.

In practice, the boundaries between self-policing and vigilantism are hazy. Concern about levels of crime in areas of kwaZulu Natal in 1996, for example, led to threats by local people to act as vigilantes. There were groups (such as neighborhood watch schemes) with special police-related interests, but there was little cooperation among groups, and few individuals were prepared to take responsibility for any form of public safety. Self-help strategies are thus limited by the problems of societal cooperation that occur when the state does not or cannot perform a coordinating function. Although key concerns tended to focus on undramatic features (such as dognapping and the roadworthiness of buses), British visitors in the early 1990s considered the main threat to policing in the area to be intolerance within a closed community: Local tyranny threatened to replace state oppression.[19] Definitions of the public good in such circumstances are sharply subjective.

Other forms of self-policing include associations set up specifically to provide security, either as part of a state strategy or as an informal means of disengagement from the state. Citizen action through a system of patrols, as developed in Bo, Sierra Leone's most important provincial town, is one such case of regime-condoned policing. The risk of rebel attack meant that this was more a military than a policing operation, but local people clearly took responsibility for their own safety. Each sector of the town arranged for its own night patrols, partly based on street-level organizations and traditional and modern forms such as ward-based soccer teams. Such patrols, known as Kamajor militia, were eventually uncomfortably absorbed into state structures in order to balance the power of the unruly army.[20]

Other types of self-policing include new phenomena modeled on the lines of traditional dance societies, threshing teams, and other forms of neighborhood organizations (and distinct from the support offered by kinship relations) that emerged in Tanzania as a means of guaranteeing the basic security that the government failed to provide. In Tanzania such groups started in certain rural areas toward the end of 1979, becoming a major feature in areas in which grassroots neighborhood collaboration was a spent force.[21] They also became a challenge to (and a criticism of) the official governmental law-and-order system. Their activities illustrate the difficulties of distinguishing self-help from vigilantism.

Taking a variety of names (suggesting they formed part of a revolutionary party or army), other Tanzanian groups, later known as *sungusungu,* patrolled villages, arresting, interrogating, and punishing those suspected of crimes such as stock theft. They regarded the police as enemies; the police in turn called them bandits, arresting and taking to court those they believed were leaders. The *sungusungu* punished policemen they suspected of crime or assisting criminals. They also arrested magistrates perceived as corrupt and killed old women accused of witchcraft.[22] Since the police were unable to deal with increasing rural crime, they may have decided to tolerate the *sungusungu,* confining their reaction to individual prosecutions.

In 1989 the People's Militia Laws Act recognized *sungusungu* and conferred on their members the powers of arrest equal to those of a police constable. And in 1990 the newly appointed home affairs minister, Augustine Mrema, encouraged the development of similar groups to support the police by bringing suspected criminals to court rather than meting out their own punishment. He had to pressure both the police and the population to accept his ideas, but it became routine for all ten-cell (or household) leaders—the lowest administrative structure in the government structure—to have policing schedules for their areas. Significantly, such self-help policing was limited by cell leaders' fear that the collusion between the police and gangs left the police virtually useless and because they believed the police to be the criminals' chief source of arms.[23] It appears that the police were unable to control their own agency.

Vigilantism

Self-policing is in practice often the equivalent of the vigilantism that so often exists in fragile societies; one person's vigilantism is another's self-help. That vigilantism tends to violence is exemplified by the so-called necklacing (execution by burning tires) in South Africa, "article 320" in Mali (which refers to 300 CFA for a liter of gas and 20 for a box of matches), and the Nigerian operation of *weet-ee,* or drinking petrol.

In her work on the Gisu of Uganda, Heald commented on the frequent examples of thief killing she encountered in the mid-1960s and the fact that the public perception of crime allowed for community mobilization in a way that nothing else did.[24] Heald believed that vigilante groups operated in the spirit of, rather than in direct opposition to, the police and represented an attempt by people to remedy local problems. The movement was not a revolt against the legitimacy of the Ugandan state so much as against its impotence. The vigilantes saw themselves as an alternative to the police or as a clandestine police force that operated with the support of the people. Heald noted, however, that nearby areas had small groups (known as 99, probably after 999, the emergency telephone number) who were not only killing thieves but also working a flourishing protection racket.

Vigilantism has implications of being a small-scale activity outside state control, but there is no reason why it cannot be exploited by the state. The Kamajor militia are linked to the state in Sierra Leone, and the Ugandan government pays armed pastoralists in Karamoja to declare themselves as state security forces. As Brogden and Shearing show in their study of township policing, vigilantes were particularly useful to the SAP in the 1980s: They were unafraid of bad publicity; they did not need to consider the legality of their actions, which could in any case be presented as another example of black-on-black violence; being black they could target activists more accurately; they could create a political vacuum into which surrogates of the National Party government could step; and they were a cheap alternative to the municipal police (into which many were recruited) for the local councils.[25]

Vigilance can be a form of surrogate social control or a controlled and politicized activity, as the People's Vigilance Brigades (BPV) in Angola in the 1980s showed. The BPV were a mass public order, law enforcement, and public service force for urban areas, created by the president in 1983 as part of an elaborate internal security establishment. The BPV even had ministerial status, with its commander reporting directly to the president. Some units were armed, but most performed public security duties (including surveillance and security patrols, as well as crime prevention and detection), welfare, and political work.

The use of vigilantes, self-policing, and the state police is shaped by African political traditions, the nature of its institutions, and social responses to political factors. The latter are important because the relationship between politics and public values establishes the boundaries of police action. And Africa's recent political traditions suggest that the limits of policing are generous.

Community Policing and Crime Prevention

A further variant of self-help policing is community policing. When local people play an active part in crime prevention, their actions are often labeled community policing, but the phrase should be used carefully and in the context of local conditions. It is often narrowly understood as policing by the community rather than a joint venture between the people and the police, but the balance should be more heavily in favor of the latter, because community policing is not necessarily self-help policing. Its application to African policing is often derided, but considered in the light of local conditions, its value lies in its encouragement of community participation in crime prevention and public safety schemes.

It has a public rather than private aspect, but no one pretends that it forms an integral part of public policing. It implies a deliberate attempt by the police or the authorities to involve the public in policing *local* areas. Projects designed to encourage participation (in Africa, as in the UK and United States) include crime-stopper schemes, auxiliary police, and special public safety schemes, such as road safety weeks and radio programs that give advice on crime prevention. Community policing also has the potential to mitigate public criticism of poor-quality policing by state forces.[26]

Community policing is designed to encourage a public acceptance of responsibility for community safety—and coincidentally to improve relationships between police and public in specific localities. Its introduction has little to do with civil society or human rights standards in the states concerned. The Zambian force, for instance, was keen to shift as early as 1993 to community-oriented policing in which communities take part in local policing, introducing schemes such as neighborhood watch, a locally based reserve constabulary, and farming networks intended to counter stock theft.

The cash-strapped Zambian government may have seen this as a cheap way to respond to community needs, but community policing was also a critical issue, as economic liberalization and creditor pressure limited government spending in 1993. Such developments are, however, undeniably fragile, for the police react to incidents as they arise, and community policing tends to be sharply focused and confined to urban areas. Chilanga police station in Zambia illustrates the limitations to community policing. It has about forty personnel serving a population of 800,000; transport is a problem; there are no radios, so patrolling officers are out of communication with the station, and there is insufficient documentation for records. The police rely on public donations for the little they have. The people criticize the police for inefficiency, but they do not provide them with adequate resources.

Liberalization and Democratization

Superimposed on the fragility and insecurity characterizing the African state have been the Western concepts of liberalization and democratization. The meaning and implications of these terms for Africa—and for policing—remain debatable. One criticism is that instead of looking for solutions to African problems based on African realities, alien concepts are imposed.[27] But concepts such as the police and self-help policing are now indigenized, and the imposition itself forms part of the reality of African coercion because African regimes appropriate concepts and practices they find useful. State policing may be an alien imposition, but it is too potentially useful (and dangerous) for regimes to disregard. The police may be neglected or weakened by regimes, but they are never ignored.

This suggests that regimes will continue to use police to regulate political activity in particular, regardless of whether or not calls for liberalization have had a fundamental affect on political participation. The police and policing are likely to remain exclusionary. If liberalization means anything in policing, its most visible impact will be in less brutal operational techniques and perhaps some degree of accountability. Western policing concepts may then be blended with African traditions as a way for regimes to maintain power.[28] What this might mean for the policed can be considered in light of the concept of civil society, for pressures for political liberalization were often seemingly driven from below by groups of students, professionals, trade unions, and business and church groups no longer willing to accept authoritarian rule.

Civil Society

In the absence of acceptable state institutions in the early 1990s, Western interest shifted away from the study of African elites to that of social groups devising survival and participation strategies in the face of continuing state repression. That this trend was then understood in political terms (that is, of liberalization and democratization) is unsurprising, for "political life in Africa is conducted through a complex web of social forces, institutional settings, and interpersonal relationships. If government structures furnish the context for official interactions in the public domain, social groups constitute the fundamental building blocks of political action and interchange."[29]

The difficulties inherent in translating liberalization into African terms encouraged a focus on the concept of civil society as a precursor or accompaniment to liberalization, with the apparent proliferation of associations and networks in Africa leading commentators to refer to civil society as a "dynamic catalyst for the advent of democracy and a crucial bulwark for the maintenance of democratic governance."[30] Much of the resulting empowerment literature was reminiscent of the earlier enthusiasm for rural socialism, but the undoubtedly vibrant associational life of Africa was generally equated with civil society by Western commentators. Both were presented as a point of understanding and a way out of the impasse of authoritarian rule and its coercive policing.

The application of the concept of civil society to Africa has involved its abstraction from its historical meaning.[31] Some authors refer to civil society as if it is a coherent whole, with a state presence, whereas others relate it to norms concerning the nature of the state, popular movements against authoritarian regimes, or autonomous societal groups interacting with the state. Each understanding is partial. It is unclear whether associational life, to take one definition, constitutes an autonomous civil society. Lewes is skeptical, suggesting that the existence of associational interests (each with their own interests) is not necessarily an indication of civil society in terms of a specific historical development. "Civil society is not automatically engendered by autonomous associations and existing private interests: *Society* (considered simply as activity external to the state) is not synonymous with *civil society* in its modern meaning."[32] The Rwandan vigilantes who took part in the mass killings of 1994 cannot be considered "civil society" in the conventionally accepted sense of the words.

The meaning remains controversial, as does the long-term value of the concept. If it has any value for contemporary policing purposes, then the strong associational life generally regarded as characteristic of Africa and often (though not necessarily) closely related to protest against authoritarian politics seems the most relevant type of (inclusive) interpretation. Yet definitions of civil society remain highly selective, and the legitimacy of police associational groups as part of that society remains unacknowledged. Indeed, most definitions of civil society are discriminatory in that the police are excluded even though they form voluntary associations of an interest group type and ascriptive or primary associations defined in terms of kinship and traditional political units. Chazan argues that the manner in which these associations interact with each other and the state is itself "what determines the substantive character and boundaries of civil society in Africa."[33]

Civil society remains at best an abstract aggregate whose members participate in nonstate activities (according to this understanding) at the same time as they exert pressure on state institutions. The structuring principle may be a complex relationship to the state, which may further complicate divisions between public and private realms.[34] Whatever the case, such critical links (which may also form a crucial tie between the economic and political interests of different social classes and groups) will need policing or, more generally, ordering in some predictable manner. And police officers (whose personal circumstances may shape their policing) will be involved as individuals or as members of kinship, local or ethnic groups whose affinities cut across conventional divisions.

It is unclear how such linkages affected the political transitions of the early 1990s. Many associational groups were able to play an intermediary role between the state and its general population (though this tended to involve defending vested interests rather than promoting democratic ideals), so there was potential for individual police involvement. In practice, however, police sympathies are generally unknown and political interventions (except on behalf of a regime) limited and personal in inspiration. Few associational organizations have in any case been able to consolidate into political organizations; success tends to dissipate energy, and leaders soon adapt to prevailing governmental norms. But even if this were not the case, Western optimism may have been misguided, for there is no simple correlation between a strong associational life and democratic government. As Bratton and van de Walle point out, "Associational groups may make demands on the state that it is incapable of processing, potentially leading to either repression or regime instability."[35]

A further alternative which deserves consideration is that a state elite may itself manipulate local traditions of associational life. This appears to have been the case in Botswana, where associations (such as churches and sports associations) are a dominant characteristic of social life in towns and rural areas.[36] However, the state elite has used the type of consultation between equals that influences many of the resulting patterns of interaction in the village assembly to legitimize and maintain its own power. It protects its interests by allowing the police (its agents) to dominate the criminal justice system at the expense of traditional law in Botswana. The elite shored up this position by defining the publication of any information the state decides is "classified" (any matter the government declared confidential) as a criminal offense according to the National Security Act. The penalty is up to twenty-five years' imprisonment regardless of public interest. Those who employ this strategy can assert control by requiring local groups to accommodate Gabarone's way of practicing and interpreting law, though such a socializing process can also be regarded as state building.

Civil society is not a coherent set of structures. A consensus on its goals—and definitions—is rare, but it appears best understood for policing in terms of associational life and public protest. The opposition movements against whom the police react are often groups of divergent (usually urban) interests. Occasionally such groups are organized into semiformal associations, such as churches, with a specific policy, but it is unlikely for them to develop into an alternative governing coalition with a sustainable social base and a coherent policy platform.

Civil society may theoretically be capable of encouraging personal rights, a respect for legal conventions, the extension of effective citizenship, and transparent and accountable policing, but there is little evidence that this has taken place in the 1990s. This is to be expected, for to achieve any form of liberalization requires specialized skills and receptive cultural norms, which are themselves scarce. A strong distrust of the police remains one of the few attributes all definitions of civil society share. Any force notorious for corruption, greed, or violence (as all are) will be seen as part of the problem by most of the population. The theory and reality of civil society appear firmly divorced, and policing remains reactive and repressive. The public police, like the associations themselves, are exclusionary. The police can easily dismiss groups as troublemakers. If civil society has any practical meaning for policing, it will be couched in terms of public order, for the police invariably watch and regulate protest.

Repression is entrenched in the African state, so the police will be involved (through intelligence, surveillance, and enforcement) whenever associations try to advance their interests. New patterns of political participation outside formal state structures and one-party systems may present problems with which regimes and their police must come to terms. The police will adapt to groups if the latter are able successfully to translate their demands into political power; otherwise they will try to contain or crush them.

In the long term, if it is understood as having a political presence, civil society will intentionally or otherwise affect policing only in terms of operations or if the nature of state coercive power is fundamentally changed. The other possibility will arise if rulers pursue popular legitimacy as a means of securing internal stability rather than through the use of force. The police can thus be taken as a barometer of the progress a government has made toward serving popular interests and needs, since such a government would presumably not fear its own population and would therefore be able to provide noncoercive policing. In the short term, however, the highly centralized, bureaucratic, and militarized nature of most police systems means that they cannot adapt to transitory or rapidly changing political events. Decisions may take weeks because they have to be made at a high command level; the junior officers who are most likely to confront protesters are not encouraged to make even simple decisions.

Even if the 1990s saw the emergence of a civil society dedicated to new opportunities for political participation, the police have not been presented with unprecedented problems. Corruption, for example, may be unchanged because resources are scarce and the public sector (always the biggest source of personal profit) is most likely to remain strong.[37] And the political expression of civil society tends to be based on loose alliances of elite factions with narrow social bases usually grounded in clientalism—lawyers are among the most prominent advocates of prodemocracy movements.

Moreover, preindependence Africanization meant the penetration of the state apparatus by sociocultural norms favorable to corruption in the 1950s and 1960s, and there is no reason why this should have changed in the 1990s. The big man is as influential as ever. Taxi drivers (representing grassroots opinion) continue to say, "Most politicians steal, kill. . . . A politician in power thinks only of his family, girlfriends and at certain opportune times, the 'tribe.' In Africa a Big Man is above the law."[38] Civil society is unlikely to redefine crime and criminality. Why should civil society be satisfied with political participation when an alternative goal may be a bigger share of resources, with the obvious potential for corruption and crime? Most big men rehearse their roles in civil society before they enter the state machinery, and civil society has, in any case, its own repressive power relations. Personalized and paternalistic relations will continue to be influential, especially where the informal sector is large and outside associational and state control. If the state is in crisis, then so must be civil society.

External Influences on the Police

As the suspension of Britain's aid program to Ethiopia in July 1997 made clear, all regimes regard policing as a sensitive issue. Ethiopia requested the program to be halted in response to British insistence on a public inquiry into the death in May of a teacher's leader whom the police said had resisted arrest. Significantly, the UK also thought the crisis sensitive, refusing even to acknowledge the suspension of aid. In practice, the external assessment and monitoring of policing is unlikely to progress beyond the consultancy aid offered by developmental or professional departments, except in reports on torture and degradation by nongovernmental organizations such as Amnesty International or international war crimes tribunals.

There is little evidence of any form of intergovernmental monitoring of policing standards. The eleven-member African Commission on Human Rights, for example, was formed to implement the Charter on Human and Peoples' Rights of the Organization of African Unity (OAU), which came into force in 1987 and has been ratified by all states except Ethiopia, Eritrea, and South Africa. But the commission lacks the resources to tackle brutal policing, which is not in any case seen as a priority. Although the commission's feebleness is partly due to the failure of some OAU members to pay their dues, it is also the result of its limited mandate.

According to article 58 of the charter, the commission's task is to draw the attention of the OAU assembly of heads of state and governments to urgent human rights situations. The assembly can then ask it to report its findings and make recommendations. In practice, the commission appears to have decided it cannot do anything, though it may have changed its mind during 1996, when it admitted that its ineffectiveness stemmed from a rigid interpretation of its mandate rather than the mandate itself.[39] The commission now appears to believe that it should investigate abuses in the absence of formal complaints (as in Sierra Leone) even if the assembly does not ask it to do so. Significantly, the commission did not act on NGO and media reports on human rights abuses in Rwanda from as early as 1990, four years before the worst massacres. Early warnings of this type have also been available on Burundi. It is most unlikely that the commission will ever restrain brutal, corrupt, or even negligent policing, and it will remain usual for human rights to be seen as fettering police work.

International intervention into policing is even rarer, though it occurred in Uganda in the 1970s and in the Congo during the 1960s, when a UN force acted as an emergency substitute for the police after Lumumba's dismissal of Belgian officers. When direct foreign or external intervention takes place within a state, it is usually the result of action to defend (or extend) national interests. A classic example of this type of intervention occurred when Belgium acted to protect the property and investments of its nationals in the Congo in the 1960s. And, during its later intervention in Zaire, Belgium consistently supported the government, sending 1,700 troops when the second Shaba war began in 1978, not only for combat duties but also specifically to police industrial sites in which Belgian nationals had interests.

National interests have continued to mold intervention in the continent in the 1990s. UNCIVPOL contributions in Somalia, for instance, included officers sent from states specifically for national reasons. And political aims prompted Operation Turquoise in Rwanda in 1994, where the most urgent issues for the French military were legal, administrative, and policing problems.[40] Policing remains secondary in such intervention, though, and is considered merely part of overall reconstruction.

Liberalization and Lesotho

The trends identified here have potentially important implications for typologies of policing, but they may not be relevant to all countries. A notable exception is Lesotho, a state with a parliamentary regime, where the security forces are under civilian control but where the government is by its own admission unable to control them.[41] Lesotho is also a special case by virtue of its size and dependence on South Africa; its inclusion in a federal South Africa remains a possibility even though it is currently recovering from South Africa's clumsy intervention in the mutiny of October 1998. Lesotho's inclusion in such a regional grouping may well prove more influential than pressures for liberalization, as regional imperatives set the agenda for the next decade. South Africa already provides some specialist policing assistance in, for example, forensic analysis, as does Swaziland and other SARPCCO countries.

Lesotho has a population of 2.2 million, many of whom are employed in the mines and other industries of neighboring South Africa; remittances are equal to just over one-third of the gross national product (GNP). Lesotho is mountainous and underdeveloped, though the World Bank's *1997 World Development Report* classes thirty African countries poorer in terms of per capita GNP. Per capita GNP in Lesotho was approximately $790 in 1997. All areas lack basic utilities; there are few radios or telephones, and the roads are decayed, so horses remain an important means of transport for the Royal Lesotho Mounted Police (RLMP). The RLMP was subordinate to the military before independence, with officers gathering political (rather than criminal) intelligence, and it retains the old hierarchical and militaristic style. Recruit training (still based on a colonial model) included four weeks of drill in the mid-1990s, while passing-out parades are still regarded as evidence of good training. The police were underresourced throughout the period of military rule (which ended with democratic elections in 1993), and this remains the case. Wages, equipment, accommodations, and conditions are set at very low levels.[42]

In 1994 the king (who cannot take political initiatives) staged a coup with elements of the army, but international and domestic pressure meant that constitutional government was soon restored. Legislation was then adopted to ensure that the RMLP reports to the minister of home affairs; the National Security Service is directly accountable to the prime minister, and the Lesotho Defence Force reports to the prime minister through the Ministry of Defence.

The effects of these events on the RLMP are interesting, not because of the elections so much as for the change to civilian rule. Relations between the police and the government were sensitive, partly because members of the present government were those against whom the police had enforced the law for more than twenty years. This meant that the government could not, said the minister of justice, law, and human rights, "stop or investigate violations [against human rights policy] because it was not in control of the police and the armed forces."[43] That the government could not control its security forces was made clear when two government ministers were kidnapped in 1994 and another had to flee to escape (undefined) security forces. One minister was abducted from his car at gunpoint after he had issued a statement criticizing a strike by police and prison guards. The police demanded a pay increase of 60 percent on that occasion, though the strike was ended when they agreed to a much lower figure.[44]

In September 1997 the deputy prime minister and home affairs minister announced a white paper containing a series of reforms in the RLMP in direct response to the strikes and mutiny earlier in the year, when complaints over low wages had led to the seizure of police headquarters in Maseru by rebel officers referred to in Chapter 1. The reforms were to include the establishment of a negotiating board designed to eliminate the possibility of police strikes, proposals for a new management system to provide better criminal intelligence, and a series of national priorities to reduce livestock theft, murder, and carjacking. The government's reform policy was prompted in part by increasing levels of violent crime, but that thirty police officers remained in prison as a result of the mutiny indicated the significance of the situation. That they were in prison rather than dead, is, however, a sign of the unusual nature of the government's admission.[45] One result of the ensuing turmoil was intervention by South Africa in October 1998.

Lesotho, along with Botswana and Mauritius, is one of the few states to have a parliamentary (rather than a presidential) regime, but this has not caused its police to deviate significantly from the familiar African pattern. The RLMP is a member of SARPCCO, but so are Angola and Mozambique. Educational standards in the RLMP are comparatively high (recruits include graduates from the National University of Lesotho), but training standards are low; the problem was acknowledged and expertise sought from the UK in the mid-1990s. Following a UK ODA review, support was offered to the RLMP for the establishment, within the Ministry of Home Affairs, of a police department able to provide policy advice to ministers, as well as some oversight and strategic guidance. Goals included increasing public confidence in the force by raising accountability and responsiveness through the development of a plan to cover management matters such as complaints and discipline, establishment and training, transport and operational policies. But such proposals have proved idealistic in the prevailing circumstances.

The main aim was to introduce the ideal of community policing in terms of communities policing themselves through the introduction of a system of neighborhood watch schemes, particularly for stock theft in rural areas. But the move was in effect an acknowledgment of the limitations of policing amid rising crime rather than the result of a desire for transparency as such. It reflects the delay and inefficiency caused by the lack of coordination among various parts of the police system. The same is true of the criminal justice system generally. In addition, there are neither laws nor procedures to deal with many forms of crime. This applies to commercial crime and money laundering and to the car thieves who cannot be pursued into South Africa. Morale is often low in the RLMP, and rusty stolen cars and seized sacks of cannabis have been reported piled outside rural police stations.

Conclusion

Perouse de Montclos's call for an unprecedented radical reform of state security apparatus in favor of self-help policing is unlikely to be heeded because the function and role of the police have little connection with community protection or crime prevention as such. State policing is adaptive, but it remains focused on order, regulatory and representational issues, and individual or group self-interest. Self-help policing shows no sign of extending beyond small bounded communities in which people take on the tasks themselves. This is a direct reflection on the capacity of the state in Africa and the relationship between elites and the population, which political trends toward liberalization in the 1990s did not fundamentally alter.

If the nature of state power has not altered, neither has the rural nature of most of the population. Thomas Laely's judgment on peasants, local communities, and central power in Burundi provides a salutary reminder of this:

> The attitudes adopted by mainstream peasantry can most aptly be summarised as pragmatic and realistic. . . . They adapt to given circumstances. Experiencing their powerlessness, they try to align themselves with the powerful as best they can. Although new concepts, such as equality of opportunity and equal rights, are not unknown, most peasants continue to let themselves be guided by traditional patterns of behaviour and values. Their reactions are in general much more often personal than collective. In short, the strategies adopted by most toward the state can be described as strongly "defensive" and "individual." . . . The state has significantly changed in the lifetime of many of its inhabitants by claiming to regulate nearly all their dealings with its agencies, as well as by its publicised mission of "development," and the activities of its expanding civil service have systematically usurped the services provided by "private" brokers. Those who looked after a broad range of concerns in the community have been replaced by representatives of various specialized functions of the state, although they also, like their predecessors, pursue their own interests as well.[46]

The police are also a supremely pragmatic and realistic organization, adapting to circumstances and aligning themselves with the powerful on whose behalf they act. They perform a specialized coercive function, reactively reinforcing the underlying political system of the 1990s as strongly as they have done for the preceding 100 years.

Notes

1. World Bank, *World Development Report 1997: The State in a Changing World* (Oxford: Oxford University Press for the World Bank, 1997). See also Jean-François Bayart, Stephen Ellis, and Béatrice Hibou, *The Criminalization of the State in Africa* (Oxford: James Currey and Indiana University Press), 1–31.

2. "Les polices africaines sont l'ombre d'elles-mêmes." Marc-Antoine Perouse de Montclos, "Faut-il supprimer les polices en Afrique?" *Monde Diplomatique,* August 1997.

3. This still leaves aside the definitional dilemma of police versus (para)-military.

4. This is particularly evident in the Lagos-based Operation Sweep of 1996–1998, when anticrime sentiment was used to mobilize popular support by the Abacha regime (with varying success) for a joint Lagos police-army sweep of criminals and dissidents.

5. The scale of the problem can be indicated by the 1995 seizure by the office of the deputy director of the Liberian national police and the head of Interpol in Monrovia of nearly $2.5 million worth of heroin and cocaine (nearly all of it from Nigeria). The colonel earned $13 a month but had not been paid for five months, and fighting the drugs trade has never been a priority for Liberia's governments. *Guardian,* 30 January 1996.

6. Richard Sandbrook, "Patrons, Clients and Factions: New Dimensions of Conflict Analysis in Africa," *Canadian Journal of African Studies* 5:1 (March 1972), 109.

7. William Reno, *Corruption and State Politics in Sierra Leone* (Cambridge: Cambridge University Press, 1995); William Reno, *Warlord Politics and African Studies* (Boulder, CO: Lynne Rienner, 1998), develops the theme further. See also David Shearer, *Private Armies and Military Intervention,* Adelphi Paper 316 (Oxford: Oxford University Press for IISS, 1998). The biggest—and most notorious—of the private military advisory firms active in Africa during the 1990s was Executive Outcomes. See Yves Goulet, "Executive Outcomes: Mixing Business with Bullets," *Jane's Intelligence Review,* September 1997, 426–430; Herbert M. Howe, "Private Security Forces and African Stability: the Case of Executive Outcomes," *Journal of Modern African Studies* 36: 2 (1998), 307–331.

8. Reno, *Corruption,* 19.

9. William Reno, "Ironies of Post–Cold War Structural Adjustment in Sierra Leone," *Review of African Political Economy* 23: 67 (1996), 14.

10. *Africa Update* 4 (1996), 5.

11. Robert Fatton, *Predatory Rule: State and Civil Society in Africa* (Boulder, CO: Lynne Rienner, 1992), 186; Frank Kunz, "Civil Society in Africa," *Journal of Modern African Studies* 33: 1 (1995), 185.

12. The privatization of prison services is further advanced. It was noticeable that every international company involved in custodial services became interested

in a South African project for financing, constructing, and operating seven prisons in 1997. Group 4 and Premier Prison Services from the UK, Wackenhut from the United States, and other companies from Australia, Canada, and Taiwan were all involved in bidding for the estimated $332.8 million project.

13. *Financial Times,* 8 May 1996.

14. Many soldiers in the security firm Executive Outcomes (EO) came from South Africa's former Reconnaissance Commandos, Parachute Brigade, Koevoet, and 32 Battalion (which was largely composed of Portuguese-speaking Angolans). Three of the company's leaders (Eeben Barlow, Laffras Luitingh, and Nic van den Bergh) had served in such elite units.

15. The scale of organized crime in South Africa has led the government to buy training from Kroll, the international business investigation and risk management agency. See the *Financial Times,* 27 May 1998. The size of the contract is no doubt as significant as it was in the case of the contract Executive Outcomes had with the Angolan government in 1997. The success of the firm's operation to protect state-owned petroleum facilities from UNITA control convinced the Angolan government to award them two consecutive one-year contracts worth $40 million a year. A DSL manager described multimillion-dollar contracts to guard mines, embassies, and oil and diamond fields as corporate colonialism. *Sunday Times,* 19 October 1997.

16. Hernando Gomez Buendia, ed., *Urban Crime, Global Trends and Policies* (Tokyo: UN University, 1989), 197.

17. It would be informative to compare the resources of such companies against those of the police. The *Guardian* (13 April 1998) reported pitched battles between private security guards and street children in Nairobi. The police ignored the guard's guns.

18. Mike Brogden and Clifford Shearing, *Policing for a New South Africa* (London: Routledge, 1993), 130–165.

19. That the more undesirable features of society may shape state policing was illustrated in South Africa in 1995, when the commissioner of police (who had deliberately changed his title from that of major general) ordered authorities in kwaZulu-Natal to abandon a police academy graduation ceremony. Of the 600 cadets to graduate, twenty-eight had serious criminal records, three were wanted by other forces, and 100 others were due to be investigated. A significant number of cadets were also thought to be members or officeholders of Inkatha, in direct contravention of the ruling that forbids police from taking part in political activity. Senior officers in the province had long had close relations with Inkatha at the expense of the ANC, and Inkatha had what was essentially its own hit squads in the police force in the old kwaZulu homeland. *Financial Times,* 7 February 1995.

20. See Ibrahim Abdullah, "Bush Path to Destruction: The Origin and Character of the Revolutionary United Front/Sierra Leone," *Journal of Modern African Studies* 36: 2 (1998), 203–235; Ibrahim Abdullah and Patrick Muana, "The Revolutionary United Front of Sierra Leone," in Christopher Clapham, ed., *African Guerrillas* (Oxford: James Currey, Fountain, Indiana University Press, 1998), 180f; Paul Richards, *Fighting for the Rain Forest: War, Youth and Resources in Sierra Leone* (Oxford: James Currey & Heinemann, 1996), 154–162. The RUF created a "police" (Clapham, *African Guerrillas,* 191).

21. Ray G. Abrahams, "Law and Order and the State in the Nyamwezi and Sukuma Area of Tanzania," *Africa* 59: 2 (1989), 359; Ray G. Abrahams, "Sungusungu: Village Vigilante Groups in Tanzania," *Africa Affairs* (1987), 179–196.

22. Abrahams, "Sungusungu," 133.

23. Aili Mari Tripp, "Governance in Tanzania," in Goran Hyden and Michael Bratton, eds., *Governance and Politics in Africa* (Boulder, CO: Lynne Rienner, 1992), 235.

24. Suzette Heald, *Controlling Anger: The Sociology of Gisu Violence* (Manchester, UK: Manchester University Press, 1989). Two chapters are devoted to Gisu vigilantism and drinking associations.

25. Brogden and Shearing, *Policing for a New South Africa*, 85–88.

26. An advertisement for an "international community policing expert" placed by Technikon SA, a provider of tertiary-level vocational education, referred to community policing as "the most credible and acceptable system to all communities." *Police Review,* 26 November 1993.

27. See Linda M. Heywood, "Towards an Understanding of Modern Political Ideology in Africa: The Case of the Ovimbundu of Angola," *Journal of Modern African Studies* 36: 1 (1998), 139–167.

28. The simplest operational methods may be the most effective, as nonviolent crowd control training provided by UK officers in a Commonwealth mission to South Africa showed. See Louise Elliston, "Marshal Training in South Africa, September to December 1993," unpublished paper presented at the University of Leicester, May 1996.

29. Naomi Chazan, Robert Mortimer, John Ravenhill, and Donald Rothschild, *Politics and Society in Contemporary Africa* (London: Macmillan, 1988), 71.

30. Peter Lewis, "Political Transition and the Dilemma of Civil Society in Africa" *Journal of International Affairs* 46: 1 (1992), 31. Some of the potential analytic flaws are pointed out in Thomas Callaghy, "Civil Society, Democracy, and Economic Change in Africa: A Dissenting Opinion About Resurgent Societies," in John W. Harbeson, Donald Rothchild, and Naomi Chazan, eds., *Civil Society and the State in Africa* (Boulder, CO: Lynne Rienner, 1994), 231–253; René Lemarchand, "Uncivil States and Civil Societies: How Illusion Became Reality," *Journal of Modern African Studies* 30: 2 (1992), 177–191.

31. See Blade Nzimande and Mpume Sikhosana, "Civil Society," Mass Organisations and the National Liberation Movement in South Africa," in Lloyd M. Sachikonye, *Democracy, Civil Society and the State: Social Movements in Southern Africa* (Harare: SAPES Books, 1995), 47–66.

32. Lewis, "Political Transition," 44. Compare "civil society continues to expand its role in demanding respect for human rights, democratic governance, and attention to a wide range of specific issues." Africa Policy Information Center, *African Policy Outlook 1997,* Comtex Newswire, 7 January 1997.

33. Naomi Chazan, "The New Politics of Participation in Tropical Africa," *Comparative Politics* 14: 2 (1982), 93.

34. Civil society is thus "situated in rules and transactions which connect state and society." Sachikonye, *Democracy,* 9.

35. Michael Bratton and Nicolas van de Walle, *Democratic Experiments in Africa: Regime Transitions in Comparative Perspective* (Cambridge: Cambridge University Press, 1997), 255.

36. See Wim van Binsbergen, "Aspects of Democracy and Democratisation in Zambia and Botswana: Exploring African Political Culture at Grassroots," *Journal of Contemporary African Studies* 13: 1 (1995), 3–34; Kenneth Good, "Corruption and Mismanagement in Botswana: A Best-Case Example?" *Journal of Modern African Studies* 32: 3 (1994), 449–521; John Holm, "Development, Democracy and Civil Society in Botswana," in Adrian Leftwich, ed., *Democracy and Development: Theory and Practice* (Cambridge: Polity Press, 1996), 97–113.

37. Liberal reforms may have increased opportunities for corruption. See Bayart et al., *Criminalization of the State.*

38. *Africa Now* 13 (June–July 1996), 12–14.

39. IPS, "Africa—Human Rights: Sharpening Teeth of . . . , " Comtex Newswire CIS: DSP-45, Nairobi, 2 August 1996.

40. R. M. Connaughton, *Military Support and Protection for Humanitarian Assistance: Rwanda, April–December 1994,* Occasional No. 18 (Camberley, UK: Strategic & Combat Studies Institute, 1996), 10.

41. For the effects of liberalization, see Khabele Matlosa, "Democracy and Conflict in Post-Apartheid Southern Africa: Dilemmas of Social Change in Small States," *International Affairs* 74: 2 (1998), 319–337.

42. The police were ranked fifteenth in importance after education, health, and the army in the mid-1990s (i.e., before the 1997 mutiny). This situation encourages officers to raise money by other means.

43. *Pointer: Jane's Intelligence Review and Jane's Sentinel,* December 1997. Amnesty International urged the government to address the arbitrary arrests, detentions, and torture that, it accepted, had taken place without government sanction. *Africa Research Bulletin* 32: 9 (1995), 11995.

44. Soldiers maintained law and order in the capital during the strike, but residents soon complained that they were undisciplined. Prison warders were also on strike. *Africa Research Bulletin* 32: 5 (1994), 11449.

45. The constitution prohibited arbitrary arrest and detention, but the mutineers were imprisoned without charges. The delay was attributed to the fact that the prosecution had not completed its investigation. The government had repealed the 1984 Internal Security Act allowing for investigative detention.

46. Thomas Laely, "Peasants, Local Communities, and Central Power in Burundi," *Journal of Modern African Studies* 35: 4 (1997), 695–716.

8

Conclusion: Modalities of Policing Africa

Whether favorable to democratization or not, significant political changes undeniably occurred in African states after 1990, with most of the resulting regime transitions happening in the first four years of the decade. With the exception of Liberia and the Sudan, where there were no transitional movements, a number of political innovations occurred, and restrictions were often lifted even when there was no real reform or increased popular participation.

Whether the nature of power was also transformed is more controversial, for the democratization movement may yet prove to represent more of a developmental phase than a turning point.[1] Both change and continuity are evident, but political continuity will probably prove to be the dominant feature in the short term because coercion and compliance remain more important than acceptance and persuasion. Amnesty International's annual reports still refer to the (often systematic) use of torture, intimidation, and harassment by police acting on behalf of the regimes managing such developments.

That the police remain an important coercive resource, no matter how tainted their status, is evident from the cynicism with which they are generally regarded. Coercion is invariably directed at the population rather than at what most people regard as criminal behavior. The Mozambican interior minister's response to a provincial governor's complaints of police harassment was "Police are police. I have never seen police who acted like saints."[2] And regimes' use of their police in the late 1990s tends to be almost as heavy-handed as it was in earlier years.

Kenyan politics, for example, have been dominated since independence in 1963 by the Kenyan African National Union (KANU). President Daniel Arap Moi finally agreed in late 1991 to end Kenya's official one-party state. His decision came shortly after Kenya's main donors applied pressure by suspending all aid, and multiparty elections took place in December 1992. Opposition parties won almost half the seats in parliament, but the elections, which returned Moi and KANU to power, were marred by irregularities. And in 1993 the New York–based Africa Watch reported that violence between ethnic groups since the advent of the multiparty system in 1991 had been "deliberately manipulated and instigated by president Daniel Arap Moi and his inner circle in order to undermine . . . political pluralism."[3] Since then, the authorities have preferred to use less overtly political charges against protesters and critics.

The Kenyan security forces appear to remain above the law. Moi explicitly authorized the police to use all the means at their disposal to deal with the civil war he claimed his opponents were prepared to unleash in 1993. Four years later, pro-reform rallies were still being disrupted by soldiers and police in riot gear firing live bullets and tear gas, clubbing demonstrators, and using mounted charges. Kenyan policing continues to be reactive and repressive, but it is more than just dysfunctional policing. It is likely that in Kenya, as elsewhere, the police are acting as state officials trying to maintain order at the same time as they retain their own hold on power. For it is not in the interests of African regimes to build strong, efficient, or "professional" forces.

Such actions are evidence of the paradoxical nature of the relationship between the police and regimes. Like police across Africa, the police in Kenya have been deliberately deprived of needed resources because they could be used against the regime. There is thus a clear distinction between the ideal and the observed relationship of the two. We need to acknowledge this if we are to understand the more general issues associated with the institutionalization of state authority in the 1990s.

This study suggests that there are few changes discernible in police systems that can be directly attributable to the political developments of 1990–1996. This is a generalization, but it is difficult to identify specific policies or courses of action in areas such as recruitment—let alone accountability—that result from political innovation in any of the forces considered here. Namibia's policy of integration is a qualitative, if flawed, transition, whereas Eritrea may also form an exception to the rule, but its circumstances are special and insurgency has had a stronger formative effect on its policing than has liberalization. The same consideration applies to Uganda, though its residual legitimacy is confined to specific regions of the country.

That few changes appear to have been imposed on—or generated by—the other police forces considered suggests that the police evaluation of the significance of recent transitions errs on the side of continuity over change. This is important because although the police are notoriously conservative, they are well placed to evaluate short-term political developments and personalities, even if their hierarchic and bureaucratic structures often make it difficult for them to respond quickly to transitory change. The only realistic alternative interpretation is that the police tend to behave like opportunistic bandits when resources are not forthcoming, no matter what course the government concerned follows in terms of reform.

Some general lessons may be drawn. It is difficult to distinguish among the public police, paramilitaries, action groups, and special units, and it is best to broaden the definition of police beyond formal civilian forces. Discussions of the public police should therefore focus on policing, as in the enforcement of order and law, so as to concentrate on the organization and what it does rather than on what it calls itself. On this basis we can say that state police systems are tenacious, reactive, and well placed to adapt to unavoidable change. They track regime developments (rather than politics as such) because their functions center on regime representation, regulatory activities, and the enforcement of order. The cycles of repression and reform identifiable in states such as Uganda reflect this, and (so far) conflict and fragmentation have had a greater impact on policing than liberalization and democratization.

Evidence shows that liberalization and democratization, as reflected in the police, have only had a superficial impact on the actual organization of states. More important, the privatization of security in states such as Sierra Leone and Angola—states that have had to deal with administrative collapse and an incapacity to provide order—has yet significantly to affect state forces, though it has the potential to do so more fundamentally than any form of increased political participation. Should this happen, the events since the 1950s suggest that state police systems will evolve to accommodate it.

The police formed part of the centralized state inherited on independence. Police systems have since evolved, not in the sense of a linear progression toward a Western model of catching criminals but through adapting to political developments and accommodating regimes. In addition, they have been shaped by the formative effects of historical inheritance, political pressure, personal ambition, and contingencies. Hence the importance of evolution, conversion, integration, and adaptation in their development. Their success in adaptation in particular is emphasized by the lack of major change, with the exception of deterioration in their reliability and capability during the first decade of independence, when they were principally influenced by the emergence of a distinctive system of personal rule characterized by coercion and corruption. The events of the 1990s leave this situation fundamentally unaltered.

The police may be weak in resources, low in status, and often sidelined or replaced by special presidential or security units, but regimes rarely ignore them. A sign of state fragmentation may occur when the police begin to act on their own behalf rather than on behalf of the regime, but no contemporary force can be described as being out of control.[4] Brutality may be permitted or excused by a regime, but that is a different matter. For possession of a police force is as much a symbol of state identity as is a national army and, for many states with internal (rather than external) threats to stability, a more pressing requirement.

Although police functions probably derive from an ambiguous mix of regime and political processes, if the political environment lacks the stability (or inertia) such a complex organization needs, there is neither the requirement nor the opportunity for the police function to operate. Police activities then contract and are devolved to localized groups providing small-scale policing. Role becomes more important than function. The resulting complexity of enforcement systems is indicated in Figure 8.1. It is, however, difficult to assess the actual and potential capacity of police systems to transform themselves to meet changed functions or roles, though we have tentative evidence of what the contours of change would look like in the limited experience of self-policing. What can be said is that processes of adaptation have resulted in identifiable cycles of progress and regression in policing since the 1950s. Current developments form part of such cycles. The dependence of the police on state or regime powers—rather than on community or local capabilities—is unlikely to change in the next decade.

Such adaptation is not unusual. A recent study suggests that half the old guard of autocratic national leaders have transformed themselves into "democratic" leaders, with most of the leaders of 1990 remaining heads of state despite all the changes.[5] Jackson and Rosberg's description of African governance as survival, of being "more a matter of seamanship and less one of navigation," remains accurate. Rulers such as Presidents Moi, Museveni, and Rawlings have successfully followed survival strategies of buying off, containing, dividing, or intimidating the opposition, at the same time they have built up their support base by mobilizing their ethnic groups or rewriting the rules of political participation in their own favor. Decisionmaking remains concentrated in the hands of elites, whereas legislatures and judiciaries are weak, and neither law nor order is easily maintained.

Despite this, the state police are likely to stay in existence in Africa for the foreseeable future. The police reinforce the political system they represent, and repression continues to be one of the few means of direct control available to regimes. The influence of neopatrimonialism persists in shaping politics, but even if liberalization had resulted in fundamental change, the police would still be representing whichever regime was in power, for they accommodate political changes. Such tenacity is not to suggest a bleak future for Africa so much as to recognize that although the

Figure 8.1 Enforcement Systems

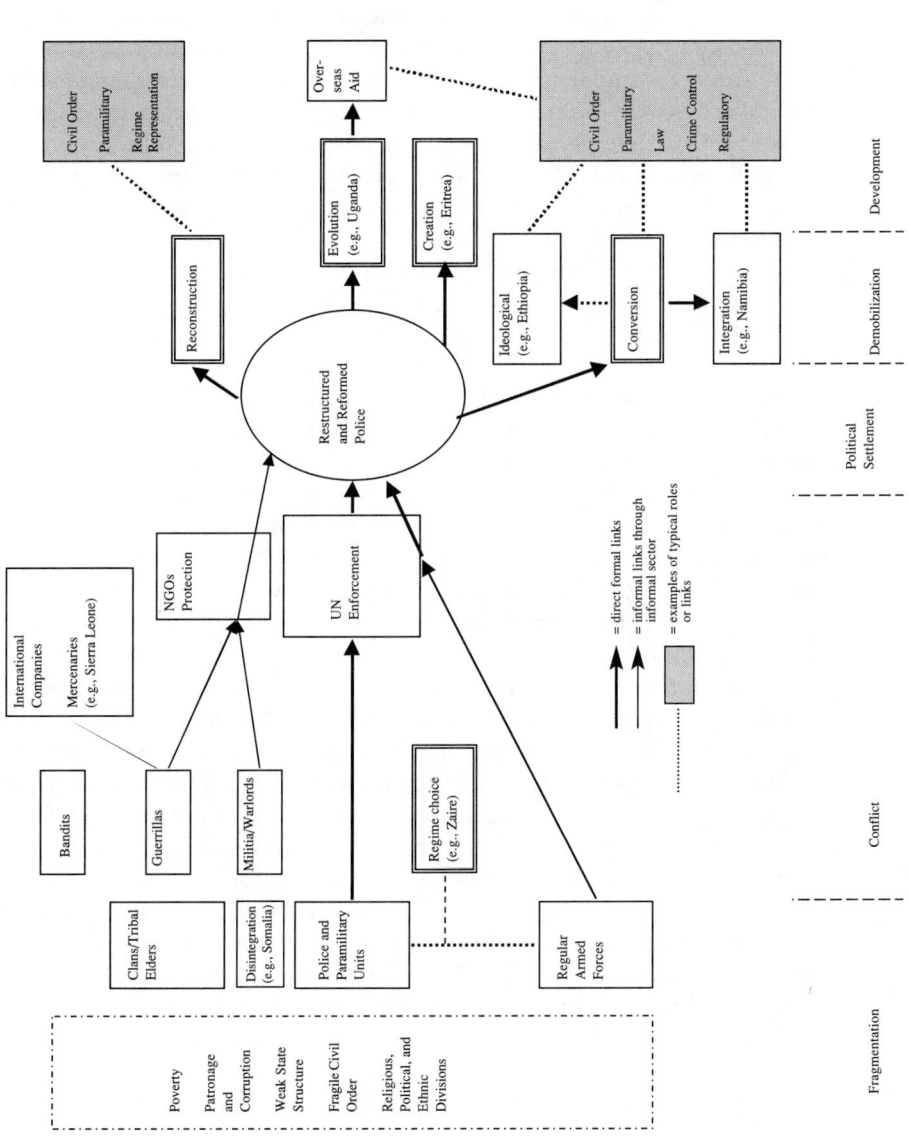

responsibility for police quality lies with political authorities, police systems are tenacious.

There is no ideal policing model appropriate to specific types of national development in Africa. As the sixfold model shows, the basic systems that can be identified in the 1990s emerged as the institutions of statehood were inherited, developed, and rearranged. And these systems will continue to operate. Debate on the nature and functioning of policing is thus useful for understanding the broader issues of state-society relations and state behavior in Africa. It casts light from two perspectives. The first concerns regime perceptions of internal security, where the emphasis is on what security means for regime survival, rather than for the provision of policing to citizens in return for the latter's acceptance and compliance. The second concerns institutional capacity, for the maintenance of internal security sheds light on the overall institutional strength of troubled states.

The model proposed in this study is sufficiently flexible to accommodate the wide range of possible approaches to policing issues, adopted in Africa, ranging from orthodox Western models to the independent approaches seen in Somalia or Tanzania. The model provides the means to discuss such policy issues as the conditions under which accountable "professional" policing can be introduced or sustained and the wide range of appropriate approaches. It shows that there is little evidence of African states' becoming more responsive to the needs of citizens in the light of proclaimed liberalization measures, and that few officials (in new or reformed states such as Eritrea and Namibia) show signs of learning from the experience of other states, so that it is doubtful whether they have the capacity to avoid their fate.

Given the relationships among the police, regimes, and society and the fact that police functions are essentially reactive and, indeed, negative, it is reasonable to see police development mirroring state development. The simplest models may yet provide the clearest insight into the linkage of policing, order, and institutional capacity, for they show the tenacity of police systems. Wars, liberalization, and international aid have left most police systems fundamentally unchanged simply because the essential nature and purpose of policing remains the same. The first major milestone in African policing was passed when politics moved from the colonial to the postcolonial state, but the second, marking a liberalization or democratization of institutional capacity, has yet to be reached.

Notes

1. It may prove to be merely one of a number of "philosophical and sociological alternatives for political legitimacy which are tested, accommodated or dis-

carded." Wim van Binsbergen, "Aspects of Democracy and Democratisation in Zambia and Botswana: Exploring African Political Culture at Grassroots," *Journal of Contemporary African Studies* 13: 1 (1995), 28.

2. *Africa Confidential* 36: 8 (1995), 7.

3. *Africa Research Bulletin* 30: 11 (1993), 11239.

4. The question was asked in Kenya after the death of a student leader. *Africa Research Bulletin* 34: 3 (1997), 12620.

5. Bruce Baker, "The Class of 1990: How Have the Autocratic Leaders of Sub-Saharan Africa Fared Under Democratisation?" *Third World Quarterly* 19: 1 (1998), 115–127.

Acronyms

ANC	African National Congress
ASEANPOL	Association of Southeast Asian National Police
BPV	Brigades Populares de Vigilância
CEAN	Centre d'Etudes d'Afrique Noire
CID	Criminal Investigation Department
CRS	Compagnies Républicaines de Sécurité
DTA	Democratic Turnhalle Alliance
EHRC	Ethiopian Human Rights Council
ELF-RC	Eritrean Liberation Front–Revolutionary Council
EPLF	Eritrean People's Liberation Front
EPRDF	Ethiopian People's Revolutionary Democratic Front
EU	European Union
FAPLA	Forças Armadas Populares de Libertação de Angola
FDRE	Federal Democratic Republic of Ethiopia
FIDH	International Federation of Human Rights Leagues
GDP	gross domestic product
GNP	gross national product
HIPC	Heavily Indebted Poor Countries
ICRC	International Federation of Red Cross and Red Crescent Societies
JCET	Joint Coordinated Equipment and Training
KANU	Kenyan African National Union
LCD	Lesotho Congress for Democracy
MPLA	Movement for the People's Liberation of Angola
NAMPOL	Namibian Police
NGO	nongovernmental organization
NLC	National Liberation Council
NPA	Nigeria Police Academy

NPF	Nigeria Police Force
NPKF	National Peacekeeping Force
NRA	National Resistance Army
NRC	National Resistance Council
NRM	National Resistance Movement
OAU	Organization of African Unity
ODA	Overseas Development Administration
OLF	Oromo Liberation Front
PFDJ	People's Front for Democracy and Justice
PLAN	People's Liberation Army of Namibia
RC	resistance council
RIP	Rapid Intervention Police
RLMP	Royal Lesotho Mounted Police
RUF	Revolutionary United Front
SADC	Southern African Development Community
SANDF	South African National Defence Force
SAP	South African Police
SAPS	South African Police Services
SARPCCO	Southern African Regional Police Chiefs Co-operation Organisation
SCEPP	Solidarity Committee for Ethiopian Political Prisoners
SNP	Somali National Police
SPF	Somali Police Force
SRC	Supreme Revolutionary Council
SWAPO	South West African People's Organization
SWAPOL	South West African Police
SWATF	South West Africa Territorial Force
TANU	Tanganyika African National Union
TGE	Transitional Government of Ethiopia
TPLF	Tigray People's Liberation Front
UNCIVPOL	UN Civilian Police
UNDHA	UN Department of Humanitarian Affairs
UNITA	National Union for the Total Independence of Angola
UNITAF	Unified Task Force
UNOSOM	UN operation in Somalia
Zanu-PF	Zimbabwe African National Union-Patriotic Front
ZNP	Zanzibar Nationalist Party

Bibliography

Abbink, Jon. "Transformations of Violence in Twentieth-Century Ethiopia: Cultural Roots, Political Conjunctures." *Focaal* 25 (1995), 55–77.
Abrahams, Ray G. "Sungusungu: Village Vigilante Groups in Tanzania." *Africa Affairs* (1987): 179–196.
———. "Law and Order and the State in the Nyamwezi and Sukuma Area of Tanzania." *Africa* 59: 2 (1989), 356–370.
Adelman, Sammy. "Accountability and Administrative Law in South Africa's Transition to Democracy." *Journal of Law and Society* 21: 3 (1994), 317–328.
Ades, Alberto, and Rafael Di Tella. "The Causes and Consequences of Corruption: A Review of Recent Empirical Contributions." *Liberalization and the New Corruption, IDS Bulletin* 27: 2 (1996), 6–11.
Adeyemi, Adedokun A. "Corruption in Africa: A Case Study of Nigeria." In Tibamanya mwene Mushanga, ed., *Criminology in Africa,* 83–103. Rome: UN Interregional Crime and Justice Research Institute, 1992.
Adeyemi, Adedokun A., et al., "Ordinary crime and its prevention strategies in Metropolitan Lagos." In Hernando Gomez Buendia, ed., *Urban Crime, Global Trends and Policies,* 137–161. Tokyo: UN University, 1989.
Africa Watch. *Accountability in Namibia: Human Rights and the Transition to Democracy.* New York: Africa Watch, 1992.
———. *Conspicuous Destruction: War, Famine and the Reform Process in Mozambique.* Washington, DC: Africa Watch, 1992.
Ahire, Philip Terdoo. "Re-writing the Distorted History of Policing in Colonial Nigeria." *International Journal of the Sociology of Law* 18 (1990), 45–60.
———. *Imperial Policing: The Emergence and Role of the Police in Colonial Nigeria 1860–1960.* Milton Keynes, UK: Open University Press, 1991.
Alden, Chris. "The UN and the Resolution of Conflict in Mozambique." *Journal of Modern African Studies* 33: 1 (1995), 103–128.
Alvazzi del Fratte, Anna, Ugljesa Zuckic, and Jan J. M. van Dijk. *Criminal Victimisation in the Developing World.* Rome: UN Interregional Crime and Justice Research Institute [UNICRI], 1995.
Amnesty International. *Report 1994.* London: Amnesty International, 1994.
———. *Kenya, Tanzania, Uganda, Zambia and Zimbabwe: Attacks on Human Rights Through the Misuse of Criminal Charges.* London: Amnesty International, 1995).

———. *Annual Report 1996*. London: Amnesty International, 1996.
Anderson, David M., and David Killingray. *Policing and Decolonisation: Nationalism, Politics and the Police, 1917–1965*. Manchester, UK: Manchester University Press, 1992.
Andrade, John, *World Police and Paramilitary Forces*. Basingstoke, UK: Macmillan, 1985.
Ankumah, Evelyn A. *The African Commission on Human and People's Rights: Practices and Procedures*. The Hague: Martinus Nijhoff, 1996.
Anyuru, Max A. "Uganda's Street Children." *Africa Insight* 26: 3 (1996), 268–275.
Arthur, John A., and Otwin, Marenin. "Explaining Crime in Developing Countries: The Need for a Case Study Approach." *Crime, Law and Social Change* 23 (1995), 191–214.
Ayoob, Mohammed. *The Third World Security Predicament*. Boulder, CO: Lynne Rienner, 1995.
Baker, Bruce, "The Class of 1990: How Have the Autocratic Leaders of Sub-Saharan Africa Fared Under Democratisation?" *Third World Quarterly* 19: 1 (1998), 115–127.
Baldwin, David A. "The Concept of Security." *Review of International Studies* 23: 1 (1997), 5–26.
Bayart, Jean-François, Stephen Ellis, and Béatrice Hibou, *The Criminalization of the State in Africa*. Oxford: James Currey and Indiana University Press, 1999.
Bayley, David. *Patterns of Policing: A Comparative International Analysis*. New Brunswick, NJ: Rutgers University Press, 1985.
———. *Police for the Future*. Oxford: Oxford University Press, 1994.
———. "A Foreign Policy for Democratic Policing." *Policing and Society* 5 (1995), 79–93.
Baynham, Simon. *The Military and Politics in Nkrumah's Ghana*. Boulder, CO: Westview, 1988.
———."Drugs Set to Become Africa's New Invaders." *Jane's Intelligence Review*, September 1996.
Berdal, Mats R. *Disarmament and Demobilisation After Civil Wars: Arms, Soldiers and the Termination of Armed Conflicts*. Adelphi Paper 303. London: Oxford University Press for the IISS, 1996.
Berdal, Mats R., and David Keen. "Violence and Economic Agendas in Civil Wars: Some Policy Implications." *Millennium* 26: 3 (1997), 795–818.
Bienen, Henry, ed., *The Military Intervenes: Case Studies in Political Development*. New York: Russell Sage Foundation, 1968.
———. *Kenya: The Politics of Participation and Control*. Princeton, NJ: Princeton University Press, 1974.
Bienen, Henry S., and Nicolas van de Walle. *Of Time and Power: Leadership Duration in the Modern World*. Stanford, CA: Stanford University Press, 1991.
———. "A Proportional Hazard Model of Leadership Duration." *Journal of Politics* 5: 4 (1992).
Bittner, Egon. *The Functions of the Police in Modern Society*. Chevy Chase, MD: National Institute of Mental Health, 1970.
Bratton, Michael. "Deciphering Africa's Divergent Transitions." *Political Science Quarterly* 112: 1 (1997), 67–93.
Bratton, Michael, and Nicolas van de Walle. *Democratic Experiments in Africa: Regime Transitions in Comparative Perspective*. Cambridge: Cambridge University Press, 1997.
Brewer, John D. *Black and Blue: Policing in South Africa*. Oxford: Clarendon Press, 1994.

———. "Some Observations on Policing and Politics—A South African Case Study." *Policing and Society* 4: 1 (1994), 175–189.
Brewer, John D., Adrian Guelke, Ian Hume, Edward Moxon-Brown, and Rick Wilford. "South Africa." In *The Police, Public Order and the State,* 157–188. Basingstoke, UK: Macmillan, 1988.
Brogden, Mike. "An Act to Colonize the Internal Lands of the Island." *International Journal of the Sociology of Law* 15 (1987), 179–208.
———. "The Emergence of the Police—the Colonial Dimension." *British Journal of Criminology* 27 (1987), 4–14.
Brogden, Mike, and Clifford Shearing. *Policing for a New South Africa.* London: Routledge, 1993.
Bryden, Matt. *Report of Trip to Cam Aboker and Rabasso Refugee Camps, 17–19 February 1995.* UN Emergencies Unit for Ethiopia, 1995.
Buendia, Hernando Gomez, ed. *Urban Crime, Global Trends and Policies.* Tokyo: UN University, 1989.
Bukurura, Sufian Hemed. "Vigilantism in Tanzania." In M. Findlay, and U. Zvekic. *Alternative Policing Styles: Cross Cultural Perspectives,* 131–138. Deventer, Netherlands: Kluwer for UN Interregional Crime and Justice Research Institute, 1993.
Bussani, Mario. "Tort Law and Development: Insights into the Case of Ethiopia and Eritrea." *Journal of African Law* 40: 1 (1996), 43–52.
Cain, Maureen E. "Trends in the Sociology of Policework." *International Journal of the Sociology of Law* 7 (1979), 143–167.
Callaghy, Thomas. "Civil Society, Democracy, and Economic Change in Africa: A Dissenting Opinion About Resurgent Societies." In John W. Harbeson, Donald Rothchild, and Naomi Chazan, eds., *Civil Society and the State in Africa,* 231–253. Boulder, CO: Lynne Rienner, 1994.
Cawthra, Gavin. *Policing South Africa: The SAP and the Transition from Apartheid.* London: Zed Books, 1993.
Center for Research on Criminal Justice. *The Iron Fist and the Velvet Glove: An Analysis of the U.S. Police.* 2nd ed. Berkeley, CA: Center for Research on Criminal Justice, 1977.
Chabal, Patrick. *Power in Africa: An Essay in Political Interpretation.* 2nd ed. Basingstoke, UK: Macmillan, 1994.
———. "The (De)Construction of the Postcolonial Political Order in Black Africa." *AI Bulletin* 35: 6 (1995), 1–3.
———. "A Few Considerations on Democracy in Africa." *International Affairs* 74: 2 (1998), 289–303.
Chabal, Patrick, and Jean-Pascal Daloz. *Africa Works: Disorder as Political Instrument.* Oxford: James Currey and Indiana University Press, 1999.
Chazan, Naomi, Robert Mortimer, John Ravenhill, and Donald Rothschild. *Politics and Society in Contemporary Africa.* London: Macmillan, 1988.
Cheek, James. "Ethiopia: A Successful Insurgency." In Edwin G. Corr, and Steven Sloan, eds., *Low-Intensity Conflict: Old Threats in a New World.* Oxford: Westview, 1992.
Clapham, Christopher. *Transformation and Continuity in Revolutionary Ethiopia.* Cambridge: Cambridge University Press, 1988.
———. "Ethiopia and Eritrea: The Politics of Post-insurgency." In John Wiseman, ed., *Democracy and Political Change in Sub-Saharan Africa,* 116–136. London: Routledge, 1995.
———. "The Horn of Africa: A Conflict Zone." in Oliver Furley, ed., *Conflict in Africa,* 72–91. London: Tauris, 1995.

———, ed. *African Guerrillas.* Oxford: James Currey, Fountain, Indiana University Press, 1998.
Clayton, Anthony, and Killingray, David, *Khaki and Blue: Military and Police in British Colonial Africa.* Athens: Ohio University Center for International Studies, 1989.
Cliffe, Lionel, with Ray Bush, Jenny Lindsay, Brian Mokopakgosi, Donna Pankhurst, and Balefi Tsie. *The Transition to Independence in Namibia.* Boulder, CO: Lynne Reinner, 1994.
Cohen, Jean L., and Andrew Arato. *Civil Society and Political Theory.* London: MIT Press, 1992.
Cohen, John M. "Decentralization and 'Ethnic Federalism' in Post–Civil War Ethiopia." In Krishna Kumar, *Rebuilding Societies After Civil War: Critical Roles for International Assistance,* Boulder, CO: Lynne Rienner, 1997, 135–153.
Cohen, R., and H. Goulbourne. *Democracy and Socialism in Africa.* Oxford: Oxford University Press, 1991.
Colleta, Nat J., Nat J. Colleta, Markus Kostner and Ingo Wiederhofer. *Case Studies in War-to-Peace Transition: The Demobilisation and Reintegration of Ex-Combatants in Ethiopia, Namibia, and Uganda.* Washington, DC: World Bank, 1996.
Collier, Paul. "Demobilisation and Insecurity in Ethiopia and Uganda: A Study in the Economics of the Transition from War to Peace." In Jackie Cilliers, ed., *Dismissed,* 104–111. Midrand, South Africa: Institute for Security Studies, 1995.
Connaughton, R. M. *Military Support and Protection for Humanitarian Assistance: Rwanda, April–December 1994.* Occasional No. 18. Camberley, UK: Strategic & Combat Studies Institute, 1996.
Cox, Thomas, S. *Civil-Military Relations in Sierra Leone: A Case Study of African Soldiers in Politics.* London: Harvard University Press, 1976.
Cramer, James. *The World's Police.* London: Cassell, 1964.
Crawford, Gordon, *Promoting Democracy, Human Rights and Good Governance Through Development Aid: A Comparative Study of the Policies of Four Northern Donors.* Leeds: University of Leeds, 1996.
Daft, R. *Organization Theory and Design.* St Paul, MN: West, 1992.
Das Dilip, K. "Comparative Police Studies: An Assessment." *Police Studies* 14: 1 (1991), 22–35.
David, R., and J. C. C. Brierley. *Major Legal Systems in the World Today.* 3rd ed. London: Stevens, 1985.
Deflem, Mathieu. "Law Enforcement in British Colonial Africa: A Comparative Analysis of Imperial Policing in Nyasaland, the Gold Coast, and Kenya." *Police Studies* 17: 1 (1994), 45–68.
de Waal, Alex. "Rethinking Ethiopia." In Charles Gurden, ed., *The Horn of Africa,* 25–46. London: UCL Press, 1994.
———. "Contemporary Warfare in Africa: Changing Context, Changing Strategies." In *War and Rural Development in Africa, IDS Bulletin* 27: 3 (1996), 6–16.
———. "Democratizing the Aid Encounter in Africa." *International Affairs* 73: 4 (1997), 623–640.
Dunn, John, and A. F. Robertson. *Dependence and Opportunity: Political Change in Ahafo.* Cambridge: Cambridge University Press, 1973.
Economist Intelligence Unit (EIU). *Namibia Country Profile: Annual Survey of Political and Economic Background, 1991–92.* London: EIU, 1991.

———. *Namibia Country Profile: Annual Survey of Political and Economic Background, 1993–94.* London: EIU, 1993.
———. *EIU Country Report: Ethiopia, Eritrea, Somalia, Djibouti.* London: EIU, 1995.
Engels, Dagmar, and Shula Marks. *Contesting Colonial Hegemony: State and Society in Africa and India.* London: British Academic Press, 1994.
Enloe, Cynthia H. "Ethnicity and Militarization: Factors Shaping the Roles of Police in Third World Nations." *Studies in Comparative International Development* 11 (Fall 1976), 25–38.
———. *Ethnic Soldiers: State Security in Divided Societies.* London: Penguin, 1980.
———. *Police, Military and Ethnicity: Foundations of State Power.* London: Transaction Books, 1980.
Eritrea. Ministry of Foreign Affairs. *Eritrea: Rising from the Ashes.* Asmara: Eritrea Ministry of Foreign Affairs, 1995.
Farrah, Ahmed Yusuf, with I. M. Lewis. *Somalia: The Roots of Reconciliation. Peace Making Endeavours of Contemporary Lineage Leaders: A Survey of Grassroots Peace Conferences in "Somaliland."* London: ACTIONAID, 1993.
Fatton, Robert. *Predatory Rule: State and Civil Society in Africa.* Boulder, CO: Lynne Rienner, 1992.
———. "Africa in the Age of Democratization: The Civic Limitations of Civil Society." *African Studies Review* 38, 2 (1995), 67–99.
Foster, Philip, and Aristide R. Zolberg, eds. *Ghana and the Ivory Coast: Perspectives on Modernization.* Chicago: University of Chicago Press, 1971.
Foucault, Michel. Trans. Alan Sheridan. *Discipline and Punish.* London: Penguin, 1991.
Furley, Oliver. *Conflict in Africa.* London: Tauris Academic Studies, 1995.
Ganzglass, Martin R. "The Restoration of the Somali Justice System." *International Peacekeeping* 3: 1 (1996), 113–138.
Ghalib, Jama Mohamed. *The Cost of Dictatorship: The Somali Experience.* New York: Lilian Barber Press, 1995.
Ghebre-Ab, Habtu. *Ethiopia and Eritrea: A Documentary Study.* Trenton, NJ: Red Sea Press, 1993.
Good, Kenneth. "Corruption and Mismanagement in Botswana: A Best-Case Example?" *Journal of Modern African Studies* 32: 3 (1994), 449–521.
———. "Towards Popular Participation in Botswana." *Journal of Modern African Studies* 34: 1 (1996), 53–77.
———. "Accountable to Themselves: Predominance in Southern Africa." *Journal of Modern African Studies* 35: 4 (1997), 547–574.
Goody, Jack. "Decolonisation in Africa: National Politics and Village Politics." *Cambridge Anthropology* 7: 2 (1982), 2–22.
Goulet, Yves. "Executive Outcomes: Mixing Business with Bullets." *Jane's Intelligence Review,* September 1997, 426–430.
Hansen, Holger Bernt, and Michael Twaddle. "Uganda: The Advent of No-Party Democracy." In John A. Wiseman, ed., *Democracy and Political Change in Sub-Saharan Africa,* 137–151. London: Routledge, 1995.
Harbeson, John, W. Donald Rothchild, and Naomi Chazan, eds. *Civil Society and the State in Africa.* Boulder, CO: Lynne Rienner, 1994.
Hardy, Wickwar. *The Place of Criminal Justice in Development Planning.* New York: New York University Press, 1977.
Harlan, John P., and Charles P. McDowell. "The Role of Police in postcolonial Sub-Saharan Africa." *Police Studies* 4: 2 (1981), 21–27.

Hashim, Alice Bettis. *The Fallen State: Dissonance, Dictatorship and Death in Somalia.* Lanham, MD: University Press of America, 1997.
Haynes, Jeff. "The State, Governance and Democracy in Sub-Saharan Africa." *Journal of Modern African Studies* 31: 3 (1991), 537.
Heald, Suzette. *Controlling Anger: The Sociology of Gisu Violence.* Manchester, UK: Manchester University Press, 1989.
Herbst, Jeffrey. "The Creation and Maintenance of National Boundaries in Africa." *International Organization* 43: 4 (1989), 673–692.
———. "Responding to State Failure in Africa." *International Security* 21: 3 (1996/97), 120–144.
Herbstein, Dennis, and John Evenson. *The Devils Are Among Us: The War for Namibia.* London: Zed Books, 1989.
Heywood, Linda M. "Towards an Understanding of Modern Political Ideology in Africa: The Case of the Ovimbundu of Angola." *Journal of Modern African Studies* 36: 1 (1998), 139–167.
Holm, John, "Development, Democracy and Civil Society in Botswana." In Adrian Leftwich, ed., *Democracy and Development: Theory and Practice,* 97–113. Cambridge: Polity Press, 1996.
Howe, Herbert M. "Private Security Forces and African Stability: The Case of Executive Outcomes." *Journal of Modern African Studies* 36: 2 (1998), 307–331.
Human Rights Watch. *Human Rights Watch World Report 1995: Events of 1994.* New York: Human Rights Watch, 1995.
Hunt, Raymond G., and John M. Magment. *Power and the Police Chief: An Institutional and Organizational Analysis.* London: Sage, 1993.
Hyden, Goran, "The Challenges of Analysing and Building Civil Society." *Africa Insight* 26: 2 (1996), 92–105.
Hyden, Goran, and Michael Bratton, eds., *Governance and Politics in Africa.* Boulder, CO: Lynne Rienner, 1992.
Igbinovia, P. E. "The Police in Trouble: Administrative and Organizational Problems in the Nigeria Police Force." *Indian Journal of Public Administration,* 28: 2 (1980), 334–372.
———. "Patterns of Policing in Africa: The French and British Connection." *Police Journal* 54: 2 (April 1981), 123–156.
———. "Police Misconduct in Nigeria." *Police Studies* 8: 2 (1985), 110–122.
International Federation of Red Cross and Red Crescent Societies, *World Disasters Report 1994.* Geneva: IFRCRC, 1994.
International Institute for Strategic Studies, *The Military Balance, 1993–1994.* London: Brassey's for the IISS, 1994.
———. "Renewed Danger in the Congo: A Year of Laurent Kabila's Rule," *Strategic Comments* 4: 6 (July 1998).
Iyob, Ruth, *The Eritrean Struggle for Independence: Domination, Resistance, Nationalism, 1941–1993.* Cambridge: Cambridge University Press, 1995.
———. "The Eritrean Experiment: A Cautious Pragmatism." *Journal of Modern African Studies* 53: 4 (1997), 651.
Jackson, Robert H. *Quasi-states: Sovereignty, International Relations and the Third World.* Cambridge: Cambridge University Press, 1990.
———. "Juridical Statehood in Sub-Saharan Africa." *Journal of International Affairs* 46: 1 (1992), 1–16.
Jackson, Robert H., and Carl G. Rosberg. *Personal Rule in Black Africa: Prince, Autocrat, Prophet, Tyrant.* Berkeley: University of California Press, 1982.
Jane's Intelligence Review. Crisis in Central Africa, Special Report 13 (1996).

Jeffries, Charles, *The Colonial Police.* London: Allen & Unwin, 1952.
Kaplan, Robert D. "The Coming Anarchy: How Scarcity, Crime, Overpopulation, and Disease Are Rapidly Destroying the Social Fabric of Our Planet." *Atlantic Monthly,* February 1994, 44–76.
Kelly, Michael J. *Peace Operations: Tackling the Military Legal and Policy Challenges.* Canberra: Australian Government Publishing Service, 1997.
Khadiagala, Gilbert M. "Uganda's Domestic and Regional Security Since the 1970s." *Journal of Modern African Studies* 31: 2 (1993), 231–255.
———. "State Collapse and Reconstruction in Uganda." In I. William Zartman, ed., *Collapsed States: The Disintegration and Restoration of Legitimate Authority,* 33–47. Boulder, CO: Lynne Rienner, 1995.
Khan, Mushtaq H. "A Typology of Corrupt Transactions in Developing Countries." *Liberalization and the New Corruption, IDS Bulletin* 27: 2 (1996), 12–21.
Kilson, Martin. *Political Change in a West African State: A Study of the Modernization Process in Sierra Leone.* Cambridge: Harvard University Press, 1966.
Klockars, Carl B. *Thinking About Police: Contemporary Readings.* London: McGraw-Hill, 1983.
Kooiman, Jan. *Modern Governance: New Government-Society Interactions.* London: Sage, 1993.
Kritz, Neil J. "The Rule of Law in the Postconflict Phrase: Building a Stable Peace." In Chester A. Crocker, and Fen Osler Hampson, with Pamela Aall. *Managing Global Chaos: Sources of and Responses to International Conflict,* 587–606. Washington, DC: United States Institute of Peace Press, 1996.
Kunz, Frank. "Civil Society in Africa." *Journal of Modern African Studies* 33: 1 (1995), 185.
Kurian, George Thomas. *World's Encyclopaedia of Police Forces and Penal Systems.* Oxford: Facts on File, 1989.
La Fontaine, J. S. *City Politics: A Study of Leopoldville, 1962–63.* Cambridge: Cambridge University Press, 1970.
Laely, Thomas. "Peasants, Local Communities, and Central Power in Burundi." *Journal of Modern African Studies* 35: 4 (1997), 695–716.
Lawson, Stephanie. "Conceptual Issues in the Comparative Study of Regime Change and Democratization." *Comparative Politics* 25: 2 (1993), 183–204.
Lee, J. M. *African Armies and Civil Order.* London: Chatto & Windus for the Institute of Strategic Studies, 1969.
Lefever, Ernest W. *Spear and Scepter: Army, Police, and Politics in Tropical Africa.* Washington, DC: Brookings Institution, 1970.
Lemarchand, René. *Rwanda and Burundi.* London: Pall Mall Press, 1970.
———. "Uncivil States and Civil Societies: How Illusion Became Reality." *Journal of Modern African Studies* 30: 2 (1992), 177–191.
———. *Burundi: Ethnocide as Discourse and Practice.* Cambridge: Cambridge University Press, 1994.
Lewis, Peter. "Political Transition and the Dilemma of Civil Society in Africa." *Journal of International Affairs* 46: 1 (1992), 31–54.
Lipset, Seymour M. "Social Conflict, Legitimacy, and Democracy." In W. Connolly, ed., *Legitimacy and the State.* Oxford: Basil Blackwell, 1984.
Lloyd, Albert B. *Uganda to Khartoum: Life and Adventure on the Upper Nile.* London: Collins' Clear-Type Press, n.d.
Lyons, Terence, and Ahmed I. Samatar. *Somalia: State Collapse, Multilateral Intervention, and Strategies for Political Reconstruction.* Washington, DC: Brookings Institution, 1995.

Maitland Jones, J. F. *Politics in Ex-British Africa.* London: Weidenfeld & Nicolson, 1973.

Makoa, Francis K. "National Security with Reference to the Lesotho Ruler's Conception." *Strategic Review for Southern Africa* 19: 2 (November 1997), 111–121.

Makumbe, John Mw. "Is There a Civil Society in Africa?" *International Affairs* 74: 2 (1998), 305–317.

Mallya, Ernest T. "Law and Order in Tanzania: The Prime Vote Winner?" *Police Studies* 17: 3 (Fall 1994), 69–81.

Marenin, Otwin. "Policing African States: Towards a Critique." *Comparative Politics* 15: 2 (July 1982), 379–396.

———. "Policing Nigeria: Control and Autonomy in the Exercise of Coercion." *African Studies Review* 28: 1 (1985), 89.

———. "The Nigerian State as Process and Manager: A Conceptualization." *Comparative Politics* 20: 2 (1988), 215–232.

———. "The Police and the Coercive Nature of the State." In Edward S. Greenberg, and Thomas F., Mayer, eds., *Changes in the State: Causes and Consequences,* 115–130. London: Sage, 1990.

Marlow, C. *A History of the Malawi Police Force.* Zomba, Malawi: Government Printer, 1971.

Maruzi, Ali A. *Soldiers and Kinsmen in Uganda: The Making of a Military Ethnocracy.* London: Sage, 1975.

Matlosa, Khabele. "Democracy and Conflict in Post-Apartheid Southern Africa: Dilemmas of Social Change in Small States." *International Affairs* 74: 2 (1998), 319–337.

Mawby, R. I. *Comparative Policing Issues: The British and American Experience in International Perspective.* London: Routledge/Unwin, 1990.

Menkhaus, Ken. "Somalia: Political Order in a Stateless Society." *Current History,* May 1998, 220–224.

Menkhaus, Ken, and John Prendergast. *Political Economy of Post-Intervention Somalia.* Somalia Task Force Issue Paper 3, www.antro.uu.se/bh/nomadnet/menkaus.html, April 1995.

———. "The Stateless State." *African Review,* May-June 1995, 22–25.

Midgley, Rob, and Geoffrey Wood. "Community Policing in Transition: Attitudes and Perceptions from South Africa's Eastern Cape Province." *Low Intensity Conflict and Law Enforcement* 5: 2 (1997), 165–181.

Migdal, Joel. *Strong Societies and Weak States: State-Society Relations and State Capabilities in the Third World.* Princeton, NJ: Princeton University Press, 1988.

Moyo, Jonathan. *The Politics of Administration: Understanding Bureaucracy in Africa.* Harare: SAPES Books, 1992.

Mushanga, Tibamanya mwene, ed., *Criminology in Africa.* (Rome: UN Interregional Crime and Justice Research Institute, 1992.

Musoke, Mubiru. "Human Rights, Politics, War and the New Constitution in Africa." *Uganda Quarterley Review* 2 (1993), 49–127.

Nathan, Laurie. *Marching to a Different Drum: A Description and Assessment of the Formation of the Namibian Police and Defence Force.* Bellville, South Africa: University of the Western Cape, 1990.

———. "From a Police Force to a Police Service: The New Namibian Police." In M. L. Mathews, Philip B. Heyman, and A. S. Mathews. *Policing the Conflict in South Africa,* 121–132. Gainesville: University Press of Florida, 1993.

Nwankwo, Clement, Bonny Ibhawoh, and Dulue Mbachu. *The Failure of Prosecution: A Report on the Prosecution of Criminal Suspects in Nigeria.* Lagos: Constitutional Rights Project, 1996.
Nzimande, Blade, and Mpume Sikhosana. "Civil Society" Mass Organisations and the National Liberation Movement in South Africa." In Lloyd M. Sachikonye, ed., *Democracy, Civil Society and the State: Social Movements in Southern Africa,* 47–66. Harare: SAPES Books, 1995.
Oakley, Robert B., Michael J. Dziedzic, and Eliot M. Goldberg, eds. *Policing the New World Disorder: Peace Operations and Public Security.* Washington, DC: National Defense University Press, 1998.
Ojo, J. D. "The Police Under the Nigerian Constitution." *African Notes* 17: 1 and 2 (1993), 13–31.
Okello, John. *Revolution in Zanzibar.* Nairobi: East African Publishing House, 1967.
Okereke, Godpower O. "Police Powers and Law Enforcement Tactics: The Case of Nigeria." *Police Studies* 15: 3 (1992), 110–117.
Okonkwo, Cyprian O. *The Police and People in Nigeria.* London: African Universities Press, 1966.
Oloka-Onyango, J. "The National Resistance Movement, 'Grassroots Democracy,' and Dictatorship in Uganda." In R. Cohen, and H. Coulbourne. *Democracy and Socialism in Africa.* Oxford: Westview, 1991, 125–141.
———. "The Dynamics of Corruption Control and Human Rights Enforcement in Uganda: The Case of the Inspector General of Government." *East African Journal of Peace and Human Rights* 1: 1 (1993), 23–51.
Omar, Mohamed Osman. *Somalia: A Nation Driven to Despair; A Case of Leadership Failure.* New Delhi: Somali Publications, 1996.
Opolot, James. "Police Training in the States of Africa." *Police Studies* 14: 2 (1991), 62–71.
———. "The Resilience of the British Colonial Police Legacies in East Africa, Southern Africa, and West Africa." *Police Studies* 15: 2 (1992), 90–99.
Ornas, Anders Hjort Af. "Pastoral and Environmental Security in East Africa." *Disasters* 14: 2 (1990), 115–122.
Overseas Development Administration. *Ethiopia: Country Aid Programme Statement.* London, ODA, [1993].
———. *Uganda: Country Aid Programme Statement, 1995–1997.* London, ODA, n.d.
Perouse de Montclos, Marc-Antoine, "Faut-il supprimer les polices en Afrique?" *Monde Diplomatique,* August 1997.
Picard, Louis A., and Michael Garrity. *Policy Reform for Sustainable Development in Africa: The Institutional Imperative.* Boulder: Lynne Rienner, 1994.
Poluha, Eva. "Democracy in Africa—An Interpretation of Priorities." *African Anthropology* 27: 1 (1995), 17–44.
Potholm, Christian. "The Multiple Roles of the Police as Seen in the African Context." *Journal of Developing Areas* 3 (January 1969), 139–158.
Prunier, Gerard. "Somaliland: Birth of a New Country?" In Charles Gurdon, ed., *The Horn of Africa,* 61–75. London: UCL Press, 1994.
———. "Somaliland Goes It Alone." *Current History,* May 1998, 225–228.
Reeve, Ros, and Stephen Ellis. "An Insider's Account of the South African Security Forces' Role in the Ivory Trade." *Journal of Contemporary African Studies* 13: 2 (1995), 226–243.
Refugee Policy Group. *Hope Restored? Humanitarian Aid in Somalia, 1990–1994.* Washington, DC: Refugee Policy Group, 1994.

Reiner, Robert. *The Politics of the Police.* 2nd ed. Brighton, UK: Harvester, 1992.
Reisman, Michael. "Towards a General Theory About African Law, Social Change and Development." In P. N. Takirambudde. *The Individual Under African Laws.* Proceedings of the First All-Africa Law Conference, 1981. Swaziland: Kwaluseni Swaziland Printing and Publishing, 1982.
Reiss, Albert J., and David J. Bordua. "Environment and Organization: A Perspective on the Police." In David J. Bordua, ed., *The Police: Six Sociological Essays,* 25. New York: John Wiley & Sons, 1967.
Reno, William, *Corruption and State Politics in Sierra Leone.* Cambridge: Cambridge University Press, 1995.
———. "Ironies of Post–Cold War Structural Adjustment in Sierra Leone." *Review of African Political Economy* 23: 67 (1996), 14.
———. *Warlord Politics and African States.* Boulder, CO: Lynne Rienner, 1998.
Richards, Paul. *Fighting for the Rain Forest: War, Youth and Resources in Sierra Leone.* Oxford: James Currey & Heinemann, 1996.
Riley, Stephen. "Africa's "New Wind of Change." *World Today,* July 1992, 116–119.
Robinson, Cyril D., and Richard Scaglion, with J. Michael Olivero. *Police in Contradiction: The Evolution of the Police Function in Society.* Westport, CT: Greenwood Press, 1994.
Rosenblum, Peter. *Ethiopia in Transition.* Washington, DC: International Human Rights Law Group, US Institute of Peace, 1994.
Rotberg, Robert I., and Greg Mills, eds. *War and Peace in Southern Africa: Crime, Drugs, Armies, Trade.* Washington, DC: Brookings Institution and World Peace Foundation, 1998.
Rotimi, Adewale, and Olufunmilayo Oloruntimehin. "Teaching and Research Network in Africa in the Field of Criminology." In Tibamanya mwene Mushanga. *Criminology in Africa,* 233–248. Rome: UN Interregional Crime and Justice Research Institute, 1992.
Sachikonye, Lloyd M., ed. *Democracy, Civil Society and the State: Social Movements in Southern Africa.* Harare: SAPES Books, 1995.
Sandbrook, Richard. "Patrons, Clients and Factions: New Dimensions of Conflict Analysis in Africa." *Canadian Journal of African Studies* 5: 1 (March 1972), 104–119.
Sangmpam, S. N. "Neither Soft nor Dead: The African State Is Alive and Well." *African Studies Review* 36: 2 (1993), 73–94.
Sayigh, Yezid. *Confronting the 1990s: Security in the Developing Countries.* Adelphi Paper 251. London: Brassey's for the IISS, 1990.
Schatzberg, Michael G. *The Dialectics of Oppression in Zaire.* Bloomington: Indiana University Press, 1988.
Shaidi, Leonard P. "Crime, Justice and Politics in Contemporary Tanzania: State Power in an Underdeveloped Social Formation." *International Journal of the Sociology of Law* 17 (1989), 247–271.
Shaw, Mark. "South Africa: Crime in Transition." *Terrorism and Political Violence* 8: 4 (1996), 156–75.
Shearer, David. *Private Armies and Military Intervention.* Adelphi Paper 316. Oxford: Oxford University Press for the IISS, 1998.
Shearing, Clifford, D. "The Relation Between Public and Private Policing." In M. Tonry, and N. Morris, eds., *Modern Policing: Crime and Justice: A Review of Research,* 399–434. Chicago: University of Chicago Press, 1992.
Siso, Gift Spho. "When Guerrillas Turn to Crime." *New African* 362 (April 1998), 20.

Tamuno, T. N. *The Police in Modern Nigeria, 1861–1965.* Ibidan, Nigeria: Ibidan University Press, 1970.
Thomas, Lynn, and Steve Spataro. "Peacekeeping and Policing in Somalia." In Robert B. Oakley, Michael J. Dziedzic, and Eliot M. Goldberg, eds., *Policing the New World Disorder: Peace Operations and Public Security,* 175–214. Washington, DC: National Defense University Press, 1998.
Tignor, Robert L. "Political Corruption in Nigeria Before Independence." *Journal of Modern African Studies* 31: 2 (1993), 175–202.
Tilly, Charles. "War Making and State Making as Organized Crime." In Peter B. Evans, Dietrich Rueschemeyer, and Theda Skocpol, eds., *Bringing the State Back In,* 169–191. Cambridge: Cambridge University Press, 1985.
Transparency International. *Transparency International: The Coalition Against Corruption in International Business Transactions.* Berlin: Transparency International, 1997.
Turk, A. "The Meaning of Criminality in South Africa." *International Journal of the Sociology of Law* 9 (1977), 31–41.
Turton, David. "Warfare, Vulnerability and Survival: A Case from Southwestern Ethiopia." *Disasters* 15: 3 (1991), 254–264.
United Kingdom. War Office. *Instructions on the Use of Armed Force in Civil Disturbances.* London, 1954.
United Nations. *The United Nations and the Independence of Eritrea.* New York: United Nations, 1996.
UN Department of Humanitarian Affairs. *Humanitarian Situation Report on Uganda.* Integrated Regional Information Network, 4 December 1996.
United Nations Research Institute for Social Development. "War-Torn Societies Project: Eritrea." Discussion paper for final national workshop, Asmara, 5–6 December 1996.
U.S. Department of State. Bureau of Democracy, Human Rights, and Labor, *Angola Human Rights Practices 1993.* Washington, DC: U.S. Department of State, 1994.
———. *Eritrea: Human Rights Practices 1994.* Washington, DC: U.S. Department of State, 1995.
———. *Ethiopia: Human Rights Practices.* Washington, DC: U.S. Department of State, published annually.
———. *Namibia: Country Report on Human Rights Practices for 1996.* Washington, DC: U.S. Department of State, 1997.
———. *Somalia: Country Report on Human Rights Practices for 1996.* Washington, DC: U.S. Department of State, 1997.
———. *Uganda: Country Report on Human Rights Practices for 1996.* Washington, DC: U.S. Department of State, 1997.
van Binsbergen, Wim. "Aspects of Democracy and Democratisation in Zambia and Botswana: Exploring African Political Culture at Grassroots." *Journal of Contemporary African Studies* 13: 1 (1995), 3–34.
van Dijk, Jan J. M., Peter Mayhew, and Martin Killias. *Experiences of Crime Across the World: Key Findings from the 1989 International Crime Survey.* Boston: Kluwer Law, 1990.
Villalón, Leonardo A. "The Moral and the Political in African Democratization: The *Code de la Famille* in Niger's Troubled Transition." *Democratization* 3: 2 (Summer 1996), 41–68.
Villalón, Leonardo A., and Phillip Huxtable, eds. *The African State at a Critical Juncture: Between Disintegration and Reconfiguration.* Boulder, CO: Lynne Rienner, 1998.

Wasikhongo, Joab M. N. "The Role and Character of Police in Africa and Western Countries: A Comparative Approach to Police Isolation." *International Journal of Criminology and Penology* 4 (1976), 382–396.

Welch, Claude E. *Protecting Human Rights in Africa: Strategies and Roles of Non-Governmental Organizations.* Philadelphia: University of Pennsylvania Press, 1996.

Williams, Christopher. "Street Children and Abuse of Power." *Africa Insight* 26: 3 (1996), 221–228.

Wiseman, John. "Leadership and Personal Danger." *Journal of Modern African Studies* 31: 4 (1993), 657–660.

———. *The New Struggle for Democracy in Africa.* Aldershot, UK: Avebury, 1996.

Woods, Dwayne. "Civil Society in Europe and Africa: Limiting State Power Through a Public Sphere." *African Studies Review* 35: 2 (1992), 77–100.

World Bank. *Sub-Saharan Africa: From Crisis to Sustainable Growth.* Washington, DC: World Bank, 1989.

———. *Demobilization and Reintegration of Military Personnel in Africa: The Evidence from Seven Country Case Studies.* Report IDP-130. New York: World Bank, 1993.

———. *World Development Report 1997: The State in a Changing World.* Oxford: Oxford University Press for the World Bank, 1997.

Young, Eric T. "Chiefs and Worried Soldiers: Authority and Power in the Zimbabwe National Army." *Armed Forces and Society* 24: 1 (1997), 133–149.

Young, John. "Ethnicity and Power in Ethiopia." *Review of African Political Economy* 70: 23 (1996), 531–542.

Zartman, I. William, ed. *Collapsed States: The Disintegration and Restoration of Legitimate Authority.* Boulder, CO: Lynne Rienner, 1995.

Index

Abacha, Sani, 42, 71
African National Congress (ANC), 59, 60, 61
Aid, international police, 4–5, 17, 22n12, 46–48, 58, 60–61, 74, 91, 102, 111n11, 114n40, 126, 136n31, 145, 159n22, 176, 177, 178, 179
Amin, Idi, 2, 90–91
Amnesty International, 97, 98, 100, 150, 176, 177, 185
ANC. *See* African National Congress
Anglophone Africa, policing in, 27, 29–30, 74. *See also* Police literature
Angola, 4, 11, 15, 47–48, 73–74, 166; People's Vigilance Brigades, 170–171. *See also* Rapid Intervention Police
ASEANPOL. *See* Association of Southeast Asian National Police
Assimilation, 29, 31, 34, 90, 172
Association of Southeast Asian National Police (ASEANPOL), 84n3

Babangida, Ibrahim, 42, 43, 46
Banda, Kamuzu, 20, 40, 49n4
Barre, Siad Mohammed, 63, 144
al-Bashir, Omar Hassan, 65–66
Baynham, Simon, 3, 33–34
Ben Ali, Zine El Abidine, 63
"Big man," 19, 86n33, 164, 176. *See also* Patron-client relationships
Binaisa, Godfry, 86n41

Botswana, 16, 18, 174–175
Bratton, M. and N. van de Walle, 1, 12, 18, 19, 20, 26n49, 174
Brutality, police, 4, 21n7, 90, 109. *See also* Human rights; Montclos
Buendia, Hernando Gomez et al., 43
Bugisu district, 44, 170. *See also* Heald
Buhari, Muhammuda, 52n36

Casino capitalism, 129–130. *See also* Namibia; Nujoma
CEAN. *See* Centre d'Etudes d'Afrique Noire
Centre d'Etudes d'Afrique Noire (CEAN), x
Chabal, Patrick, xn4, 19
Chad, 68, 79, 85n30
Children, street, 114n44, 121
Chissano, Joaquim, 58
Civil-military relations, 3, 76–77
Civil order, 67–70
Civil society, 172–176
Civilianization, 123
Cobbina, John, 64
Coercion, 6–7, 8, 37–38, 163, 185. *See also* Marenin
Colonial, policing, 27, 29–30, 50n6
Colonization, 49n2
Commercial security, 7, 51n14, 163–164, 165, 166–167, 181n7, 181n12, 182n14, 182n15
Community policing, 87n53, 171–172, 179–180, 183n26

207

Compliance, 24n24. *See also* legitimacy
Congo (Zaire), 4n8, 23n20, 36, 140, 153–155, 166. *See also* Mobutu
Consensus, international, 12, 30, 31
Construction, 82–83, 115. *See also* Eritrea
Conversion, 11, 82–83, 99, 125, 132. *See also* Ethiopia
Corruption, 24n37, 36, 49, 122, 166, 181n5, 182n19. *See also* Drugs; Good; Montclos; Nigeria; Transnational crime; Transparency International
Counterinsurgency, 4, 7, 30, 42, 47, 48, 73, 93
Coup: Burundi, 66; Zanzibar 64. *See also* Ghana
Crime, x, xiin4, 18, 20, 26n51, 36, 42–43, 44–45, 52n29, 52n39, 59–60, 61, 62, 77, 78, 102, 121, 124, 131–132, 137n46, 145, 161–162, 174, 182n15. *See also* Buendia
Crime prevention, 3, 29, 124
Criminalization, xiin4, 48, 108
Crowd control, 21n5, 183n28
Culture, senior officers, 67. *See also* Occupational culture; Sandhurst

Demobilization, 5n14, 73, 113n31, 114n38, 117, 126, 135n24, 172
Democracy, "no-party," 92–94. *See also* National Resistance Movement
Democracy, participatory, 65
Democratization, x, 75, 86n41, 163, 172, 185, 187
Dergue, 10, 102, 113n28
Discipline, 24n36
Discretion, 5, 9, 56, 66, 75. *See also* Paramilitarism
Disorder, political, xiin4, 77–78. *See also* Order
Drugs, illegal, 16, 52n29, 57, 60, 61, 63, 78, 84n13, 85n18, 108, 132, 180, 181n5. *See also* Liberia; *Qat*

Egal, Mohamed Ibrahim, 152–153, 155–156
Emergency powers: Sudan, 111n3; Uganda, 90
EPLF. *See* Eritrean People's Liberation Front

EPRDF. *See* Ethiopian People's Revolutionary Democratic Front
Eritrea: crime, 121–122; demobilization, 117; effects of insurgency, 116; human rights, 122–123; policing developments, 118–123; political developments, 83, 115–118, 123. *See also* Insurgency
Eritrean People's Liberation Front (EPLF), 115, 116–117, 118, 121, 123
Ethiopia, 10, 83; authoritarianism, 100; police force, 101–110; political developments, 99–101; violence, 108–110. *See also* Conversion; Demobilization
Ethiopian People's Revolutionary Democratic Front (EPRDF), 99, 100, 101, 102–103, 104, 106
EU. *See* European Union
European Union (EU), 55, 60. *See also* Police aid
Evolution, 82–83, 89–90. *See also* Uganda

Foucault, Michel, 8–9
Fragmentation, 139–141, 142, 144–145, 149–151, 155, 157n7, 158n9; Congo (Zaire), 153–155; Somaliland, 151–153. *See also* Somalia
Francophone Africa, policing in, 4, 26n49, 50n5, 74. *See also* Chad

Ghana, 30; colonial policing, 32–33; coup (1966), 33–34, 63–64, 65, 74. *See also* Baynham; Nkrumah
Gime gema, 106
Good, Kenneth, 18, 61, 133
Governance, 23n17, 71–72, 165; good government, 14–15

Harlley, J. W. D., 33–34
Heald, Suzette, 44, 170
Human rights, 74–76, 87n51, 177; in Eritrea, 122–123; in Ethiopia, 109–110; in Namibia, 127, 132; in Uganda, 97–98, 111n16
Hussein, Shawgi, 70

Insurgency, 82, 83, 85n29, 91, 92, 94, 99, 100, 106, 115–116, 186

Integration, 82–83, 125. *See also* Namibia
International intervention, 64, 176–177
Interpol, 55, 58, 63, 181n5

Jackson, Robert H., 12, 13. *See also* Jackson and Rosberg
Jackson, Robert H., and Carl G. Rosberg, 23n17, 188. *See also* Jackson

Kabila, Laurent, 155. *See also* Congo (Zaire)
Kamajor militia, 169. *See also* Sierra Leone
Kenya, 30, 36, 58, 89, 97–98, 167, 185–186
Koevoet, 4, 73, 87n47, 182n14. *See also* Namibia; South Africa; Special units

Law, 29, 34, 51n28, 74–75, 87n50, 87n51, 90, 91, 99, 111n16. *See also* Policing and law
Lee, J. M., 69, 142–143
Legitimacy, police, 10, 17, 24n24, 37–38. *See* Marenin
Lesotho, police mutiny, 13–15, 25n39; Royal Lesotho Mounted Police, 47, 178–180
Liberalization, x, 1–2, 3, 13, 17, 19, 25n43, 62, 71, 75, 77, 78, 82, 163, 172, 173, 178–180, 186, 187, 190. *See also* Civil society; Lesotho
Liberia, 159n33, 181n5
Lusophone Africa, policing in, 4. *See also* Angola; Mozambique

Malawi, 9, 30; Malawi Police Force, 38–40
Marenin, Otwin, 1, 3, 17, 37–38
Masire, Ketumik, 18
Mauritius, 24n36. *See also* Paramilitarism
Meles, Zenawi, 99, 100, 106, 110
Mengistu, Haile Mariam, 99, 100, 112n22. *See also* Dergue
Military forces, 3
Military police, 23n20
Militia, 151, 152, 159n33, 160n37, 169, 170. *See also* Kamajor militia; Somalia; Somaliland

Mobutu Sese Seko, 36–37, 153, 154, 164
Moi, Daniel Arap, 19, 185–186, 188
Montclos, Marc-Antoine Perouse de, 161–163, 180
Mozambique, 4, 22n11, 58, 59, 73, 185
Museveni, Yoweri, 91–93, 97, 98, 188

Namibia, 77–78, 83, 124; crime, 131–132; human rights, 32; ideals, 132–133; reconciliation 125–126, 132; SWAPO's security, 129. *See also* Casino capitalism; Good; Integration; NAMPOL; Presidentialism; SWAPO
Namibian Police (NAMPOL), 11, 124–128, 132–133
NAMPOL. *See* Namibian Police
National Resistance Movement (NRM), 92–95
Neopatrimonialism, 19–20, 75, 188
Nigeria, 25n37, 89; colonial policing, 31; Nigerian policing units 7; Nigeria Police Force, 35–36, 41–42, 45–46
Ninjas. *See* Rapid Intervention Police
Nkrumah, Kwame, 32–34, 36
NRM. *See* National Resistance Movement
Nujoma, Sam, 129, 130–131

Occupational culture, 22n12, 56–57, 67. *See also* Ben Ali
Operation Sweep, 7, 43, 52n36
Order, 29, 47; political order, 77–79, 162, 165–166. *See also* Civil order
Osman, Khojali, 65

Paramilitary, 7, 9, 15, 22n8, 23n20, 24n36, 35, 61, 73–74, 76–77, 102, 114n35, 114n41. *See* Rapid Intervention Police
Participatory democracy, 65
Patron-client relationships, 20, 25n41, 69. *See also* "Big man" Neopatrimonialism
Peasantry, 180
Police, adaptation by, 5, 12, 20, 31–32, 51n28, 55, 66, 82–83, 99, 175–176, 181, 186–188

Police budgets: Eritrea, 119; Namibia, 127; Uganda, 96. *See also* Under-resourcing
Police definitions, 6–7, 161, 187
Police functions, 7, 41, 65, 188
Police literature, 2–5, 27n9
Police-military relations, 2–3, 7, 9, 13–14, 18, 29–30, 41–42, 48, 51n14, 51n16, 62, 76–77, 90
Police, models of, 5, 79–83, 189. *See also* Adaptation; Construction; Conversion; Evolution; Integration; Transition
Police, politics and, 3, 8, 13, 32, 55–56, 62, 64–65, 66–67; Ethiopia, 110; Lesotho police mutiny, 13–14; Malawi Police Force, 38–40, 63–65, 66–67, 77–78; Zanzibar, 63. *See also* Ben Ali; Ghana; Malawi
Police, public, 7, 15
Police, rationale for, 6
Police, as regime, 34. *See* Ghana; Tunisia
Police repression, 5, 8, 17, 21n7, 24n27, 37–38, 87n47, 90–91, 144, 161–162, 175, 185, 187. *See also* Repression
Police roles, 7, 15, 188
Police, stagnation of, 39, 41, 45–46
Police, strategic statements, 8, 133; Uganda, 95
Police systems, 27, 187, 189; conversion, 11; definitions, 10–11; legitimization, 10; organization, 15–16; resilience, 5, 12, 17; value, 20, 79–83. *See also* Adaptation
Police under-resourcing, 40, 41, 45, 96–97, 108, 110, 119, 123, 127–128, 186–187
Policing, characteristics, 15–17, 19, 41; definition, 7–10. *See also* Police under-resourcing
Policing, exclusionary, 163, 164–165. *See* Commercial security; Policing, privatized
Policing, law and, 27, 29, 75, 111n16. *See also* Human rights
Policing, by military, 11; Burundi, 66n27; Chad, 68; Ethiopia, 102–106; Ghana 74. *See also* Operation Sweep

Policing, postcolonial, 30–32, 34–35, 40–41, 44–45, 49
Policing, privatized, 149–150, 163–164. *See also* Policing, exclusionary; Security; Self-policing; Shadow states; Somalia
Policing, regional, 56–57. *See also* SARPCCO
Potholm, Christian, 7, 64–65
Presidentialism: Malawi, 20; Namibia, 130–131. *See also* Nujoma
Prison, 29, 49n4, 90, 111n5, 181n12. *See also* Assimilation
Professionalism, xiin2, 5, 32n11, 50n11, 56–57
Promotion, police, 16
Public good, 155–156, 161, 162–163, 165, 167, 168, 169. *See also* Commercial security; Policing, exclusionary

Qat (quat), 151, 159n34

Rapid Intervention Police (Ninjas), 58, 68, 84n6. *See also* Rapid reaction forces; Special units
Rapid reaction forces, 15, 24n36, 42, 68, 84n6, 114n41, 155. *See also* Special units
Reconciliation, 116, 117, 123, 124, 125, 135n23. *See also* Namibia
Reconstruction, 73–74, 82–83, 95. *See* Ethiopia; Namibia; Somalia; Uganda
Recruitment, police: Eritrea 119; Ethiopia, 106–107; Namibia, 125–126; Uganda, 90, 142
Regime, 8, 12, 13, 23n17, 31, 34, 41, 55, 72, 78, 165–166, 172; police relations with, 4, 6–7, 12, 186, 188
Regional policing. *See* SARPCCO; Transnational crime
Reno, William, 165–166. *See also* Shadow states
Repression, 175. *See also* Police repression
Revolution, police, 10
RLMP. *See* Royal Lesotho Mounted Police
Royal Lesotho Mounted Police

(RLMP), 178–180. *See also* Aid, international police
Rural policing, 31, 43; in Burundi, 180; in Ethiopia, 107; in Uganda, 44–45
Rwanda, 68

SANDF. *See* South African National Defence Force
Sandhurst, Royal Military Academy, 62. *See also* Occupational culture
São Tomé, 51n16
SARPCCO. *See* Southern Africa Regional Police Chiefs Cooperative Organization
Security: internal, 2, 15, 35, 70–71, 78, 94, 112, 124, 133n7, 152, 175, 189–190; national, 2, 25n39, 35, 66; physical, 73, 108, 113n31; regime, 21n2, 35, 94, 109; security sector, 2, 10. *See also* Commercial security; Policing, privatized
Security sector reform, 5
Self-policing, 120, 149–153, 164, 165, 166, 167, 168–169. *See also* Community policing; Militia; Vigilantism
Shadow states, 12, 163, 165–166, 187. *See also* Policing, exclusionary; Reno
Shari'a, 150
Sierra Leone, 141–142, 166, 169, 170. *See also* Kamajor; Shadow states
Somalia: localization, 149–150, 156–157; localized public policing, 144–149, 157; militia, 151; private policing, 149–151, 156; reconstruction, 74, 146–148. *See also* Somali Police Force
Somaliland, district policing, 148–149, 151–153, 162–163
Somali Police Force (SPF), 143–144
South Africa, x, xiin3, 4, 6, 8, 14, 21n5, 58, 59–61, 77–78, 85n18, 168, 170. *See also* South African National Defence Force; Township policing
South African National Defence Force (SANDF), 14
Southern Africa Regional Police Chiefs Cooperative Organization (SARPCCO), 57–59, 60
South West Africa People's Organization (SWAPO). *See* SWAPO
Special units, 15, 25n38; Congo (Zaire), 36, 155; distinctions, 161; Namibia, 4, 87n47, 127, 132, 135n26; Nigeria, 2, 7, 42, 43; South Africa, 60–61, 87n47; Sudan, 65–66; Tanzania, 68; Uganda, 2. *See also* Ninjas
SPF. *See* Somali Police Force
State, 12; collapse, 141; failure, 142–143; fragmentation, 140–142, 187–188; power, 3
SWAPO. *See* South West Africa People's Organization
Sudan, 65–66, 70, 73. *See also* Bashir
Sungusungu, 169–171. *See also* Self-policing; Vigilantism
Suppression facility, 76

Tanganyika, 64. *See also* Zanzibar
Tanzania, 2, 58, 60, 68, 91, 97–98
Tigray People's Liberation Front (TPLF), 99–100
Togo, 9, 31
Township policing, 6, 169, 170. *See also* Self-policing
TPLF. *See* Tigray People's Liberation Front
Traffic police, 15, 74, 96, 97, 121
Training, police: Nigeria, 45. *See also* Uganda
Transition, 82, 139–140, 157, 186. *See also* Congo (Zaire); Somalia; Somaliland
Transparency International, 25n37
Transnational crime, 52n29, 57, 59–60

Uganda, 50n6, 58, 83; under Amin, 90; under Obote 31, 91; resources, 96–97; rural policing, 44–45; Uganda Police Force, 94–98; vigilantism, 170. *See also* Heald; Human rights; Museveni
Unified Task Force (UNITAF), 146–147
UNITAF. *See* Unified Task Force
United Nations in Somalia (UNOSOM), 145–148, 150, 152, 153, 177
UNOSOM. *See* United Nations in Somalia

Urbanization, 41–43, 48, 107. *See also* Rural policing

Vigilantism, 44, 168. *See also* Self-policing

Witchcraft, 45, 61
World Bank, 17, 18, 71, 75, 163, 178

Zaire, 23n20, 36–37. *See also* Congo (Zaire)
Zambia, 57, 58, 98, 167, 171–172
Zanzibar, 64
Zartman, I. William, 141
Zimbabwe, 16, 23n20, 24n41, 51n28

About the Book

The use and abuse of political power in Africa has been closely related to the role and function of the police. Alice Hills explores the impact of the cautious moves toward liberalization across the continent both on policing systems and on the relationship between those systems and national development.

Hills engages contemporary debates on security sector reform, governance, law and justice, and civil society to examine the environment within which Africa's police forces operate. She also addresses the special problems confronting reconstructed states: the prevalence of low-intensity conflicts, reintegration programs, UN and NGO involvement, the nature of policing, and differing concepts of professionalism and liberalization.

A series of case studies—from Congo (Zaire), Eritrea, Ethiopia, Namibia, Somalia, and Uganda—inform this original book, which offers an important prism through which to view state-society relations in Africa.

Alice Hills is senior lecturer in defense studies at the Joint Services Command and Staff College.